Exploring Creation

with

Zoology 1

Flying Creatures of the Fifth Day

by Jeannie K. Fulbright

Exploring Creation With Zoology 1: Flying Creatures of the Fifth Day

Published by
Apologia Educational Ministries, Inc.
1106 Meridian Plaza, Suite 220
Anderson, IN 46016
www.apologia.com

Manufactured in the United States of America
Seventh Printing: April, 2011

ISBN: 978-1-932012-61-3

Printed by Courier, Inc., Kendallville, IN

Cover photos © Rusty Trump, © Stuart Elflett, © Marco Kopp, © Brand X Photos, © Digital Vision

Cover design by Kim Williams

Need Help?

Apologia Educational Ministries, Inc. Curriculum Support

If you have any questions while using Apologia curriculum,
feel free to contact us in any of the following ways:

<u>By Mail</u>:   Curriculum Help
Apologia Educational Ministries, Inc.
1106 Meridian Plaza, Suite 220
Anderson, IN 46016

<u>By E-MAIL</u>:   help@apologia.com

<u>On The Web</u>: http://www.apologia.com

<u>By FAX</u>:   (765) 608 - 3290

<u>By Phone</u>:   (765) 608 - 3280

Illustrations from the MasterClips collection and the Microsoft Clip Art Gallery

Scientific Speculation Sheet

Name _____ **Date** _____

Experiment Title _____

Materials Used:

Procedure: (What you will do or what you did)

Hypothesis: (What you think will happen and why)

Results: (What actually happened)

Conclusion: (What you learned)

Introduction

Congratulations on choosing *Exploring Creation with Zoology 1: Flying Creatures of the Fifth Day*. You will find this to be an easy to use science curriculum for your whole family. The text is written directly to the student, making it very appealing to kids from six to thirteen. The material is presented in a conversational, engaging style that will make science enchanting and memorable for your students, creating an environment in which learning is a joy.

Lesson Increments

The lessons in this book contain quite a bit of scientific information. Each lesson should be broken up into manageable time slots depending on your children's age and attention span. This will vary from family to family. There are 14 lessons in this text, covering birds, bats, pterosaurs, and insects. The insect segment, beginning in Lesson 9, would best be done when the weather is warm and insects are easy to find. The book does not have to be done in order, but you should do lesson 1 first. After that, you can do the insect segment whenever it is most convenient for you. Most lessons can be divided into two-week segments.
You can do the reading and the notebook assignments during the first week, and you can do the experiments and the data recording during the second week. If you do science two or three days per week, you can read four to six pages a day to finish a lesson and begin the experiment. This will give you 32 weeks for the entire book. Older students can work through the book more quickly if they wish.

For record keeping and evaluation, narrations and notebooking replace the traditional and less effective method of filling in blanks in a workbook. We believe notebooking and narrations are a superior method of facilitating retention and providing documentation of your child's education.

Narrations

Older elementary students can do the entire book and most experiments on their own, while younger students will enjoy an older sibling or parent reading it to them. Each lesson begins with a reading of the text. Throughout the reading, the students will be asked to retell or narrate the information they just studied. This helps them assimilate the information in their minds. The act of verbalizing it in their own words propels them forward in their ability to effectively and clearly communicate with others that which they know. It also serves to lock the information into their minds.

Communication skills are necessary no matter what interests your children pursue, so please don't skip the narrations. Though they may seem to take up valuable time, they are vital to your child's intellectual development. Persevere through the first attempts; the more narrating the child does, the better at it he will become. The better at narrating the child becomes, the better at writing, researching, and clearly communicating his beliefs he will be. Some parents encourage their child to take notes as they listen to them read. You may or may not want to try this.

Notebooks

At the end of each lesson, notebook activities are used to give the child further experience with the material. The notebook is an important tool that will provide you and your child with a record of what was learned. The notebook activities generally occur at the end of a lesson, but they are sometimes used to break up lessons. Older students are given additional assignments in some of the notebooking segments for more challenge. You have the option of creating your own notebook, or purchasing the *Zoology 1 Notebooking Journal* that accompanies this book. The notebooking journal includes all the templates for every notebook assignment in the text, as well as additional project ideas, book and DVD suggestions, Vocabulary Crosswords, Scripture Copywork and much more. Also included are colorful lapbook style miniature books.

Projects and Experiments

In this text there are a wide variety of projects and experiments. Every single lesson ends with an opportunity to further ground your child in real science using the scientific method. The last lesson culminates with the children designing and conducting their own experiment based on their own hypothesis about caterpillars. This will help you evaluate whether your child genuinely understands the necessary components for designing an experiment.

The projects and experiments in this book use mostly common, household items. As a result, they are fairly inexpensive, but you will have to hunt down everything that you need. To aid you in this, pages viii-xi contain a list of the materials that you need for the experiments and projects in each lesson.

The Immersion Approach
Is it Okay to Spend a Year on Just a Part of Zoology?

Many educators promote the spiral or survey approach to education, wherein a child is exposed over and over again to minute amounts of a variety of science topics. The theory goes that we just want to "expose" the child to science at this age, each year giving a bit more information than was given the year before. This method has been largely unsuccessful in public and private schools, as National Center for Education Statistics (NCES) data indicate that eighth graders are consistently less than 50% proficient in science.

This method assumes the young child is unable to understand profound scientific truths. Presenting a child with scant and insufficient science fails to develop a love for the subject. If the learning is skimpy, the subject seems monotonous. The child is simply scratching the surface of the amazing and fascinating information available in science. Sadly, students taught in this way are led to believe they "know all about" that subject, when in reality the subject is much richer than they were allowed to explore. That is why we recommend that kids, even young children, are given an in-depth, above their perceived grade level exploration into each science topic. You, the educator, have the opportunity to abandon methods that don't work so that your students can learn in the ways that have been proven effective. The immersion approach is the way everyone, even young kids, learn best. That is why we major in one field in college and take many classes in that field alone. If you immerse your child in one field of science for an entire year, he will develop a love for that subject and a love for learning in general.

Additionally, a child that has focused on one subject throughout an entire year is being challenged mentally in ways that will develop his or her ability to think critically and retain complex information. This will actually benefit the child and give him an advantage on achievement tests. He will be able to make more intelligent inferences about the right answer on science questions, as God has created an orderly world that works very similarly throughout all matters of science. A child who has not been given the deeper, more profound information will not understand how the scientific world operates.

Course Website

If your child would like to learn more about the animals discussed in this course, there is a course website that allows the student to dig even deeper into these aspects of zoology. To go to the course website, simply type the following address into your web browser:

http://www.apologia.com/bookextras

You will see a box on the page. Type the following password into the box:

Godmadethemfly

Make sure you capitalize the first letter, and make sure there are no spaces in the password. When you hit "enter," you will be taken to the course website.

Items Needed To Complete Each Lesson

Every child will need his own notebook, blank paper, lined paper, and colored pencils.

Lesson 1

- Cup full of water
- Four straws (Two could be paint stirrers which are given away at hardware stores.)
- Scissors
- Pen
- Cardboard box (A pizza box or cereal box works well.)
- Clay
- Tape
- Tape measure (or some other device for measuring distance, like a yardstick or someone's feet)
- Several sheets of plain white paper
- One sheet of thicker, colored paper (such as construction paper) or a thick decorative paper like you would find in a scrapbook store
- A long-arm stapler (If you don't have one, you can go to an office supplies store or copy center and use theirs. They might charge you a small fee, but most places allow you to use it for free.)

Lesson 2

- Colored pencils
- Outline of a bird (available on course website)
- An adult with a knife
- Two bamboo skewers
- An empty plastic bottle with a wide mouth opening, such as a juice jug. You can use a plastic soda pop bottle instead, but the narrow mouth opening will make it hard to fill with seeds.
- Wire or string
- Bird seed
- Small plastic zippered bags
- Mesh bag or suet basket (A suet basket can be purchased in lawn and garden stores and some pet stores.)
- 2 cups crunchy peanut butter
- 2 cups lard (not shortening)
- 4 cups rolled oats (not quick oats)
- 4 cups cornmeal
- $\frac{2}{3}$ cup sugar
- 1 cup raisins
- Stove

- Pot
- Stirring spoon
- Freezer
- Two identical bird feeders (You can make them both or purchase them both, but they must be the same)
- Two types of bird seed

Lesson 3

- Umbrella
- At least two feathers (Make sure they come from game birds like ducks, chickens, or geese. It is illegal to collect the feathers of many other kinds of birds.)
- A magnifying glass
- An umbrella
- Water
- Oil (like vegetable oil)
- Two terracotta, ceramic, or plastic saucers from large planters (Make sure they are exactly the same size, shape, color, etc.)

Lesson 4

- Chicken bone
- Cow bone (like one from a t-bone steak)
- Two bird feeders that are exactly the same and can be painted (We used wooden tangerine crates to make our feeders, but you can use any kind of feeder, even a soda pop bottle feeder like the one you made in Lesson 2.)
- A scale to measure the weights of the feeders and seed each day.
- Spray or acrylic paint: red and green (You can use a color besides green, but be sure that one of the colors you use is red.)
- Bird food

Lesson 5

- Mud (about a handful)
- Twigs (any will do)
- Grass (Just pull some from your yard.)
- String (any kind)
- Cotton balls (a few)
- Leaves (Just pull some from a tree.)

- Real estate advertisements from the newspaper
- A 1-in x 6-in piece of lumber at least 5 feet long. Use cedar if you can find it. (Many lumber stores will cut the board for you. If they do you will need four pieces 9 inches long, one piece 8¾ inches long, and one piece 7 inches long).
- Outdoor nails or wood screws that won't rust
- Screwdriver and hammer if you are using nails
- Drill
- Drill bits: one ¼-in and one $\frac{7}{64}$-in. They don't have to be exactly this size, but something close.
- Hole saw attachment for drill (1½ inches for a birdhouse this size)
- Two 1½-in x 1-in middle hinges (should come with screws to attach the hinges)
- 1 gate hook and eye assembly (1-in assembly)
- Tape measure (or ruler)
- Two outdoor wood screws that will not rust, 2 inches long

Lesson 6

- Five eggs from the refrigerator
- A bright lamp with the shade removed
- A darkened room
- A large box or low table
- A pencil
- A bowl (It should be deeper than the height of an egg on its side.)
- Water

Lesson 7

- A sheet of notebook paper
- A square inch of paper or a math manipulative that is a square inch
- A blindfold
- 20 cotton balls
- 20 different agents with characteristic smells such as vanilla, toothpaste, dish soap, hand lotion, coffee, juice, vinegar, oils, and perfumes.

Lesson 8

- An old photo of a family member the students knows little about but someone else in the family knows a lot about
- A page of notebook paper
- Masking tape

- Strapping tape (the kind with reinforcing fibers)
- A shipping box made of corrugated cardboard
- A hardboiled egg
- A paper plate
- A piece of wax paper
- Clay or Play-doh®
- Plaster of Paris
- Water
- A paint brush
- A tea bag
- Hot water
- An old toothbrush (optional)

Lesson 9

- Two live insects (catch them from outside)
- Jar with holes in the lid
- A dead insect
- A bowl
- Water
- A spoon
- Salt
- Paper towels
- Magnifying glass
- A small plastic or glass aquarium with a lid (A plastic storage container with holes punched in the lid will work.)

Lesson 10

- Magnifying glass
- Cigar box or shoebox
- A rectangle of Styrofoam® that will fit in the box listed above
- Pins
- Dead insects you collect
- A wide-mouth jar
- Clean sand
- Liquid disinfectant (Lysol® a similar product or household cleaner)
- Cardboard
- Water
- Measuring cup
- Scissors
- Two soup cans
- Something to punch holes into the soup cans
- Fruit, meat, or other possible insect baits
- Cheesecloth

- ◆ A small board or boards that will cover the openings of both soup cans with room to spare

Lesson 11

- ◆ Two glass jars (One needs to be large enough to fit a soda pop can into. Ideally, the can should fit into the jar with just a little room to spare.)
- ◆ Jelly
- ◆ A soft drink can
- ◆ A piece of netting (or cheesecloth)
- ◆ Black construction paper
- ◆ Two rubber bands
- ◆ Sand (dirt or peat moss is fine)
- ◆ Paper plate
- ◆ A piece of sponge
- ◆ Bread and honey (to feed the ants)
- ◆ A few small plates

Lesson 12

- ◆ A banana
- ◆ A glass jar with a lid
- ◆ A small sewing needle
- ◆ Scissors
- ◆ A small square of tissue paper (or a square of toilet paper)
- ◆ A bowl of water
- ◆ A large funnel with a pretty large drain hole (It is best to cut off the top of a plastic, 2-liter soda pop bottle to make one of these.)
- ◆ A lamp with the shade removed (A bendable-necked desk lamp works best.)
- ◆ A clear glass jar in which the funnel rests comfortably
- ◆ A trowel or very large serving spoon
- ◆ A couple of containers in which to collect your dirt
- ◆ A set of measuring cups

Lesson 13

- ◆ A tall drinking glass
- ◆ A small spoon
- ◆ Water
- ◆ At least one cricket (You can either catch them yourself or buy them from a live bait or pet store.)
- ◆ Spray bottle of water

- ◆ Four different types of materials that you will test. Here are some suggestions: grass clippings, dried leaves, moss, bark mulch, pine shavings, a piece of a black plastic bag.
- ◆ A knife
- ◆ A shoebox or plastic box with a lid
- ◆ Sand
- ◆ A fresh potato

Lesson 14

- ◆ Caterpillars (You can either find them outside or order them from a supplier. Several suppliers are listed on the course website I discussed in the introduction to this book.)
- ◆ A potted plant that the caterpillar likes to eat
- ◆ Two coat hangers
- ◆ Tulle or netting (found at any fabric or craft store)
- ◆ Rubber band
- ◆ Sugar
- ◆ Water
- ◆ Clean lid from a jar
- ◆ Cotton balls

Exploring Creation With Zoology 1: Flying Creatures of the Fifth Day
Table of Contents

Lesson 1
What is Zoology?

Welcome to **zoology**! Did you know that you've actually done zoology before? When you examined an insect or watched a squirrel in your yard, you were, in fact, doing zoology, because zoology is the study of the animals that God made. All animals are included in zoology, even fleas, ants, and spiders. Some people don't realize that critters like these are animals, but they are!

Try to picture in your mind all the animals that God created. You could probably spend years trying to study every animal. Instead of trying to study all the animals in one book, then, we will focus on a special group of animals fashioned by God on the fifth day of creation: the flying creatures. Did you realize that the flying animals God created on the fifth day

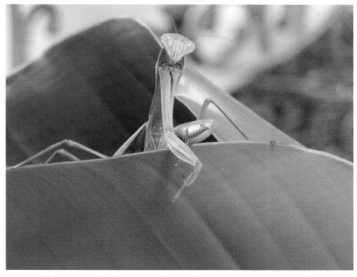

All insects (including this praying mantis) are animals.

included much more than just birds? The Bible was originally written in a language called **Hebrew**, and in Hebrew, the word used for the flying animals in Genesis is *owph*. The Hebrew word *owph* means "flying creatures." Read the Bible verse below:

> Then God said, "Let the waters teem with swarms of living creatures, and let birds fly above the earth in the open expanse of the heavens." God created the great sea monsters and every living creature that moves, with which the waters swarmed after their kind, and every winged bird after its kind; and God saw that it was good. God blessed them, saying, "Be fruitful and multiply, and fill the waters in the seas, and let birds multiply on the earth." There was evening and there was morning, a fifth day. (Genesis 1:20-23)

Even though this English translation of the Bible (New American Standard) refers to the flying creatures as "every winged bird," the original Hebrew simply says "flying creatures." So the Bible tells us that on the fifth day God made every flying creature, even insects and bats.

Are you wondering which animals, exactly, will be covered in this book? Our study of zoology begins with birds, then bats, then flying reptiles, and it ends with insects. It will be more fun if you can do the insect lessons in early fall, spring, or summer when insects are out and about; so feel free to read the insect lessons when it works best for you. Before you learn about specific types of animals, however, I want you to learn a little about a few general topics such as how zoologists organize the animals they study, how certain animals fly, where animals live, and that some animals go extinct. That's what I'm going to cover in this lesson.

Classification

Scientists who study animals are called **zoologists** (zoh awl' uh jists). They have a tough job, because there are a *lot* of animals in creation. In order to help them organize all of these animals, scientists put them into several groups based on how similar the animals are to one another. After they put animals in groups, they then name each animal. Do you remember one of the jobs that God gave Adam in the Garden of Eden? Adam had to name all the animals. Even today, people are still doing what Adam did. Whenever a new animal is discovered, it is put into several groups and then named. This process is called **taxonomy** (taks ahn' uh mee), and it is used to group and name all living things. The names they choose are not English "common" names, but Latin scientific names.

When scientists learn of a newly-discovered animal (there are new animals discovered every year, especially in the insect world), they study it to see how to classify, or group, it. If it has all the features of a butterfly, for example, it is put into the butterfly group, which is called **Lepidoptera** (lep uh dahp' tur uh). That's Latin for "scale wings." It gets even more specific than that, however. If it has tiny front legs, it's put in a special group of butterflies with tiny front legs. Then, if it also has orange coloration, it's placed with other butterflies having tiny front legs and similar colors. On and on it goes, so that the animal is put in smaller and smaller groups until all the butterflies in a group look almost exactly alike. That group is called a **species**, and it is the most specific grouping used when scientists classify animals.

Are you wondering why scientists do all of this grouping? There are many reasons, but one is because when you have animals divided into groups, it is easier to learn about them. If one species of butterfly lays eggs on a certain plant, maybe other similar species lay eggs on a similar plant. If you wanted to attract a certain species of butterfly, you would want to know what kind of food it eats. You might learn what food it eats by studying similar butterflies that are in the same group. In other words, it's easier to study animals when they are divided into groups based on their similarities. Since zoologists spend a lot of time classifying animals into groups, we need to learn about how they do this.

All animals are first put into one big group called the **Animal Kingdom**, or **Kingdom Animalia** (an' uh mahl' ee uh) in Latin. Then, each animal in the Animal Kingdom group is put into a smaller group, called a **phylum** (fye' lum), with other similar animals. That group is then given a scientific name. For example, all animals in the Animal Kingdom with a backbone (also called a "spine") are separated and placed into phylum **Chordata** (kor dah' tuh). Do you have a spine? Yes, you do. You can feel it if you run your fingers over the middle of your back. This means you are in phylum Chordata along with all creatures that have a spine. The easy way to remember this phylum name, Chordata, is to remember that inside of the spine is a special cord of nerves. That nerve cord is so important that if you were to injure it badly, you might never be able to move your arms and legs. No wonder God put it inside the bones in your spine. That cord really must be protected!

Animals that have backbones are often called **vertebrates** (vur' tuh brayts), and animals without backbones (like insects) are called **invertebrates** (in vur' tuh brates). It turns out that there are *a lot* more invertebrates than vertebrates in the Animal Kingdom. Because of this, all vertebrates can be fit into one phylum, but there are so many invertebrates that they must be put in several phyla (plural of phylum). Look at the diagram below. **Arthropoda** (are thruh' pah duh) is one phylum of animals that don't have a backbone. Crabs, lobsters, spiders, and insects are in this phylum. Another phylum that contains animals without a backbone is phylum **Annelida** (an uh lee' duh). Earthworms are put in this phylum. There are other phyla of invertebrates, but I don't want to go into them now.

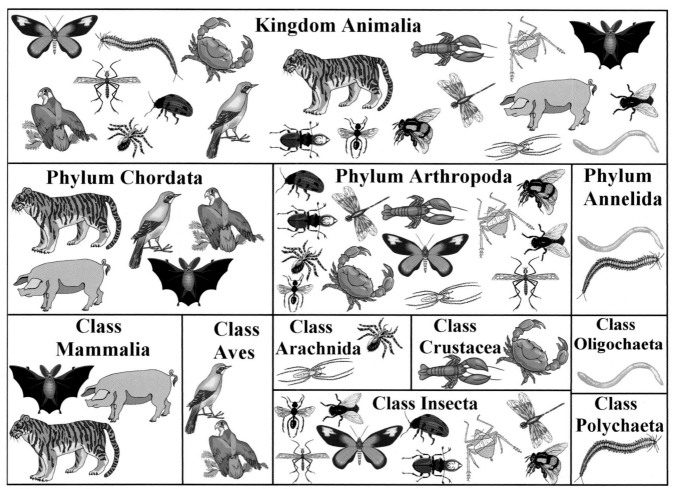

This drawing illustrates part of the process of classification. The creatures in the top box are all in the Animal Kingdom. They are then grouped into phyla based on their similarities. Then, they are grouped into classes. This is only a partial illustration, as there are many more groups, ending in species, which is the smallest of all the groups.

After being divided into phyla, the animals in each phylum are further divided into groups called **classes**. For example, birds are put in their own class, called **Aves** (aye' veez). Animals that have fur, give birth to babies, and nurse their babies with mother's milk are put into a class called

Mammalia (muh mail' ee uh). Each class is further divided into **orders**, so birds in class Aves are divided into orders based on the special characteristics of each bird. Birds of prey that have a hooked beak, like falcons, are in the order Falconiformes (fal' kuhn uh for' meez); birds that sing are in the order Passeriformes (pass' er uh for' meez); and birds that look like pelicans are in the order Pelecaniformes (pel ih kahn' uh for' meez).

Of course, this happens with all phyla. The creatures in phylum Arthropoda, for example, are further divided into classes like **Insecta** (arthropods with similar features, such as six legs) or **Arachnida** (uh rak' nih duh – arthropods with similar features, such as eight legs). These classes are also further broken down into orders. Can you believe that we are not done yet?

Scientists divide the animals in each order into groups called **families**. For example, in order Falconiformes, we have hawks, eagles, falcons, and other birds of prey. Well, hawks and eagles are in one family because they are pretty similar, while falcons are put in another family. After animals are divided into families, they are then each put in a group called a **genus** (jee' nus). Hawks and eagles are in the same family, but they are each put into their own genus.

These two birds are very similar and therefore belong to the same genus (Falco). However, they cannot mate and have babies, so they belong to different species.

Finally, scientists divide the animals in a genus into different **species**. For example, the picture to the right shows two falcons. Because they are so similar, they both belong in genus *Falco*. However, they are not similar enough to be in the same species. As a result, they each belong to separate species. The important thing to remember about animals in the same species is that a male and female from the same species can mate and have babies. Even though the two falcons in the picture have a lot of things in common, they cannot mate with one another, so they belong in different species.

Latin

You might have noticed that the names for many of the classification groups are long and hard to pronounce. That's because a lot of them come from a language called Latin. Why do scientists use Latin? Well, Latin is a language that no one speaks but many people learn. Therefore, it never changes. English, on the other hand, changes all the time. Several years ago, the word "cool" was only used to describe the temperature. Now, "cool" also means "neat," or "great." The word "neat" once meant "tidy and clean." Now the word "neat" also means "great."

Latin is helpful to scientists because the Latin words they use to name things do not change. So scientists all over the world can work together to try to understand nature even though the scientists may not all speak the same language. For example, a butterfly that we call the "mourning cloak" is called the "Camberwell beauty" in England, and in Germany it is called the "trauermantel." Its scientific name, however, is *Nymphalis antiopa* (nihm' fuh lus an tee oh' puh). Since this name comes from Latin, it doesn't change from country to country. Scientists from every country will know what butterfly is being discussed if it is called by its scientific name.

Binomial Nomenclature

Did you notice that the butterfly I talked about had two names? It turns out that all animals have two names, because when a scientist talks about an animal, he uses the animal's genus and species to name it. This helps scientists know the classification, because by just seeing an animal's name, you know what genus and species it is in. The butterfly I was talking about above, then, is in genus *Nymphalis* and species *antiopa*. Notice that its name is written in italics and that the genus name is capitalized but the species name is not. This is the way all scientists write the scientific names of animals. This two-name system is called **binomial nomenclature** (bye no' mee ul no' mun klay chur).

Try This!

To help you remember the system of classification that scientists use, you can remember this sentence: "**K**ings **P**lay **C**hess **O**n **F**ine **G**lass **S**ets." That's a mnemonic (nih mahn' ik) phrase. It helps you remember the order of classification groups because the first letter in each word is the same as the first letter of each classification group from the largest to the smallest: **K**ingdom, **P**hylum, **C**lass, **O**rder, **F**amily, **G**enus, and **S**pecies.

Can you make your own mnemonic phrase to help you remember the order of the classification system? You will want to make a sentence that makes sense to you and will be easy to remember. The sentence must have seven words that start with the letters given in the diagram below:

Kingdom	Phylum	Class	Order	Family	Genus	Species
K	P	C	O	F	G	S

If you have an animal field guide (or a set of encyclopedias), look up some animals that you already know. Look at the Latin name for each animal and try to pronounce it. Notice that it is written in italics and that the first word (the genus) is capitalized but the second word (the species) is not.

Explain what you have learned about taxonomy and binomial nomenclature.

Flight

Five days after God said let there be light, there were handsome creatures speckling the sky with their majesty and declaring the glory of God with their amazing ability to fly. Today, these creatures remind us how wonderful God is to have made such beautiful, astonishing animals.

We see birds, bats, and insects flying, gliding, soaring, and sailing through the air with ease. How do they do it? How come we can't just flap our arms really fast and join them in the air? Well, God designed these creatures with wings, which we don't have, and a very key ingredient for flight is the *shape* of those wings. The shape of its wings is what gives a creature the ability to lift off the ground. Have you ever heard the terms **lift** and **drag**? These are flight terms which explain why a bird can fly with its wings and why we can't fly with our arms. I will explain these terms in a way that will help you understand what they mean, but you will really have to listen closely.

Long ago, in the 1700s, a man named Daniel Bernoulli (bur new' lee) did some experiments with objects under water. Those experiments help us understand how things fly. You might be asking yourself what water has to do with lifting things up into the air. Well, you are going to learn about one of God's invisible creations and how He made the air so that birds could fly. Air, just like water, applies pressure on everything it touches. This is because air is not just empty space like it appears to our eyes; it actually weighs something, just like water. Air really has a lot of stuff in it; microscopic stuff that is in the air all around you. So, when you walk through the air, the stuff in the air is actually pressing against you. Of course, it's a lot easier to walk through air than to walk through water because water is much heavier than the stuff in the air. Nevertheless, walking through air is just like walking through a swimming pool, only easier.

Uplifting Pressure

So the air all around you presses upon you. It doesn't press on you as much as something heavier like water in a swimming pool, but it does press upon you even though you can't feel it. The pressing of air against you is called **air pressure**. If there is a lot of air pressure, the air is pressing hard. If there is only a little air pressure, the air isn't pressing as hard.

Well, Daniel Bernoulli (the scientist I mentioned before) discovered that when he made water move quickly against things that were in shape of a bird wing (this shape is called an **airfoil**), the water moved differently on top of the wing compared to the bottom of the wing. As the water moved along the top of the wing, it actually sped up, which caused it to push with less pressure. The water that moved along the bottom of the wing did not speed up, so it pushed on the wing with the same pressure as always. So the water on the bottom of the wing pushed up more strongly than the water on top of the wing pushed down. What happens if you push up on something more strongly than you push down on it? It rises, doesn't it?

The same thing happens with air and a bird's wing. Faster-moving air on top of a bird's wing pushes down on the wing with low pressure, and the slower-moving air on the bottom of the wing pushes up with higher pressure. As a result, the air pushes the wing up harder than it pushes the wing down. This causes the wing to rise. In other words, it *lifts* the wing. Because of this, scientists say that the difference in air pressure on a wing provides *lift* for the wing.

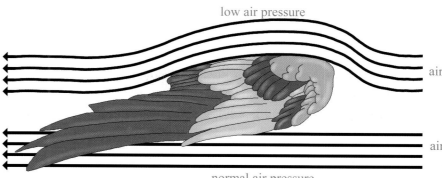

When air flows across a bird's wing, the air that travels above the wing moves more quickly than the air that travels below the wing. This causes more pressure on the bottom of the wing than on the top, which lifts the wing, making the bird fly.

Try This!

Here is a fun experiment that shows you how air pressure works. You will need a cup completely full of water, two straws, and scissors. Put one straw in the water and cut it so that it sticks

out of the water by only about ½ inch. Now, put the cup with the straw in it next to the edge of a counter or table, and squat down so your eyes are level with the cup. Using your fingers to hold the small straw next to the edge of the cup, blow through the other straw at an angle towards the top of the straw in the cup. Angle the straw upwards so that the air coming out of it passes right over the top of the straw in the cup. Keep blowing and blowing. This will make the air move faster over the top of the straw in the water. As a result, the air pressure above the straw in the water will decrease, and when there is less air pressure above the straw, what do you think will happen? Try it and see.

Did a stream of water squirt out the straw that was in the cup? It should have, if you blew at the right angle. Be sure you weren't trying to blow on the water in the cup; blow only on the tip of the straw in the cup. Keep trying until it works. What explains this result? Well, when you blew air over the top of the straw, the moving air could not press down as hard on the water in the straw. The air over the rest of the water in the cup was not moving, so it continued to press down on the water with its full pressure. Since the water in the cup was being pressed down harder than the water in the straw, water was forced up and out of the straw! This is a lot like what happens to a bird's wing. Just as the difference in air pressure over the straw and the rest of the cup lifted water out of the straw, the difference in air pressure between the top and bottom of a bird's wing lifts the wing into the air.

Airfoil

Let's talk more about the shape of a bird's wing so you can understand how God created the wing and the air to work together. Look at the diagram of the bird's wing on the previous page. The shape of the bird's wing is why it experiences lift. As the bird's wing (with its airfoil shape) moves through the air, some air goes above and some air goes below the wing. Because the wing is curved, the air moving over the top of the wing has to go farther than the air moving underneath the wing. In order for the two air flows (the one going below and the one going above) to make it to the end of the wing at the same time, the air on top of the wing must move faster because it has a longer way to go.

As your experiment showed, fast-moving air cannot exert as much pressure as slow-moving air. That pressure difference on a wing lifts the wing (and the whole bird) into the air. As the bird speeds up, the air travels over the wing even faster. As the air travels faster and faster over the wing, less and less pressure is placed upon the top part of the wing. This gives the wing more and more lift, causing the bird to go higher and higher. That is why birds flap their wings – to move faster so that the air travels faster over their wings. Speed is very important in making lift. When a bird flaps its wings, the wings provide a force that makes the bird go faster. Scientists call this force **thrust**. The more thrust that the wings give the bird, the faster the bird goes, and the greater the lift on its wings.

What a Drag

Although the speed of the air over an airfoil gives lift, staying in the air is difficult because there is another force that tends to slow a flying creature or object. That force is called **drag**. Drag resists or pushes against an animal or object as it travels through the air. You have probably felt this drag when you ran against the wind on a very windy day. If you were shaped like a knife, it would be easier for you to run through the windy air, because the air would not drag against you as strongly while you ran. When something can travel through the air without a lot of drag, we say that it has an

Even if it had wings, a pig could not fly. This is partly due to the fact that it doesn't have an aerodynamic shape.

aerodynamic (air' oh dye nam' ik) shape. The reason an airplane isn't shaped like a chair is because it wouldn't be very aerodynamic. It would experience a lot of drag as it traveled through the air. This same thing is true for submarines that travel through water. Even swimmers want to reduce drag; they make themselves as smooth as possible by wearing swim caps and shaving their legs.

A bird is not shaped like a pig, and a bat is not shaped like a dog. There is a reason for this. God created each flying creature with a body shape that is aerodynamic. Even the long-legged storks and other water birds can trail their legs behind them in such as way as to make themselves aerodynamic.

Explain in your own words what you have learned about lift, thrust, and drag.

Mid-Lesson Break
Your Notebook

Today you will begin a very important notebook in which you will put your own creations, illustrations, images, and artifacts you collect concerning zoology. You will always want to do your best work for your notebook, because it will contain information and data that you will want to keep for the rest of your school years. When you are in high school and want to remember how an experiment turned out and what materials you used, you will check this notebook. When you want to remember something specific you learned about birds, bats, insects, or pterosaurs, you will also check this notebook. Use your best handwriting, and always record as much information as possible. In science, you can never have too much information.

At the end of every reading segment, write down what you learned that day. Speaking it out loud is also helpful, so if you are not yet able to write quickly, you can dictate it to your parent or teacher to write it down for you. In this way, you can make your own zoology book that contains your own knowledge!

You can also put pictures of projects you did in your notebook, or you can record the extra things your family did to enhance your learning, such as going on a field trip or a nature walk. You can add anything you want to your notebook – pictures of flying creatures, feathers (though there are laws about what kinds of feathers you can collect), or insect parts you find out in nature that would lay flat and fit inside your notebook. Remember the mnemonic you did earlier in this lesson? You should put that in your notebook.

Every experiment you do will need to be recorded. You can make copies of the Scientific Speculation Sheet found at the beginning of the book (page iv) to record all your data. Keep this in your notebook as well.

After you have put your classification mnemonic in your notebook, write down what you learned today about classification and flight. Be sure to include a drawing to explain how a wing gets lift, such as the one on page 7.

Optional exercise for older students: Use the library or internet to learn about Carolus (sometimes called "Carl") Linnaeus. He is considered the founder of the classification system you learned about in this lesson. The course website I mentioned in the introduction to this book has some links to information about this very interesting Christian man.

Mid-Lesson Experiment
Experimenting With Glider Design

To better understand how lift works, you will conduct an experiment with two gliders that you will build out of cardboard, straws, clay, and tape. You will make two gliders that are exactly alike except for the size of the wing. One will have a shorter, wider wing; one will have a longer, narrower wing. Based on the knowledge you have about flight, you will make guesses about which glider you expect will fly farther.

Every science experiment has what we call **variables**, which are things that change in the experiment. A good science experiment will have only one variable, so that anything different that happens during the experiment can be assumed to be the result of that one variable. The variable in this experiment will be the size of the glider's wings. We want that to be the *only* variable. As a result, we need to make sure that everything else is the same. The size of the two gliders, for example, must be exactly the same. The way you cut and build each glider must be done in exactly the same way. Both gliders must be made from the same material. Where you test the flying of your gliders must be exactly alike; don't test one in the living room and one in the garage. The reason all these things must be kept the same is because we want to know the effect that wing size has on the distance a glider flies. If other things are different besides the wings, one of those factors may be what makes one of the gliders go farther. To make sure that any difference between the flights of the gliders is due only to the wing size, everything else between the gliders must be the same. This is how you conduct a real scientific experiment.

You also need an accurate way to measure your data. Measuring is an important element for many science experiments. How will you measure which glider flies farther? You can measure how far it goes before it lands. You will need a good place to fly them, as well as an accurate way to measure how far they went. A tape measure that can stretch out would be a good indicator. You could also have the same person measure the distance by putting one foot in front of the other over the entire distance of the glider's flight. It needs to be the same person each time. Why do you think that is?

Another key to getting accurate results in an experiment is repeating the experiment enough times to make sure your results are consistent. You need to throw the gliders over and over, measuring again and again to find out if you get the same results most of the time. If the experiment is done only once, it may have been affected by factors that you didn't think of, such as how you threw it, the wind direction at the time, or other things that you didn't consider. All scientists forget to consider a few things here and there, and repeating an experiment over and over again will help make these forgotten factors less important.

Every experiment begins with a hypothesis, or a guess. You need to guess which wing design (a short, wide wing or a long, narrow wing) will enable your glider to fly the farthest. Record your guess on a Scientific Speculation Sheet. Now it is time to perform the experiment and see whether or not your guess is right!

You will need:

♦ The Scientific Speculation Sheet (with your hypothesis recorded)
♦ Pen
♦ Cardboard box (A pizza box or cereal box works well.)
♦ Straws (You could use paint stirrers which are given away at hardware stores instead.)
♦ Clay (two small chunks about the size of grapes – both exactly the same size)
♦ Scissors
♦ Tape
♦ Tape measure (or some other device for measuring distance, like a yardstick or someone's feet)

1. Cut two rectangles for the wings: one long and thin (perhaps 1 inch by 8 inches) and the other short and wide (perhaps 2 inches by 4 inches).
2. Cut two smaller rectangles of exactly the same size (one inch by two inches) for the glider's tails. You can color or decorate them if you wish, as long as they are exactly the same.
3. Use tape to attach the tails to the end of each straw in the exactly the same place. Be certain to center the tail on the straw so that it will be balanced.
4. Attach each wing about 2 inches from the front of the each straw. Again, be certain you have the straw right in the middle of the wing so that it is balanced. You may need to use a tape measure to see where the middle is on each wing and tail.
5. Place a small clump of clay on the front of each straw to balance out the weight. This will help your airplane to sail farther as well.
6. If possible, choose a place outside to test your gliders.
7. Throw one of the gliders and measure the distance it travels. Record the result on the Scientific Speculation Sheet.

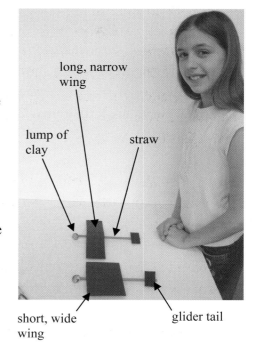

long, narrow wing

lump of clay

straw

short, wide wing

glider tail

8. Throw the other glider, trying to do everything exactly the same as you did with the first glider. Once again, measure the distance it travels and record the result on the Scientific Speculation Sheet.

9. Repeat steps 7 and 8 at least ten times, recording each distance on the Scientific Speculation Sheet.

10. Now you need to **average** the results you have for each glider. When you average the results of several different experiments, you are hoping that any variables you couldn't keep the same will cancel each other out. For example, suppose the wind was blowing one way during one of your throws and another way during another throw. This would affect the distance that the glider traveled, but hopefully, if the wind caused the glider to travel farther while it was blowing one direction, it would cause the glider to travel shorter when it was blowing in the other direction. In the end, averaging the results of the throws will hopefully get rid of the wind's effects. To average the results, add them all together and divide by the number of times that you threw the glider. For example, suppose I threw a glider 10 times and got the following results: 12 feet, 13 feet, 11 feet, 9 feet, 10 feet, 11 feet, 12 feet, 13 feet, 10 feet, and 9 feet. I would average them by adding them all together: $12 + 13 + 11 + 9 + 10 + 11 + 12 + 13 + 10 + 9 = 110$. Then, I would divide 110 by 10 to get 11 feet. This means that on average, the glider traveled 11 feet.

11. Write the average for each glider on the Scientific Speculation Sheet and compare the two. The glider with the larger average had the wing design that allowed for the longest travel in the air. Was your hypothesis correct?

12. On your Scientific Speculation Sheet, write down the materials you used to make the gliders, the procedure you used to test how well they flew, and what you learned about the best wing design for a glider.

Were you surprised by your experimental results? In general, a long, narrow wing will allow a glider to travel farther than a short, wide wing. This is mostly due to drag. The ends of a wing experience a lot of drag due to the way air travels around them. The longer and narrower the wing, the less the drag, so the farther the glider can travel.

Habitats

Many penguins live in Antarctica, where it is cold. They have been designed to live well in such a habitat.

God's amazing creation is filled with many places that are very different from one another. Some places (like the southern parts of Florida) stay warm all year, while others (like Antarctica) stay cold most of the time. As you probably already know, some kinds of animals prefer a certain part of the earth over other parts of the earth. Penguins, for example, are usually found in colder places, like Antarctica. We call the places animals live **habitats**. I'm sure you have heard that word before. When we keep an animal in a container of some kind, we try to make it as close to its natural habitat as possible. We even call the place we keep the animal its habitat.

God gave each animal special features that help it survive in its habitat. A bird that lives near the ocean, eating creatures found under the water, has feet that can walk on sand or swim in the water. Animals that live in grasslands often are not very colorful so that they are not easily seen and eaten by other animals. God created each animal in the special way that would be best for its habitat. Parrots are brightly colored, matching the fruit that grows on the trees in the forest where they live. Bats are usually darkly colored and hard to see in the dark caves where they dwell. Even the eggs of birds are often perfectly colored for their habitat. Some animals actually blend in so

Do you see the lizard in this picture? He is hard to see because he blends in with his surroundings. In other words, he is camouflaged. If you can't find the lizard in this picture, visit the course website.

well that they are amazingly hard to see. We say that they are **camouflaged** (kam' uh flahjd). This helps them hide from other animals that want to eat them.

Oftentimes, people will change the habitat that an animal prefers, making paved roads, parking lots, and buildings. When this happens, animals will either move to another place that is more natural

These are bird nests in the letters of a large sign that is on the outside of a local library.

or try to adjust to the changes that have been made. If you drive around the city, you will see birds that once made nests in cliff walls or trees. They now build their nests in the large letters of signs. As another example, Purple Martins[*] naturally nest in holes they find in trees or rocks. People like to hear them sing, however, so they began making birdhouses to attract them. Purple Martins adapted to these new homes, and now most will only nest in birdhouses that people build for them.

As a general rule, you will find a greater variety of animals in a more natural habitat, such as a park or forest area. If you leave a segment of your backyard to nature, not mowing or spraying it with pesticides, you will find that more birds and interesting insects will make your yard their home or visit it frequently. This is because you are providing them with water, food, and shelter, and that's really all an animal needs in its habitat!

[*]Please see the note about bird names at the bottom of page 20.

Instinct

"Is it by your understanding that the hawk soars, stretching his wings toward the south?" -Job 39:26

All of God's creatures have been given a special gift called **instinct** (in' stingkt). Instinct is a built in need to do something for survival. It's not something a creature thinks about; it's just something the creature does automatically. A baby bird automatically throws its head back, opens its mouth wide, and hollers for food. It is an instinct. Mother cats instinctively wrestle and bite their kittens, teaching them how to fight. Baby bats automatically cling to the cave wall. Birds begin building nests in the spring, even before there are eggs to put in them. Many birds automatically fly towards special places where birds of their kind congregate to have their young. Grasshoppers naturally spit out the contents of their stomach on predators that try to eat them. Emerald moths naturally chew off bits of flowers and stick them to their bodies in order to camouflage themselves. Bees naturally work to take care of the hive and make honey. Butterflies naturally "know" which plant their young need

This butterfly (*Agraulis vanillae*) knows by instinct that its young will want to eat the plant on which it is laying its eggs.

to eat, and that's where they lay their eggs. Birds, bats, and insects are given many instincts, and they follow their instincts without even thinking about it. We will study many such instincts in this book.

Instincts are evidence that there is a God who created the world around us. They point to an Intelligent Designer who gives animals the ability to do smart things that will help them to survive. If animals with very limited intelligence can do very intelligent things that keep them alive and well, there must be an Intelligent Designer who gave them such an ability.

The Bible says that man can choose to do what is right or what is wrong. This is a gift God gives to no other creature – the ability to choose how to behave. When we choose to follow God and live for Him, He will lead us and guide us, helping us to make the right decisions for our lives. Animals aren't given this option, because animals aren't made in the image of God. Therefore, they must be given automatic "instructions" that they can follow in order to survive. Those instructions are the instincts that God gave them. Those instincts demonstrate that God takes care of His creation, including the animals.

Extinction

Have you ever heard that some animals are **extinct**? This is very true. We live in a world that is damaged by sin. And because of this sin, the beautiful world that God made, the world that He declared excellent, is not as good as it once was. The result is that people and animals die. Animals become extinct when every single one dies out and there are no longer any of them living on earth. We know of these animals either because they were photographed or described in books before they all died out or we find their preserved remains in the ground. The preserved remains of creatures that were once alive are called **fossils**.

Many animals have become extinct throughout the history of the world. We have recorded a few, but there are many more that have not been recorded. It is a sad thing when this happens, but it is part of living in a world that is captive to sin. One day, there will no longer be any death or destruction. The Bible talks about animals that will live on the earth during that time. Perhaps when God brings down the new heaven and the new earth, animals that were once extinct will be on the new earth.

How does an animal become extinct? There are many ways this can happen. Sometimes, a change in its habitat will cause an animal to die. These changes could be an environmental change like a drought (a long time with no rain) or a long time of cold weather. They could also be the result of a catastrophe like the worldwide flood described in Genesis. Many kinds of animals became extinct after the flood because the conditions of the earth after the flood were not as warm and friendly as they had been before. Many species did not survive the new harsh climates, and we only know about them because we have found their fossils.

This is a drawing of Passenger Pigeons. They are now extinct because people hunted them until there were no more left.

Some animals die out because people hunt them or destroy their habitats. The **Passenger Pigeon**, for example, was a common pigeon that traveled in huge numbers. Scientists believe that at one time there were more Passenger Pigeons than any other type of bird on the earth. They estimate that in the 1800s, there were over two billion of these birds. When traveling from one place to another, they flew in huge flocks that were up to a mile wide and *300 miles long*! When these flocks passed over an area, the sky would be covered with birds, darkening the sun.

That's a lot of birds, and they ate *a lot* of food. When they descended on a place to eat, they would gobble up all the seeds in sight. They were shot and killed by the millions each year. Pigeon hunting was very profitable, because back then people ate pigeons the way we eat chicken today. These pigeons, which only laid one egg per year, soon began to die out. The last wild one was shot in 1900 by a 14-year-old boy who had it stuffed. It is now in a museum.

The **Dodo Bird** also went extinct. We know about this bird because when sailors found this flightless bird on an island in the Indian Ocean, they wrote about how strange it was. It would come right up to the sailors, as friendly as could be. The sailors named it the Dodo Bird because they thought it wasn't very smart for being so friendly. They were mighty hungry for meat after traveling the open seas, and they would kill these friendly birds so they could eat their meat. The Dodo Bird also laid its eggs on the ground, which was fine until people brought pigs, monkeys, dogs, and rats to the island. These animals were not a natural part of the island habitat, and they either ate or crushed the Dodo Bird eggs. Within eighty years of its discovery, the Dodo Bird was extinct.

This is a drawing of a dodo bird, which is now extinct.

Animals that are dying out and might become extinct are called **endangered species**. These days, people try to protect endangered species so that they won't go extinct. At one time, the **Trumpeter Swan** was an endangered species. There were once millions throughout North America, but Native Americans and European settlers hunted them for their beautiful feathers and good meat. By the 1900s, there were only a few left on the earth. The United States government made it illegal to hunt them, and people helped them by placing eggs from swans in the zoo into the nests of those in the wild. Soon, the population grew back and they are no longer endangered.

Bald Eagles, once an endangered species, are now thriving.

The Bald Eagle has a similar story. There were once Bald Eagles all over North America. No one is certain why they began to die out. Some believe that it is because the settlers competed with them for the same food. Some believe it is because they were killed by salmon fishermen who didn't want the birds eating the salmon they were trying to catch. Some believe they didn't have enough areas to nest in once people moved in. This is unlikely, since they nest on cliffs and in high trees. Whatever the cause, in the 1960s, there were only a few hundred in the entire world. To protect them, the U.S. government made it illegal to kill them or destroy their nests. If you find that you have an eagle's nest on your property, you are not allowed to disturb it in any way. Even if you were planning to build a house right next to it, you are not allowed to, no matter how much money you paid for the land. Such laws helped the Bald Eagle population to recover and increase. Now there are thousands of Bald Eagles in North America again. Do you have any living near you?

Have you read any books about **dinosaurs** (dye' nuh sawrz)? What about flying reptiles like the **pterosaurs** (tair' uh sawrz)? The pterosaurs and other flying reptiles were created on the fifth day, just like all the other flying animals. We will study them a bit later in this book. They and the dinosaurs are now extinct. We know that they lived on earth at one time because we find their fossils. However, we cannot find any living dinosaurs or pterosaurs today. There are many different ideas about what caused them to go extinct, but the most likely reason is that they died out because of changes to the earth that were caused by the worldwide flood that is discussed in the Bible. Although Noah's ark probably had young dinosaurs from each kind on it (there was plenty of room for them), many creation scientists believe they couldn't handle the new climate that the earth most likely experienced after the flood. As a result, they probably died out.

Extinction Errors

Usually, scientists say they believe an animal is extinct when no one has seen it for a while. When this happens, scientists often begin an expedition to see if they can find the animal in its natural habitat or where the last living one was seen. If they are unable to find the animal after years of searching, they consider it extinct. Sometimes, however, a supposedly extinct animal will turn up again in a different place. For example, the **Blackburn's sphinx moth** (*Manduca blackburni*) was thought to be extinct, because it could not be found in any of its normal habitats. However, in 1984, a small population of this moth was found on a Hawaiian island.

The **Miami blue butterfly** (*Hemiargus thomasi*) is another example of an extinction error. Everyone thought that this butterfly became extinct after Hurricane Andrew wiped out the last known group of the butterflies. In 1999, however, a person interested in butterflies found a whole colony of them in the Florida Keys.

The **Takahe** (tuh kah' ee) was also once thought to be extinct. This bird (its scientific name is *Notornis mantelli*) once thrived in New Zealand. However, in the 1800s, settlers brought red deer to New Zealand, and the deer began eating the grass that was the Takahe's main food source. Also, weasels were brought in to try to control the rat population, and the weasels began eating Takahe eggs. By 1900, it was thought that the Takahe population had been wiped out. However, nearly fifty years later, someone found a group of them living in the valleys of the Murchison mountains in New Zealand. Maybe you will one day rediscover a bird or insect that is currently thought to be extinct!

This is a photo of a Takahe, which was once thought to be extinct.

What Do You Remember?

Explain what you learned about animals and habitats. What is instinct? Can you think of any animal instincts? Explain what you learned about extinction. What is one reason the dinosaurs may have become extinct?

Notebook Activities

In your notebook or your *Zoology 1 Notebooking Journal*, write down all the fascinating facts that you remember about habitats, instinct, and extinction. You may also want to include some illustrations.

Older Students: Scientists often classify animal habitats just like they classify the animals themselves. The largest category in habitat classification is called a **biome** (bye' ohm). Most scientists recognize five basics kinds of biomes on earth. Conduct some research to learn about these five kinds of biomes, their environment, and the animal life found in each. The course website I mentioned in the introduction to this book has links to information on these biomes. After you have done this, record what you learned in your notebook. The *Zoology 1 Notebooking Journal* includes a page for you to complete this activity.

Make a Field Notebook

You are going to make a notebook for when you are outdoors studying nature. You will draw and write down your observations about the wildlife you see. This notebook needs to be lightweight and small enough to fold and put in your pocket. You can buy nature journals, but making one is a simple process, and when you use all the pages, you can just make a new one.

You will need:

- Several sheets of plain white paper
- One sheet of thicker, colored paper (such as construction paper) or a thick decorative paper like you would find in a scrapbook store
- A long-arm stapler (If you don't have one, you can go to an office supply store or copy center and use theirs. They might charge you a small fee, but most places allow you to use it for free.)

Instructions:

1. Put the plain white sheets of paper into a pile.
2. Place the thicker, colored paper on the bottom of the pile.
3. Make a neat pile out of all of the papers, and turn it over so that the colored page is now on top.

4. Once again, make the pile neat.
5. Use a long-arm stapler to staple the pages together right in the middle. Put one staple close to the bottom, another near the middle, and another near the top.
6. Fold the papers right along the staples.
7. Now you have a field notebook that you can carry with you whenever you are outside!

Project
Nature Scavenger Hunt

Nature walks are wonderful and fun. The more often you do it, the more you will enjoy it. You will also begin to notice things you've never noticed before. The more you learn about nature in this book, the more you will know what to look for when you are outdoors.

Today, you will plan an outdoor adventure somewhere that has a natural environment. Parks that allow foliage to grow, fields, or forests are perfect. Be certain the place you choose is not private property. Parks, public land, or nature preserves are best. Read the Scavenger Hunt List on the next page; it lists things that I want you to find. You will probably not be able to find *all* the things on this list. In fact, it would be very unusual for everything to be in one habitat. However, you will use this list whenever you go out on nature walks. Each time, you will look for the things on this list. If you have the *Zoology 1 Notebooking Journal*, a page with the Scavenger Hunt List is included. If you do not have the notebooking journal, you may want to print the Scavenger Hunt List on the next page and staple it into your field notebook so that you always have it while you are out studying nature.

Scavenger Hunt List

☐ Three feathers found on the ground (To keep any feather, it must be from a game bird like a duck, goose, pheasant, chicken, dove, etc. Many other birds are protected as endangered species, and it is illegal to keep their feathers.)
☐ A bird with red coloring on it
☐ A bird with blue coloring on it
☐ A bird's nest (Do not take it home.)
☐ A hole in a tree high above the ground
☐ A bird soaring through the air
☐ A flock of birds
☐ A beetle
☐ An ant hill
☐ A bumblebee
☐ A butterfly with yellow colors
☐ A butterfly with brown colors
☐ A butterfly with orange colors
☐ A butterfly that is mostly white
☐ A caterpillar (This is the young version of a moth or butterfly.)
☐ A bird egg shell on the ground (best found in spring or early summer)
☐ A type of bird (other than a duck or goose) that is using water in some way
☐ A bat flying through the sky (Look for bats in the evening around dusk.)
☐ The sound of a bird singing (See if you can find it by following its sound.)
☐ The sound of a woodpecker drumming
☐ A grasshopper that has wings and can fly (best found in late summer)
☐ A bird carrying food or nesting material
☐ A praying mantis or one of its egg cases
☐ The cocoon of a moth or the chrysalis of a butterfly
☐ An insect or cocoon wrapped inside a leaf
☐ A dragonfly
☐ A Japanese beetle or June beetle
☐ A leaf with eggs laid on the underside
☐ A leaf with eggs laid on the upper side
☐ A gall (an unusual growth) on a leaf or a plant (oak leaves and branches commonly have them)

For those of you living in Arizona or other desert regions, a different scavenger hunt is available on the course website that I mentioned in the introduction to this book.

A Note about Bird Names

As you go through this course, you will find the names of many different species of birds. Interestingly enough, those who study birds (ornithologists) do not follow the rules that other biologists follow when it comes to the *common* (non scientific) names of bird species. In all other areas of biology, the common name of a species is not capitalized unless it contains a proper noun. Thus, "moon snail" is not capitalized, but the first word of "African elephant" is capitalized. In ornithology, however, common species names *are* capitalized. In this book, then, you will find the common species names for birds capitalized, but the common species names for all other creatures not capitalized. Of course, even ornithologists follow the rules for binomial (scientific) names, capitalizing the genus name and not capitalizing the species name.

Lesson 2
What Makes a Bird a Bird?

Everywhere you go on this big, beautiful earth, you see birds. You see them in the sky, in the trees, even out at sea. This makes studying birds easy and fun. If you don't have many birds in your yard right now, you will soon. In this book, we will do projects that will attract birds for you to study. You will see how easy it is to make your yard a bird paradise. You will also keep a bird journal and record all the birds that visit your yard. It will be exciting for you as you come to know which birds are regulars to your yard and which birds are just visitors on their way through town. You may even get to know your regular visitors so well that you can give them names!

So what makes a bird a bird? Could it be the beak? All birds have beaks, but a duck-billed platypus, which is not a bird, has a beak. The octopus and the squid also have beaks, so it's not the beak that makes a bird a bird. We also know that it isn't that they fly, because other creatures, like insects, also fly. In addition, some birds, like

The duck-billed platypus has a beak (called a "bill"), but it is not a bird. It is a mammal.

ostriches, don't fly. If you haven't already guessed yet, the thing that makes a bird a bird is its **feathers**. Every bird has feathers, but no other type of animal does.

Birds are vertebrates. We learned about vertebrates and invertebrates in Lesson 1. Do you remember what it means to be a vertebrate? All vertebrates have backbones, or spines. Since birds have backbones, they are vertebrates, which makes them a part of phylum **Chordata**.

Birds make up a special group of vertebrates that belong in class **Aves**. Aves is a Greek word that means "bird." All birds, like bats and other mammals, are **warm-blooded**. This means God gave their bodies the ability to keep a steady body temperature (a pretty warm temperature) even if the air around them is freezing. Not all animals are warm-blooded. In fact, there are a lot more cold-blooded animals than there are warm-blooded animals. If an animal is cold blooded, its body temperature changes depending on the temperature outside. The only way it can only control its body temperature is to move to a place that is warmer or cooler, depending on its needs.

The magnificent feathers of a peacock tell you that it is a bird.

Bird Watching

Many people, young and old, rich and poor, are enthusiastic bird watchers. In fact, there are huge organizations that are completely devoted to bird watching or the study of birds. Anyone, even you, can be a member. These organizations are important because we don't know everything there is to know about birds. There is still so much to learn about where birds live, when birds come and go, what birds do and do not eat, what makes birds sick, and what keeps birds healthy. Bird organizations rely on their members to keep them informed about the birds they see. Often, fascinating and important discoveries are made by people just like you, who began to be interested in the birds in their area and noticed something interesting to report to their bird organization. You can even begin reporting the birds you see in your backyard today! There are many different programs like eBirds, the Great Backyard Bird Count, the Christmas Bird Count, Autumn Hawk Watch, and Classroom Feeder Watch that use bird watchers just like you to help scientists learn more about the birds in your area. If you go to the course website I mentioned in the introduction to this book, you will find links to programs like these.

Bird watching is fun and interesting.

Have you ever watched a bird hopping around your yard or singing in a tree? Have you ever tried to copy a bird's song and sing back to it? As you study birds, you will make great discoveries about your very own backyard birds: where these birds spend the summer, where they spend the winter, what kind of nest they build, what you can feed them, how old they are when they leave the nest, and much, much more. Observing bird behavior is part of being a scientist.

As you observe bird behavior, you will find that some birds (like the chickadee) move around almost constantly, while other birds (the Mourning Dove) are slow moving and often still. When birds begin to visit your yard, write in your field guide everything you notice about their behavior. Then, when you read your field notebook, you will notice that many of the very things you wrote down are also written in field guide books that are written by the experts. Soon, you will become a local bird expert, and you too could write a bird book for your county or town. Would you like to do that?

Every scientific field has its own **vocabulary**. Do you know what vocabulary words are? Bird vocabulary is made up of words that are not often used by people, unless they are interested in birds. In this course, you will learn a lot of vocabulary words. Scientists who study birds for a living are called **ornithologists** (or' nuh thol' uh jists). Many people who are interested in birds become amateur ornithologists. They study ornithology even though they are not paid for it. People who enjoy watching and studying birds are often called **birders**. One birder might say to another birder, "Where did you bird last week?" or "Have you been birding lately?" If, after studying this book, you decide to make bird watching a hobby, you can call yourself a birder!

Benefits of Birds

Did you know that you need birds? That might surprise you, but it is very true. Have you ever seen birds pecking at trees? What do you think they are looking for? They are trying to find insects, because most birds find them quite yummy. They eat insects because insects are full of protein, and birds (in fact, all animals) need protein to survive. If birds didn't eat all those insects, just imagine how many insects there would be! One of the jobs God gave to birds is to keep the insect population from getting too large.

Many birds (like this Western Bluebird) eat insects, which helps to keep the insect population in check.

Throughout history, when insect populations grew out of control, they destroyed plant life in the area, ruining food crops as well as flower gardens. Huge areas of forests and valleys have been killed by large insect populations. Without birds, insect populations would just keep getting bigger and bigger, growing out of control and perhaps causing **famines** on the earth. A famine is when there is almost no food available, causing people to starve.

Did you know that God designed birds to increase the number of eggs they lay whenever there are more insects than usual? Perhaps God designed it so that whenever the bird eats more protein than usual, the bird's body is given the extra energy it needs to produce more eggs. We aren't sure, but that would make a great science experiment, wouldn't it?

Birds eat other things besides insects. They also eat seeds, berries, and fruit. However, when the insect population gets really big, some birds start eating nothing but insects. Birds will even change the normal location of their habitat from the ground to the trees or from the trees to the ground, depending on where the insect outbreak is located. Isn't God's design of birds amazing?

Some birds just love insects. It is their favorite thing to eat. Do you have a lot of annoying insects in your yard? If so, you may want to attract the Whip-poor-will and the Purple Martin to your yard. Both of these birds eat a lot of insects. These special birds fly through the air and swallow the insects as they are flying around. In order to find out if these birds would be interested in your yard, however, you will first need to learn about the habitats of the Whip-poor-will and the Purple Martin.

Keeping the annoying insect population down is a great reason to begin attracting birds to your yard. You can do this by placing bird houses, feeders, and bird baths in your yard. Some birds, such as the Purple Martin, like the birdhouses we make for them so much that they have become dependent on them. Since they like to swoop through the air to catch the insects, however, it is hard to get them to live in an area with a lot of trees. They need more open space. If your yard has a lot of trees in it, you will probably not be able to attract Purple Martins. After making your yard more attractive to birds, get ready to see what new species start visiting.

A birdhouse can attract birds to your yard.

Tell someone what you have learned about birds today. What makes a bird a bird? Why do people need birds?

Identifying Birds

Believe it or not, it won't take you long to be able to quickly know which birds are in your yard. In a few short weeks, you can learn how to identify them, what kind of nest they make, and what they

When studying birds, a field guide is essential, and binoculars can be very helpful.

eat. First, you will need a good bird field guide. It is better if you can find a field guide that is specific to your area so you won't have to look through pages and pages of birds, many of which don't even come to your state. You can also access free online field guides. You can find links to free online field guides on the course website I discussed in the introduction to this book. Once you get your field guide, you must spend some time studying it, understanding it, and even making notes in it to help you. You may not be used to writing in books, but you can make an exception in this case. Just as some people write in their Bibles, underlining and making notes to help them remember important things, you will also mark up your field guide in this way. If you share the field guide with your siblings, be sure everyone agrees on how to mark it. In addition, having a pair of binoculars is helpful when trying to study the details of a bird that is not very close to you.

Field Guides

Study your field guide so that you are familiar with how the birds are organized in the book. This is important because it will help you more easily find them when you spot one in your backyard. Otherwise, when you see a bird, you'll grab your field guide and begin looking in the back, then in the front, frantically flipping through the pages looking for the bird you see. Then, you'll glance out to look at the bird again and it will be gone. This is why you need to know the general layout of your field guide, so that when you see a little brown bird, you can immediately flip over to the section that contains little brown birds.

Becoming familiar with your field guide will make it easier to identify birds.

How does your field guide separate the birds? Some bird field guides simply use size as the dividing factor; putting the smallest birds in the front of the book and the biggest birds in the back. Some bird field guides separate birds by color, using color coded tabs based on the birds' most striking or dominant colors. Some bird field guides separate birds by similarities. For example, black birds, crows, and grackles will be in one section because they are all similar to each other. Ducks, loons, and other water birds will be in another section, because once again, they are similar to one another.

Do You Reside Here?

The Sandhill Crane (*Grus canadensis*) lives in Canada and the northern U.S. in summer and migrates to Mexico and the southern U.S. for the winter.

Probably the most important thing to focus on when you look through your field guide is which birds you will find in your area. Unless a bird is listed in the field guide as being common to where you live, you probably won't see it. So it is important that you make your field guide work better for you by marking birds that you will see in your area. Usually, there is a little map next to the bird, showing whether or not it visits your area. Often this map has different colors showing where the bird can be found during specific seasons. Some birds live year round in one location; others travel to different places during different seasons. When birds travel from one habitat to another for different seasons, we say that they are **migrating** (my' gray ting). Field guides generally tell you whether a bird is a permanent resident of your area or just spends one or two seasons near you. Some birds may not even spend a season in your area. They may just travel through your city, staying only a day or two before heading north or south, depending on the season. These are called **migrant** (my' grunt) or **transient** (tran' zee unt) birds.

A good way to mark your field guide is to use color coded markers to mark birds that are permanent residents, summer residents, winter residents, or birds that just pass through as they are traveling. Use a different color marker for each type of bird and place a conspicuous dot next to the bird in your field guide. This will help you greatly as you flip through the book trying to identify the birds you see. Another tip is to make a black slash near birds that never come to your area. Don't mark them out, because you may see those birds when you are on vacation. Simply put a slash somewhere near the bird. That will tell you to ignore this bird when you are identifying birds in your area.

Field Marks

At first glance, it might seem that it would be hard to tell one bird from another. Many birds seem to look a lot alike. This is especially true with female birds. Many female birds are brownish gray and have fewer colors than the males. That's because they need to be camouflaged when they sit on their eggs in their nest. The muted colors help them blend in with their nest so that they are hidden from predators. This makes it hard for us to identify them, but there is a trick to it.

These birds look similar, but they are different species. The top one is a Purple Finch, while the bottom one is a House Finch.

If we closely observe each bird, knowing where to look, we start to notice little differences that separate one bird from another. These little differences are called a bird's **field marks**. Every bird has field marks. What are these field marks? They are the colors, shapes, and features of each section of the bird. Two birds might look the same, but on a section of the wing, one might have a white stripe of feathers. That may be the only difference that separates it from the other bird. Of course, the bird will also have a different song, and it might have different behavior patterns, but those things are hard for beginners to notice.

Study the picture on the left. It shows you the parts of a bird. Each part has a special name. It will help your memory if you point to each part and say its name. Better yet, teach a younger sibling or a parent about the different parts of a bird by using the picture.

This diagram shows you the names for different parts of a bird. It is important that you learn them so that you can look for field marks.

Why is it important to learn the different parts of a bird? When you learn them, you will know where to look for a bird's field marks. A Ruby-throated Hummingbird, for example, looks very similar to the Calliope Hummingbird. However, most field guides will tell you that the Ruby-throated Hummingbird has a red throat, while the Calliope Hummingbird has a throat that is striped with magenta (a deeper color of red). If you don't know where the throat of a bird is, you will not know where to look to identify these birds. In the same way, the Rufous Hummingbird looks a lot like the Ruby-throated Hummingbird, but its throat is darker (orange-red to brown), and its back is brown.

Based on what you have learned, identify each of these birds as a Ruby-throated Hummingbird, a Calliope Hummingbird, or a Rufous Hummingbird. Check the answers to the narrative questions at the back of the book to see if you are right.

If you know the parts of a bird, you know how to identify the bird. Some birds are very easy to identify, while others are not. Some birds have obvious features, while others have less noticeable characteristics. Notice the Tufted Titmouse in the picture on the right, for example. This bird is easy to identify because of the tuft of feathers on its crown. The titmouse also has a rusty colored spot on its body. By studying the diagram, can you tell which part of the body has the rusty colored spot on it? Look closely at the diagram and at the picture. Did you figure out that it is the flank?

The titmouse in this photo is easy to identify because of the tuft of feathers on its crown.

The gray stripe through the eye is a field mark that helps to identify this bird as a Black-whiskered Vireo.

Have you ever noticed how different people have different eyes? My eyes probably look different from yours. Your friend's eyes look different from yours as well. You have very special eyes that are probably similar to those of others in your family. Well, birds are no different. Eye color or marks around the eyes are especially important to birders, because the eye color or the marks alone can be the easiest way to identify a bird. Many birds will have a dark patch around the eye, a stripe on both sides of the eye, a stripe above the eye, or some other distinguishing eye mark. Check your field guide and notice how many birds have eye-related field marks.

Try This!

Can you tell the differences between these three vireos (vuh' ree ohs)? Their differences are very slight, almost unnoticeable to the untrained eye. If you glance at them quickly and look away, they may look like the same bird. If you begin to think about the different parts of a bird that you saw on the diagram, however, you will notice differences. Try to explain the differences before you read on.

Red-eyed Vireo   Yellow-throated Vireo   White-eyed Vireo

Did you notice that the bird on the left has no white bands on its wings, but the other two have them? The bird on the right has a white eye, while the eyes of the other two are darker. In addition, the one in the middle has yellow on its throat, while the other two have white throats. The bird on the left has a bluish gray crown, while the other two birds have crowns that are greenish yellow. These are small differences, but they separate each species from the other.

As you can see, knowing the different parts of a bird is helpful when you are trying to identify one bird species from another. In addition to special markings, birds also have distinctive body parts that may differ from other birds. We will study these more closely in a later lesson.

Wings

The wings of a bird often carry important field marks, so it is important that you study them carefully when you look at a bird. Often, the location of a color band on a bird's wing is the only thing that separates one species from another. If a strip of color crosses the bird's wing horizontally, we call it a **wingbar**. The white wingbars pointed out on the bird on the right are field marks that help us recognize it as a Pine Warbler, whose scientific name is *Dendroica* (den' droy cuh) *pinus* (pie' nus). If a similar looking bird does not have such wingbars, it might still be a bird from genus *Dendroica*, but it is not from species *pinus*.

wing bars

The wingbars on this warbler help to identify it as species *Dendroica pinus*.

Crests

As you can see from the diagram on page 26, the top of a bird's head is called the **crown**. Some birds have a tuft of feathers that stand up on the crown, and that tuft of feathers is called a **crest**. The titmouse shown on page 27, for example, has a crest. Many birds, such as the Northern Cardinal and the Black Crowned Crane, also have crests. It is important to note, however, that not all crests stand up on the crown. A Wood Duck, for example, has a crest, but as you can see from the picture on the right, the crest lies down over the back of its head. The scientific name for the Wood Duck is *Aix* (ayks) *sponsa* (spon' zuh). If a bird has a crest, it is usually easy to identify.

crest ———

The Wood Duck has a crest that lies down over the back of its head.

What's in a Name?

The common names given to birds often refer to their colored markings. The Ruby-throated Hummingbird, for example, gets its name because of the red throat on the male of the species. The Yellow-rumped Warbler looks like other warblers, except it has a small yellow spot right on its rump. Since this mark is actually under its wings, you can only see it when the bird is flying away from you. That's because while it is flying, its wings aren't covering the yellow spot on its rump.

Some common bird names are confusing. The purple finch, for example, is not purple at all; it's strawberry colored. The Purple Martin actually looks rather black at times. So you can't always use a bird's name to help you identify it. It is best to look for field marks and refer to your bird field guide.

Passerines

Most of the birds you will see in your yard are **passerines** (pas' uh rynes). This means they are in order **Passeriformes** (pass' er uh for' meez). More than half of the birds in the world are passerines. All passerines have feet that allow them to perch on branches, with three toes pointing forward and one toe pointing backwards. All passerines are singing birds as well, though some have songs that are not quite as lovely as others. All passerine chicks are born without feathers, blind, and completely dependent on their parents for food and protection.

Though the passerines are similar in many ways, there is a big difference in their eating habits and sizes. Some (like ravens) are very large, while others (like chickadees) are tiny. Some (like the flycatchers and martins) are insect eaters with mouths that open like giant nets. These passerines make amazing swoops through the air, "netting" flies and mosquitoes by the thousands. Their wings are pointy and short to help them twist and turn in the air. Some passerines (like nuthatches) peck around on trees, collecting insects, eggs, cocoons, and spiders. Some (like sparrows and grosbeaks) have strong bills that can crack open even the toughest seed. Others (like shrikes) eat mice and large insects. Some passerines (like honeycreepers and orioles) even drink nectar from flowers.

From Large to Small

When you begin to attract birds to your yard with bird feeders, bird houses, and bird baths, you will notice that they come in many shapes and sizes. Size is very important in identifying birds, so scientist divide birds into seven basic sizes. Birds are measured while lying on their back, from the tip of the bill to the end of the tail. Find a yard stick or measuring tape and measure out the following seven sizes: **very small** (4" or less), **sparrow-sized** (about 6"), **robin-sized** (about 10"), **pigeon-sized** (about 13"), **crow-sized** (about 17"), **goose-sized** (about 25"), and **very large** (greater than 20"). Most of the birds you will see in your yard will range from very small to crow-sized.

Try This!

You are going to play a game with a partner to see if he or she can guess which bird it is you are describing. Look through a book, magazine, or the internet for photos of birds. Choose one to describe to your partner, but do not show your partner the picture. Just describe the bird.

Your partner should look through your field guide to see if he or she can find the bird you described. Use field marks to help your partner identify the bird, and use the proper terms from the bird diagram on page 26. For example, say "The crown is red, the nape is black, and the back and rump are gray." After you have described a bird to your partner, switch places and have your partner describe a bird for you to find in the field guide.

Bird Behavior

As you know, field marks are important for identifying birds, but noticing the bird's characteristics, behaviors, and habits is also valuable. Some birds hop from tree to tree and from feeder to tree; moving here there and everywhere within seconds. Other birds, like the Mourning Dove, bob their heads as they slowly and carefully walk around the yard. A chickadee will not usually sit and eat at a feeder. Instead, it takes a seed and hops over to a nearby tree limb to peck at it. Some birds stay at the feeder until they've eaten their fill. The goldfinch does this when pecking at a thistle feeder.

Most birds have very different ways of behaving. If you watch carefully, you will begin to notice these differences. Some run along the ground. Some prefer worms from the yard to bird feeders. Some flash their wings now and again. Some move their tails up and down. Some walk up trees. If you take time to notice the different actions of the birds, it will help you identify them.

Habitats

Perhaps the most distinguishing characteristic of birds is that each bird prefers to stay within its habitat. You probably won't find a duck in the desert or a roadrunner in a pine forest. This is because a duck's habitat is water, while roadrunners prefer open, dry, shrubby deserts. Whenever you are determining what kind of bird you are looking at, an important thing to notice is the habitat around you. Remember that a habitat is a place that provides food, shelter, water, and living space for the bird. With very few exceptions, a bird will not be found outside its natural habitat. When you read your field guide, pay attention to the habitat the bird prefers.

Some birds even prefer certain types of trees in which to nest. An ornithologist looking for a Black-backed Woodpecker, for example, might look in a forest that had a recent fire because these birds like to nest in dead trees. On the other hand, the Red-cockaded Woodpecker likes a pine forest that has very few dead trees, since they nest in living pine trees. You will find that birds are very picky when it comes to where they live.

Bird Banter

The flowers have already appeared in the land; The time has arrived for pruning the vines, and the voice of the turtledove has been heard in our land. -Song of Solomon 2:12

As you become even more familiar with birds, you will begin to identify which birds are nearby from their songs and calls. Birds talk to one another by songs, calls, and other noises like tapping and drumming.

This Western Meadowlark *(Sturnella neglecta)* is singing.

Birds do not have vocal cords like you and I. To make sounds, vibrations are sent across the bird's voice box, called the **syrinx** (sihr' inks). Usually, the more muscles a bird has attached to its syrinx, the more sounds it can make. Mockingbirds can make many, many sounds. In fact, they can copy the sounds of other birds and even machines. A pigeon or dove, on the other hand, is only able to make a few cooing noises. Which of those two birds do you suppose has the most muscles attached to its syrinx?

Learning a bird's song is a wonderful way to begin to identify birds. If you know a bird by its song, you can know which birds are around even if you can't see them. In addition, a bird's song is sometimes the best way to identify it. The Willow Flycatcher (*Empidonax traillii*) and the Alder Flycatcher (*Empidonax alnorum*) look almost exactly alike, but they can be identified by their songs, which are noticeably different.

This brings us to an interesting point about classifying birds. Scientists put birds in different species according to their song. But is this a reliable method? Does this really separate one bird from another? Let's use a real example. In the 1800s, some blackbirds were taken from Europe to Australia and New Zealand. These blackbirds came from a species of blackbirds that had a particular song. Now, two hundred years later, the offspring of these blackbirds actually have very, very different songs from the original species of blackbirds still living in Europe. Does it really make sense to say the blackbirds in Australia and New Zealand are now a different species? There is no definite answer to this question.

The best time to begin learning a bird's song is in the winter and early spring, when there are few leaves on the trees. As soon as you hear a bird singing, quietly creep up to a place where you can see the bird and identify it. As time goes on and more birds begin to appear in your yard, you will easily recognize new bird songs from those of your regular visitors.

Blue Jays got their name because they sound like they are saying, "Jay."

Sometimes the noise that a bird makes can be described with words. When a Blue Jay makes noise, it sounds like it is saying, "Jay." The Whip-poor-will sounds like it is saying, "Whip poor will." The sounds these birds make give them their names.

Try This!

When you are outside listening to birds, try to see if you can "hear" any words in the noises they are making. Write down in your journal what words you thought you heard, and if you can see the bird, identify it. If a bird makes noises that don't sound like words, that's okay. Many birds make noises that don't sound like words.

Songs and Calls

Early on a spring morning, you can hear birds calling and singing with vigor. A bird **call** is a single sound that a bird makes, while a **song** is a series of notes that have a pattern. About half of all birds are able to both sing and call. The other half can not sing; they can only call.

There are many reasons that a bird sings or calls. For example, a bird sings to attract a mate. This means that early spring is a time of much singing, since this is when birds are mating. Each species has its own specific songs and calls. Some birds have a whole repertoire of songs, all different from one another. The cardinal has over twelve different songs. Some birds, like the mockingbird and the catbird, imitate or copy the songs of other birds and other things. In fact, the scientific name for the Northern Mockingbird is *Mimus* (mim' us) *polyglottos* (pah lee glot' us), which means "mimic of

Mockingbirds like the one in this photo can imitate many sounds.

many tongues." Many of you have seen parrots that can say words they have been taught. Scientists believe that perhaps the female bird chooses a mate depending on how long or loud he can sing. They also believe the more songs the male has in his repertoire, the more likely he is to win the mate.

Birds of the same species may sound exactly alike to us, but birds have excellent hearing and have the ability to hear even the slightest difference in the songs of different birds. A parent can find its chick in a crowd by its call alone, though to us, it would sound like every other squawking chick.

Claims to Territory

This Red-winged Blackbird (*Agelaius phoeniceus*) is marking its territory.

Songs are also used to mark the territory where a bird will raise its young. Once a bird has begun to build its nest and lay its eggs, it will very loudly proclaim that this is its territory. This is the bird's way of communicating to other birds that they should not come into its living area. This appears to work because birds seem to respect the continual songs of other birds. A bird's territory can be very small (like the size of its nest), or very large (like the size of an entire city block). Each bird knows where its territory ends and another begins.

Most birds fight over territory only with members of the same species. They usually don't mind the arrival of another species. A male bird that sits at your feeder and sings is letting other birds know that this is its feeder. It will share the feeder with female birds of the same species, but will not share the feeder with any male bird of the same species. You may even see the male bird offer food to the female as part of their courtship. Interestingly, he often doesn't care if birds of other species come to the feeder.

A bird will usually find a favorite singing spot and return to the same spot again and again. For example, a robin once chose the very tip top corner of our roof as its spot to sing each day. Has a bird picked a place in your yard as its favorite singing post?

The Purpose of Calls

Do you remember what a bird call is? It's a short sound, not a series of sounds. Birds call when they are alerting others to danger, or when they are feeding or migrating. Some newborn chicks communicate with their parents using a call. Some birds also have gathering calls, which give the other birds information about where and when to gather and migrate. Communication is very important to birds. Without being able to communicate, many birds would starve, lose their way during migration, or be unable to defend their territory or find a mate.

Other Communications

Calls and songs are not the only communication tools bird use. Birds like the woodpecker, for example, also communicate by tapping trees, drainpipes, poles, tin roofs, or anything else that makes a loud noise. This is called **drumming**. The continual rat-tat-tat-tat-tat lets other woodpeckers know to stay away. "This is my territory!" the bird says. Both the male and female woodpecker drum on objects to establish territory.

Woodpeckers like this one (*Dryocopus pileatus*) communicate by drumming on trees, poles, etc.

Body motions can also communicate information from one bird to another. For example, hungry baby birds will peck at their parent's beaks or open their mouths widely to ask for food. When an adult bird thrusts its head forward and opens its mouth, it is saying that it is angry and ready to fight. Birds that have a crest on their head will raise their crest to show that they are the boss. When a bird spreads its wings and puts its head and beak up into the air, this also communicates that it is not happy. This often happens at a bird feeder. A bird will also fluff out its feathers when it is upset.

A male grouse does a very strange and unusual maneuver to communicate. He beats the air with his wings to make a sound similar to that of a heartbeat. This "heartbeat," however, can be heard a half mile away!

Bird Banding

One reason we know so much about birds is that people have been **bird banding** for a long time. Have you ever heard of bird banding? It is the practice of putting tiny bracelets on the legs of birds. These bracelets help us to learn all about where the bird goes, how long it lives, and what its habits are.

Bird banding is a very important part of bird science, but the whole process actually began by accident. It started in about 1595, when King Henry IV of France lost one of his Peregrine (pehr' uh grin) Falcons. Believe it or not, falcons have a long history of being well-loved pets. He was very distressed to have lost his beloved bird, but thankfully, the king had all of his beloved birds marked. The next day, people all over the country knew of the king's loss. As a result, people were watching for the falcon so that they could return it to the king. It was later found more than 1,300 miles away on the island of Malta!

About a hundred years later, a Turkish man placed a ring on a Gray Heron's leg. It was later caught in Germany by someone's pet falcon. What a surprise it must have been to learn that the bird had come from Turkey!

As time went on, a new idea began sprouting in the minds of those who loved and wanted to know more about birds. Once such person was **John James Audubon** (aw' duh bon), who was a real bird lover. He lived in Kentucky and sailed down the Mississippi River painting birds in an attempt to draw every bird in North America in its natural habitat. In 1803, Audubon tied a silver wire to the leg of some phoebes (fee' bees), a species of migrating bird, to test his hypothesis that migrating birds return to the same place year after year. His beliefs were confirmed by the fact that the birds he banded kept returning to the same place time and time again. After that, bird banding began in earnest. Today, bird banding is an important method used to learn things like where birds live, where they travel, how fast they get to where they are going, what routes they take, and how long they live.

When a bird is banded in one location, information such as the date and location is recorded. If it is found in another place, the ornithologists there will be able to understand some important information about that bird such as where it migrates and how long it has lived since it was banded.

The U.S. Department of the Interior and a specific division of the U.S. Geological Survey (the Patuxent Wildlife Research Center) are in charge of all bird banding in the United States. The Canadian Wildlife Service is the Canadian counterpart.

Bird bands like this have helped us learn a lot about birds.

These organizations keep records of all the birds banded in both countries, and that information is shared with ornithologists to help them understand birds better. Each band put on the bird has a number. No two bird bands have the same number. Only people who have a banding license are allowed to put these little metal bracelets on the birds.

Banders (people who band birds) use nets to catch birds for banding. The nets are very soft so that they do not hurt the birds. Banders are trained in how to hold a bird in a way that calms it. The bander is also trained in how to attach the band around the bird's leg. Using pliers, a bander carefully attaches the bracelet. He then weighs the bird, measures its length and wing span, and writes down this information in a special book. Everything is then sent to the wildlife organizations, where it is entered into a database. If a banded bird is captured by someone else, he or she can use the information on the band to notify wildlife organizations or even the person who first banded it.

More than 56 million birds have been banded in the last 100 years. Millions and millions of these birds are caught again and again by banders, who record the bird's whereabouts and condition and then release it. If you want to learn more about bird banding or learn how you could become licensed to band birds, go to the course website that I mentioned in the introduction to this book. There you will find links that you can use to learn all about this interesting activity.

What Do You Remember?

What are the benefits of birds? Why is it important to know what habitat a bird prefers? What are some reasons a bird sings? What are some reasons a bird might call? What is the history of bird banding? What are passerines?

Nature Points

Begin to keep a record of the birds you see in your yard. Have a notebook next to the window ready to use. Always write the date, the field marks you see, the bird's behavior, and the identity of the bird (if possible). As the seasons change, you will notice that some birds no longer come to your yard. When their season returns, however, you'll be excited to see them again. Record the date you first see a new species or last see a species. These types of records are important for birders and could even help ornithologists a great deal. Do you notice any territorial behavior in the birds you see? Do they seem to be friendly towards one another? If one bird arrives at the feeder, does another bird of the same species also arrive with it? If so, does the one immediately leave? Which one is the more powerful bird? Which bird gets its way at the feeder? Do smaller birds wait for bigger birds to leave? Do the birds fuss at birds of the same species? Do they also fuss at birds of a different species?

Notebook Activities

Write down all the fascinating facts you want to remember about birds and birding in your notebook. If you are using the *Zoology 1 Notebooking Journal*, write these observations on the Fascinating Facts pages provided.

Map a Bird

Have you ever studied a map? In most maps, you can find a section that is called the map's **key**. The key usually has special colors, symbols, or patterns that refer to different things on the map. For example, on a map of the United States, you might see black lines that separate the states. These black lines, called **borders**, are not there in real life, but they help us to see where one state ends and the other begins. The map key might say that the color black means a border.

You are going to make a different kind of map. To make this map, you will need colored pencils and an outline of a bird. If you are using the *Zoology 1 Notebooking Journal*, a template is provided for you with an outline of a bird. If you are creating your own notebook, you can trace the bird in the diagram on page 26, or you can go to the course website I mentioned in the introduction to the book. You will find a link there that will lead you to a bird outline.

You will map out the parts of a bird. Your bird map will have a key that represents the different parts of the bird. You will draw lines between each part of the bird you want to identify, as the child has done in the picture above. Use the bird diagram on page 26 to help you. On your key, make a small box with each color and then write the part next to the color. Then, fill in each part with the color you chose. For example, you might choose the color red to indicate the crown. If so, your key should have a little box colored in red with the word "crown" next to it. Then, you need to color the crown on the bird outline. When you are done with your bird map, put it in your notebook.

Project
Build Two Bird Feeders

Creating a bird-friendly yard will make bird watching especially enjoyable. A good way to start making your yard inviting to birds is to provide bird feeders. Birds that eat seeds will come to seed feeders, and birds that prefer insects will come to suet feeders. In this project, you will make one of each kind of feeder.

Let's start with a seed feeder. To make a seed feeder, you obviously need seeds. Sunflower seeds are a songbird favorite, but they can be expensive. Using a variety of seeds will attract many

In this part of the project, you will be making a seed feeder like this one.

birds (and squirrels) to your yard. Small birds usually bring lovely chirps and songs with them. Large birds usually caw or make other loud noises, and are less desirable to some people.

You will need:

♦ An adult with a knife
♦ Two bamboo skewers (They will serve as perches for birds.)
♦ An empty plastic bottle with a wide mouth opening, such as a juice jug. You can use a plastic soda pop bottle instead, but the narrow mouth opening will make it hard to fill with seeds.
♦ Wire or string
♦ Bird seed

1. Have an adult cut two holes on opposite sides of the jug, about two and half inches from the bottom. The holes should be about the size of a nickel or quarter, depending on the size of the seed you bought. The holes should be large enough for a bird to access the seed, but not so large that the seed just spills out. If you buy very small seeds like those from a thistle, for example, you will need to make the hole the size of a pea. Thistle seeds will tend to attract finches.

2. Have the adult use the knife to make a small slit at the bottom of the bottle on each side, about 2 inches below each hole.

3. Slide the bamboo skewers through these slits to make a perch under each hole.

4. Make a small hole on each side of the bottle, near the mouth.

5. Slide the wire or string through the holes and tie the ends together above the feeder's mouth.

6. Fill the feeder with seeds and replace the lid.

7. Secure your feeder to a tree that birds are likely to see when passing through your area.

Now it is time to put a suet feeder in your yard. Suet is a favorite among many birds. Some birds will prefer it to bird seed and will make a regular visit to your yard if you have suet available. In the winter, birds that usually eat insects will prefer suet as it provides their need for protein. You can buy suet and suet feeders rather cheaply at discount stores, but birds seem to prefer the "Smart Suet" recipe below over the suet you can buy in the store. Woodpeckers will flock to this recipe for Smart Suet.

You will need:

♦ Small plastic zippered bags
♦ Mesh bag or suet basket (A suet basket can be purchased in lawn and garden stores and some pet stores.)
♦ Stove
♦ Pot
♦ Stirring spoon
♦ Freezer
♦ 2 cups crunchy peanut butter
♦ 2 cups lard (not shortening)
♦ 4 cups rolled oats (not quick oats)
♦ 4 cups cornmeal
♦ $\frac{2}{3}$ cup sugar
♦ 1 cup raisins
♦ 1 cup bird seed (You can also add whole wheat kernels or other unprocessed grains.)

Start by making the "Smart Suet."

1. Melt the lard and peanut butter in a pot over low heat.
2. Stir in the rest of the ingredients.
3. Scoop the mixture into small plastic zippered bags.
4. Place the bags in the freezer so that the suet will harden.

Once the suet has hardened, you are ready to use it in a suet feeder.

5. Remove the suet from one of the bags and place it in the mesh bag or suet basket.
6. Hang the mesh bag or suet basket on a tree outdoors.
7. Wait, watch, and enjoy.

Scientific Experiment
Which Food Do the Birds in Your Yard Prefer?

You will conduct an experiment to see which feed your birds prefer. Do you remember the important elements of conducting a good scientific experiment? The best kind of experiment has only one variable (one thing that changes), and all of the other things are held constant, which means that they stay the same. You also need a way to measure the data.

In this experiment, you will use identical bird feeders and fill them with different kinds of food.

In this experiment, the only variable should be the type of food you use. Everything else will need to be constant. This means that the feeders you use should be the same. The amount of food in each container should be the same, because a full container may attract more birds than one that is half empty. You should put them both in the same location. After all, if one feeder is closer to the trees or further from the house than the other one, it may affect which feeder the birds visit. The feeders should also be put out at the same time.

You also need to measure your data. You will do this by observing the feeders and counting the birds that visit each feeder. The feeder that has more visitors probably contains the food that the birds in your area prefer.

You will need:

♦ Two identical bird feeders (You can make them both or purchase them both, but they must be the same)
♦ Two types of bird seed

1. Choose which two types of bird seed to test in your experiment. Choose only two. You can choose between thistle seeds, sunflower seeds, peanuts, or any other bird seed that is available for purchase near you. You can even test two different kinds of sunflower seeds.
2. Make a hypothesis as to which food will be preferred by the birds in your area. Use a Scientific Speculation Sheet to write down your hypothesis.
3. Put the feeders very close to one another in your yard.
4. Put one type of food in one feeder and the other type in the other feeder.
5. Watch the feeders so that you can count the birds that visit them. The times that you watch the feeders should be another constant. You should choose a couple of times per day to watch and record your results. In general, birds are active in the early morning and the late afternoon, but you need to choose times that you are available.
6. Use the Scientific Speculation Sheet to record what the weather was like (raining, cloudy, sunny, etc.) each time you watch the feeders. These details may turn out to be important.
7. As you watch the feeders, count the birds that come to visit them, and record the total number of birds that visited each feeder.
8. After you have watched the feeder for a few days, try to see which feeder had more visitors. The food in that feeder is what the birds in your area prefer.
9. Compare your results to your hypothesis. Was your hypothesis correct or incorrect?
10. Fill out the rest of the Scientific Speculation Sheet, indicating what you used, what you did, and what you concluded from the experiment.

Lesson 3
Birds of a Feather
"He will cover you with his feathers, and under his wings you will find refuge…" – Psalm 91:4

Have you ever heard the expression "birds of a feather flock together?" It means that people are attracted to other people who have similar interests. Can you think of an example of this? The expression began because birds are attracted to other birds with feathers of the same shape and size.

You might think that a bird recongizes another bird of its same species because it learned to recognize its parents when it was a **hatchling** (a baby bird that just hatched), but this is not so. Let's consider the cowbird, which lays its eggs in another bird's nest and allows the other bird to hatch and raise its young. When the cowbird hatchling grows up and leaves the nest, it joins up with other cowbirds, even though it has never seen another cowbird. Isn't that amazing?

The cowbird has an instinct to look for and flock with other birds that have feathers the same shape and size as its own. Do you remember what instinct is? It is the special inner wisdom that God gave to animals. Instinct causes many female birds to look for male birds with the best feathers and song. For some birds, good feathers are the most important feature to look for in a partner!

The feathers on these pelicans are light enough to allow for flight but strong enough to withstand the stress of flight.

Feathers are incredible works of God. They are tough and strong, yet light and bendable. If God made feathers too heavy, a bird would not be able to fly. If God made feathers too weak, however, a gust of wind could break them and throw the bird to the ground. Instead, God made them light enough to allow birds to fly but strong enough to keep them from breaking. Let's take a closer look at feathers. I think you'll be amazed at what you find. You will need to gather some bird feathers to study. Any feathers will do, but make sure they come from game birds like ducks, chickens, or geese. It is illegal to collect the feathers of many other kinds of birds. Be sure to wash them before handling them with your bare hands!

Feather Facts

Did you know that a bird actually has different types of feathers? Each feather type has a purpose, or reason, for being on the bird. Its shape and structure fit that purpose. There are five basic types of feathers: **contour feathers**, **down feathers**, **semiplumes**, **filoplumes**, and **bristles**. Feathers can be tiny (such as the feathers on a bird's eyelid), or they can be several feet long (such as the beautiful feathers making up the tail of a peacock).

Some birds have a lot of feathers because they live in very cold climates. The Tundra Swan [*Cygnus* (sig' nus) *columbianus* (koh' lum bee an' us)] that nests in the arctic has about 25,000 feathers to keep it warm. Some birds don't need quite as many feathers as the Tundra Swan. The birds that live in tropical areas have no trouble staying warm, because the weather is always warm. The hummingbirds that live in South America, for example, might only have a thousand feathers. That's still a lot of feathers, but it is a lot fewer than what the Tundra Swan has. A few birds that stick around when the cold weather comes will actually grow extra feathers just for the winter.

Molting

Do you know what **molting** is? Many of God's creatures, including birds, molt. When a bird molts, it loses its old feathers and replaces them with new ones. Why would a bird do that? Well, after a while, a bird's feathers begin to get a little ragged. Just think about all the wear and tear on those feathers when the bird flies through trees, builds nests, fights other birds, and flies across the country. So, one by one, worn-out feathers begin to fall out as new ones grow to replace them.

If a bird didn't molt, its feathers would get so worn out that it wouldn't be able to fly very well. Eventually, its feathers would be no good for flying at all. Having perfectly shaped feathers is important for proper flight, so molting is a necessary part of a bird's life.

God designed most birds to molt just before it is time to find a mate. Most birds molt gradually, shedding a few feathers at a time. Believe it or not, however, some birds (like geese) shed all their wing feathers at once. Of course, once that happens, the geese are unable to fly until the new ones grow to replace the old ones! Most birds tend to molt all of their feathers in a year, but large birds (like eagles) take two years or longer to molt every feather

Sometimes, when a bird molts, the new feathers that grow back are a completely different color. Often the new color is designed to help the bird blend into its environment. For example, the ptarmigan (tar' muh gun) has summer feathers that are brown (blending in with the ground) and winter feathers that are white (blending in with the snow). The photos on the right show a Yellow-rumped Warbler, which also has different summer and winter feathers.

The top photo shows a male Yellow-rumped Warbler (*Dendroica coronata*) in winter. The bottom photo shows a male of the same species in summer. Note the differences in color and markings.

God designed birds to lose their feathers in a very orderly way. Have you ever heard the phrase, "God is a God of order?" Because He is a God of order, His creation is orderly. Even the way birds molt is orderly. The order in which a bird loses its feathers is called the bird's **molt sequence**, and many bird species have their own specific molt sequence. Different species of birds also molt at different times. Some birds may begin molting during the spring, while others will molt during the winter. During molting of the wing feathers, each feather on one wing usually falls off with another feather located in the exact same place on the opposite wing. This is called **symmetrical** (suh met' trih kuhl) **molting**. Why do you think birds molt in this way? What do you think would happen if a bird lost feathers on one wing but didn't loose them on the other wing at the same time? It would be very difficult to fly straight, because the wings would not be balanced.

Because of symmetrical molting, most birds can fly perfectly well while they molt. However, those birds that lose the feathers they use for flight all at once cannot fly while they molt. After geese molt, for example, they have to wait a few weeks for new feathers to grow before they can take to the air again. They usually find a nice lake or pond to wait for their feathers to grow back. That place can become littered with feathers, which makes it a great place to collect feathers.

Explain in your own words what you have learned about God's design for bird feathers and molting.

Feather Features
The Shaft

Study one of the feathers you collected for a moment. Look at the middle of the feather. Do you see a thick, hard pole? That is called the **shaft**. It is usually hollow and can be easily bent. It is made of a material called **keratin** (kair' uh tin). Look at your fingernails; they are also made of keratin. Some animal horns (like those of a rhinoceros) are made of keratin, as are animal claws. A bird cannot feel the shafts on its feathers, but the place where the feather is attached to its body is sensitive. Because of this, a bird's wings can be clipped without pain, just as your fingernails can. In fact, pet store owners sometime clip a bird's wings to keep it from flying away or injuring itself in the store. It doesn't hurt the bird at all.

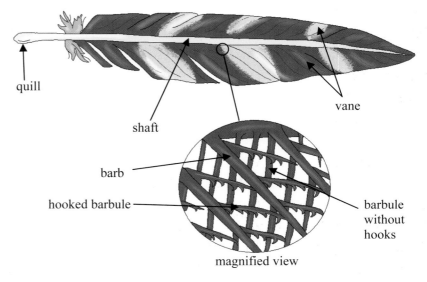

This is the basic structure of a feather. You will want to refer back to this drawing as you read the next page.

The bottom part of the feather's shaft is where it is attached to the bird. This is called the **quill**. Many years ago, people used quills to write. They dipped a quill in ink, and the ink moved a little ways up the hollow shaft. Then, they could write with the quill until the ink ran out, and when it did, they would dip it in the ink again.

Where the quill is attached to the bird, there are special muscles that can raise or lower the feather. Without these special feather muscles, birds would not and could not fly! This is because these muscles raise and lower the feathers so that they can adjust to the changing conditions that the bird experiences during flight.

The Vane

The rest of the feather, the soft part, is called the **vane**. Look closely at the vane on the feather you have. It is made up of hundreds of **barbs** that look like skinny hairs. These barbs stick out from the shaft. At first glance, you might think the feather is very simple. If you use a magnifying glass to look closer, however, you will see the complicated design of a bird's feather. Use a magnifying glass to look at one of the barbs very carefully. You should be able to see that each barb has another set of tiny little "hairs" on it. They are called **barbules** (barb' yoolz).

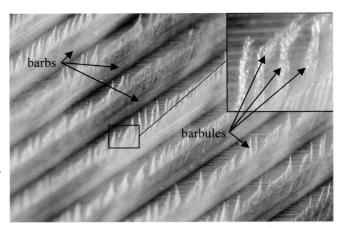

A magnified view of the barbules on the barbs of this feather is shown in the upper right corner of this picture.

These barbules are like little hooks and latches. Some of the barbules have hooks, and they hook to the barbules that don't have hooks (see the drawing on the previous page). This makes them act like little "zippers" that zip the feather's barbs together. These "zippers" are flexible, however, so that the feather can bend during flight.

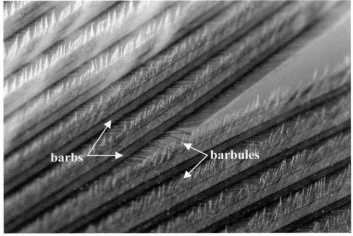

This feather has a barb that is "unzipped." It can be "rezipped" by putting it back where it was and pressing the barbules together.

Can you "unzip" a barb on the feather you have? Now put it back where it was and press the barbules back together. Isn't that wonderful that they simply hook back together?

Have you ever noticed a bird using its beak to poke at its feathers? God designed birds with the ability to know when the barbules on their feathers become unhooked. When this happens, a bird will run its beak across its feathers, which hooks the barbules back together. This is called **preening**. Preening helps birds fix their feathers and get them back in shape for flying.

What do you remember about the parts of a feather? Show someone one of the feathers that you collected and name as many of its parts as you can. Why does a bird molt?

Contour Feathers

Now we're going to talk about the five basic types of feathers, starting with the **contour feather**. If you have a contour feather, it will look similar to one of the feathers pictured on the right. It may have a solid vane all of the way down the shaft, or it may have a solid vane near the top of the shaft with fuzzy feathers near the bottom of the shaft. Where the vane is solid, the feather has hooked barbules that "zip" the barbs together. Where the feather is fuzzy, there are no hooked barbules, so the barbs do not stay together.

Contour feathers give the bird its shape and form and allow it to fly.

Have you ever heard the word "contour?" It means "shape" or "form." Contour feathers are the feathers that give the bird its shape and form. As you already know, some birds (like the titmouse) have tufts on the top of their head. These tufts are made with contour feathers. Peacocks and turkeys have contour feathers on the tail that can fan out. In addition to giving a bird its shape and form, many contour feathers are used for flight. I want to spend some time talking about these special contour feathers.

The contour feathers that a bird uses in flight (often called **flight feathers**) are stiffer than the other contour feathers, and they usually have a solid vane all of the way down the shaft. In the picture above, the contour feather on the left is not a flight feather, but the contour feather on the right is. Can you guess where the flight feathers are located? They are on the wings and the tail! The flight feathers on the wings are called **remiges** (rem' uh jeez), and the ones on the tail are called **retrices** (reh' truh seez). A bird actually has three different types of remiges: **primary flight feathers**, **secondary flight feathers**, and **tertiary** (tur' she air' ee) **flight feathers**, depending on where they are located on the wing.

The feathers you see on the wings and tail of this Bald Eagle (*Haliaeetus leucocephalus*) are its flight feathers.

The Remiges

"Primary" usually means "first" or "most important." These flight feathers are the most important feathers on a bird's body, because they provide the thrust needed to get the air moving across the wings. If the primary flight feathers are damaged, the bird may not be able to produce enough thrust to fly. Pet stores often clip these feathers to keep a bird from flying away.

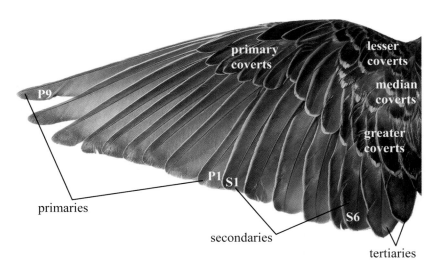

When a bird has its wings stretched out, the primary feathers are the furthest from the bird's body. They are towards the outer tip of the wing. The primary feathers begin at the joint of the arm and end at the furthest stretch of the wing. Ornithologists number them beginning with the one closest to the bird's body, P1, and ending with the last one at the tip of the wing. Different species have different numbers of primary feathers.

The secondary feathers are closer to the bird's body, and they form the airfoil shape of the wing that allows the bird to lift up in the air when it is thrusting forward. They are also numbered, beginning with the one right next to the primary feathers. Once again, different species of birds have different numbers of secondary flight feathers. The tertiary feathers are the closest to the bird's body, and they also help to provide lift to the wing.

Notice in the photo of the wing that there are other feathers called **coverts**. These are contour feathers that are not used for flight. Instead, they cover the bases of the flight feathers.

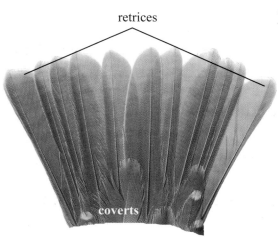

This is the tail of a bird, showing the retrices and coverts.

The Retrices

As I told you before, the tail feathers are called the **retrices**. They are stiff and firm flight feathers, but they are smaller than the flight feathers on the wing. Notice that the bases of the retrices are covered with coverts, just as the bases of the remiges are. The retrices steer and balance the bird as it flies through the air, allowing the bird to turn. A bird can also use its tail feathers (and its wing feathers) to act like a big brake that catches the air like a parachute, slowing the bird down.

Using Flight Feathers

Flight feathers must be strong so that when a bird uses them to catch the air like a parachute, they don't get blown apart. The swan in the picture on the right is doing that so that it can land safely. What do you think it feels like to do that? Some people know what it feels like because they jump out of airplanes and pop open a parachute that catches the air so that they can make a slower landing.

This swan is using its wing and tail feathers like parachutes to slow down as it lands.

Most birds can land softly if they catch the air just right, but one bird that God created to spend most of its life at sea, the albatross, has a terrible time landing on the ground. It often crash lands on its nose and does several somersaults before stopping. Because it has such trouble landing on the ground, it only comes to shore to nest and lay eggs. Sailors nicknamed this bird the "gooney bird" because of its silly stance on land and its crazy landing technique.

Try This!

Before we talk about the other types of feathers, try to run outside while holding an open umbrella behind you. You will feel the air getting caught in the umbrella, slowing you down. Now you can see why God created the birds with the ability and need to catch the air when they land. Try to imagine what would happen if a bird was unable to use its wing and tail feathers as parachutes when it landed. It wouldn't be too long before flying birds became extinct!

Down Feathers

A down feather has no shaft and no hooked barbules. It is very soft.

People who live in very cold regions often buy down jackets and down comforters to keep themselves warm. These jackets and comforters are stuffed with down feathers. A down feather does not have a shaft, only a small quill at the bottom. The hairs of the feather puff out in all directions at the top of the quill. They do not hook at all. They are fluffy, fuzzy feathers that feel soft to the touch.

Every bird has down feathers under its contour feathers, close to the skin. That's a nice place to have such soft, cozy

feathers. Down feathers keep the bird warm.
What birds do you think have the most down
feathers? Birds that live in the coldest regions of
the world have a thick coat of down feathers
underneath all their other feathers. That is how
they survive the terribly cold temperatures in their
habitat! Some birds pluck the down feathers off
their chest and line their nests with it to make a
cozy bed. Some newly hatched birds have a
warm coat of down feathers but no contour
feathers at all. As a result, they look a lot
different from their parents. Chickens and most
water birds hatch that way.

The baby geese (goslings) in this picture have down
feathers but no contour feathers. That's why they look so
"fuzzy" and so different from their parents.

There is a special kind of down feather called a **powder down feather**. This kind of feather
grows all of the time, and its tip crumbles into a very fine powder. The bird spreads this powder across
its feathers while preening, which helps to waterproof feathers. It also gets rid of food and slime that
gets stuck to the bird's body when it eats. Not all birds have powder down feathers.

Semiplume Feathers

This semiplume feather is fuzzy, but it is not a down
feather, because it has a shaft.

Semiplumes are another kind of feather.
They are usually tiny white feathers hidden
underneath a bird's contour feathers. They are like
down, but they have a shaft running up the middle.
Because of the shaft, they look a bit like contour
feathers, but they don't have any zippered barbules.
Like down feathers, semiplumes help to keep a bird
warm. They also give the bird a little bit of form
and shape, smoothing out the contours of the body.

Did you figure out which kind of feathers
you collected? Most likely, you had contour
feathers. There are still two more types of feathers to study, but they are so small that you probably
haven't ever seen them.

Filoplume Feathers

Have you ever seen a plucked chicken? A hundred years ago, almost everyone had seen a
plucked chicken at some time in their lives. Nowadays, most people don't have the opportunity to see
chickens right after they are plucked. Well, a plucked chicken doesn't look exactly naked. If you

plucked all the contour, semiplume, and down feathers off any bird, it would still look like it was covered with a thin coat of hair. Those tiny little hairs are actually feathers, which are called filoplumes (fil' uh ploomz). Filoplumes are teeny, tiny feathers that look like hair on a bird.

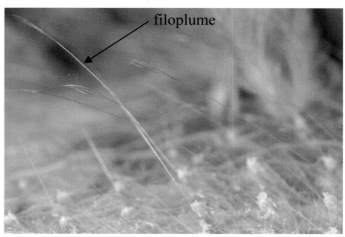

The filoplumes are little sensory feathers that can tell if a flight feather is positioned properly. They relay messages to the bird's brain so the bird knows if it needs to adjust the position of a feather. They also tell the bird if something is touching its feathers.

Filoplume feathers look like hairs, but they are not. They have the physical structure of a feather, not hair.

Bristles

Bristles are almost like eyelashes that a bird has near its mouth, nostrils, and eyes.

Bristle feathers look more like animal hair than any other feather on a bird. However, they are very stiff, like our eye lashes. And just like our eyelashes, bristle feathers are found near the eyelids of a bird. They are also found near the mouth and nostrils. A bird uses its bristle feathers like a cat might use its whiskers; they help it sense very light touches. For example, the bristle feathers can help a bird feel an insect that hits it. If the bird feels an insect on its bristles, it can turn its head in the direction of the touch that it feels and catch the insect. Not surprisingly, then, this type of feather is most common on insect-catching species such as the flycatcher, warbler, and nightjar.

Explain in your own words all that you remember about the five different kinds of feathers.

Preening

Do you remember what preening is? I mentioned it earlier. It is what a bird does when it hooks its barbules back together with its beak. To preen, the bird gently strokes or nibbles along the barbs of each feather, starting at the quill and working towards the tip so that the barbules are properly hooked together. Watch the birds in your yard for signs of preening.

Zipping barbules isn't the only reason a bird preens. It preens to clean and straighten its feathers as well. When a bird preens, it carefully cleans, rearranges, and oils its feathers with its bill. How can a bird oil its feathers? Where does a bird get the oil? God equipped many birds with a sac of oil, called a **preen gland**. This little sac of oil is located at the base of a bird's tail feathers. The bird uses its beak to push oil out of the sac onto its bill and then rubs its bill along its feathers. The oil helps clean and waterproof the feathers. Have you ever noticed a bird pushing at its tail feathers? It's probably squeezing oil out of its preen gland.

Waterproofing feathers is especially important to birds that live near water. Ducks, geese, penguins, and many other water birds (called **waterfowl**), keep their feathers coated with oil so they do not become soaked. If these birds didn't waterproof their feathers, the soaked feathers would get so heavy that the bird would likely sink down below the surface of the water! Also, if waterfowl did not waterproof their feathers, the water would be able to reach their skin and make them cold.

Try This!

Let's see what happens when you waterproof a feather. You will need two feathers, a cup of water and some oil (like vegetable oil). Dip your finger in the oil and rub it onto one feather, covering the feather in oil. Don't pour it on or soak the feather. Simply rub a thin layer over it. Once the feather has a thin coating of oil on it, set it aside. Take the feather that does not have oil on it and dip it into the cup of water. Pull it out and set it down. Next, dip the feather that has oil on it into the water cup. Set it next to your other feather. What happened? The water should have beaded up on the oil-covered feather, while the water soaked through the other feather.

Can you explain why this happened? It has to do with the chemicals the make up the oil. Oil does not mix with water and therefore repels the water, keeping the feather from absorbing it. It makes a "shield" around the feather, keeping the water out. Many birds use their oil gland to place such a "shield" around their feathers when they preen.

Cormorants

There is actually one kind of water bird that does not waterproof its feathers. It likes to get its feathers nice and soaked so it will sink down to the bottom of the lake, river, or ocean where it can find lots of fish. This kind of bird can dive much deeper than ducks and geese, because its heavy, waterlogged feathers help it sink. This kind of bird is called a **cormorant** (kor' moor ant). If you have ever read *The Story About Ping*, you have heard of this kind of bird.

For thousands of years, cormorants have been used as fishing birds in China. Chinese fishermen train a cormorant by placing a metal ring around its neck so that it cannot swallow the big fish that its instinct causes it to dive down to catch. When a cormorant brings a large fish that it catches up to the waiting fisherman, it is rewarded with a small scrap of fish that can fit through the metal ring around its throat. All day long, the cormorant dives down and brings up fish for someone else because it is never quite satisfied by the little scraps it gets as its reward. At the end of the day, the ring is removed, and the bird is finally given a decent meal.

This cormorant is holding its wings out so that they can dry.

Cormorants can often be seen sunning themselves on rocks with their wings outstretched. This helps them dry their wings so that they can fly. These birds can be found near lakes, rivers, and oceans all over the world, including in the United States! Are there any cormorants in your area?

Feather Color

Birds are the most colorful of all the vertebrate animals that God created. Their feathers are colored by various **pigments** (pig' muhnts), which are chemicals that have specific colors. **Melanins** (mel' uh ninz), for example, are pigments that are brown and black. These account for the gray, black, and browns in a bird's feathers. Melanin is also found in people! The darkness of a person's skin is related to the amount of melanin found there. However, melanin can't be the only pigment in birds, since they are much more colorful than we are! Birds also have **carotenoids** (kuh rot' en oydz). These pigments, also found in carrots, are in the foods that birds eat. They produce the beautiful reds, oranges, pinks, and yellows that we see in some birds. In order to get these carotenoids, birds must eat the right kinds of food. For example, flamingos are pink because of carotenoids in the foods that they eat. In a zoo, the food that flamingos eat does not always contain carotenoids, so zookeepers artificially add carotenoids to their food so that the flamingos will be pink. Even so, they are generally not as vividly pink as those in the wild. Finally, some birds get their color from **porphyrins** (por' fuh rinz), which are red and green pigments that birds make themselves. Most birds have only certain pigments, which is why they have only certain colors.

Flamingos are pink because of carotenoids in the food that they eat.

Some very colorful birds do not get their colors from pigments. Instead, they get them from the way the sunlight reflects off their feathers. Some greens, some whites, and all blue colors on birds are produced through a coloring effect similar to what happens when light reflects off a CD. Have you noticed that when you shine light on a CD, a rainbow of colors is produced? That's because the structure of the CD causes light to reflect in a way that makes those colors. The same thing happens when light shines on certain feathers. For example, Blue Jays are blue, but they have no blue pigments. Instead, their feathers are made so that light reflecting from them is blue. If you crush up a Blue Jay feather or just look at it with light shining from behind the feather, you will see no blue color. The blue color shows up only when light reflects off the complete feather.

The brilliant colors on this peacock feather are the result of iridescence.

Some feathers are even more like a CD. When light shines off them, they produce a display of several colors. Feathers like this are called **iridescent** (ir uh des' unt). Most iridescent feathers have melanins that make them black or brown. However, they are structured so that they are able to reflect light in such a way that they appear to have dazzling gemlike colors. Most hummingbirds are iridescent, as are some cowbirds and grackles. They appear black when in the shade, but as soon as the sun is able to shine on their feathers, a beautiful iridescent color shines back at us. As the picture illustrates, peacock feathers are iridescent.

Interestingly enough, there are some animals that are born with no pigments. This is not supposed to happen. In other words, it is an accident of nature. Because they have no pigments, these animals are white. They don't even have coloring in their eyes, so their eyes are red because of the way light reflects from them. Animals like this are called **albinos** (al bye' nohz).

Bird Baths

Because birds like to keep their feathers clean and nice, you will often see a bird sitting on its favorite perch preening away to keep its feathers clean and ready for flight. Another way a bird keeps clean is by taking a bath. Many birds enjoy bathing in little pools of water to keep their feathers in tip-top condition. Bathing also helps birds keep cool on a hot summer day.

Once in the water, a bird fluffs its feathers to expose its skin, submerges its belly and breast in the water, rolls back and forth, and creates a shower by flicking its wings. When finished, the bird shakes off and then flies somewhere to dry and preen.

Some birds do the unthinkable and roll around in the dirt after they have had their bath! Why on earth do birds take dust baths? The easy answer is that we don't know for sure. Some scientists think the dust gets rid of extra preen oil or perhaps removes lice, a kind of insect that harms birds (and other animals) by biting their skin and feeding on their blood.

Sunbathing

Although many people know that birds like to take baths in water, did you know that some birds also like to sunbathe? To do this, some birds will lay down on the ground with their wings and tails outstretched, soaking up the sun. Other birds don't lie down on the ground, but instead find a sunny perch and stretch out their wings to soak up the sun's rays. The vulture in this picture is doing just that.

This vulture is soaking up the sun. How many primary and secondary feathers can you count on its wings?

Amazingly, some birds (like blackbirds, starlings, and jays) sunbathe right on top of an anthill. If you've ever stepped on an anthill, you know that ants don't like to have their home disturbed. They scurry out, crawling on whatever offended their home. Well, when birds sunbathe on anthills, the ants crawl all over the birds. Sometimes a bird will even pick up the ants with its beak and rub them on its feathers. This is called **anting**. The bird does this because ants release a chemical called formic acid that other little creatures like mites and lice really don't like. So, the birds use the ants to get rid of the mites and lice.

Since I have mentioned lice a couple of times now, it is important for you to understand that the lice which live on birds and feed on their blood is different from the lice that live on people and feed on their blood. Because of this, you don't need to worry about getting lice from birds. The kind of lice that likes bird blood has no desire to feed on your blood.

What Do You Remember?

What does it mean for a bird to molt? What is the hard, stick-like structure that runs the length of some types of feather? What part of the feather attaches to the bird's body? What is the soft part of a feather called? What does it mean to have hooked barbules? What is preening? Where are flight feathers located? What are the five basic types of feathers? What do some birds bathe in other than water? Why do scientists think they do this?

Notebook Activities

Record the amazing things you learned about bird feathers for your notebook. If you have the *Zoology 1 Notebooking Journal*, record your observations and drawings on the Fascinating Facts pages. Then, draw a diagram of a feather and label its parts. You can use a box on one of your Fascinating Facts pages to do this. Be sure to include the vane, barbs, and barbules in your diagram.

Make a Bird Guide

In many places, you can buy field guides that list only the birds that reside in your area. You will make a smaller version of this; yours will include only the birds that visit your neighborhood. This book will take a while to make, but you can work on it each time you see a new bird at a feeder or elsewhere in your neighborhood. It will be a book you can share with your neighbors so that they too will know the birds in the area. Make your field guide the same way you made your field notebook in Lesson 1. Each time you see a new bird in your neighborhood, use a new page in your field guide to describe it. Take a picture of the bird or find a picture that you can cut out and put on the page. You could draw the bird if you can't take or find a picture. Use the field guide you have been using or do research at the library or on the internet so that you can identify the bird and write some important facts about it in your bird guide.

Older Students: You can make a bird field guide that encompasses your entire city. Make yours very detailed with a lot of information about each bird's habitat, nesting practices, etc.

Begin a Life List

Most birders keep a **life list**. This is a list of all the bird species they've ever identified and seen with their own eyes. The life list is extremely important to birders. In fact, many birders will go on trips to Alaska or the Amazon rain forest just to add rare birds to their life list. However, even if you never leave your home state, your life list can have hundreds of species. If you were able to see every species of bird in North America, for example, you would have a life list with over 800 birds on it. Birders who get at least 600 species on their life list are said to be a part of the "600 Club." Many birder organizations celebrate when one of their members reaches this milestone.

When making your life list, use both the common and Latin names when recording a bird you have seen. Make certain you are identifying the bird correctly before adding it to your life list. If it is a kind of bird that has many species that look similar and you are unsure exactly which one it is, do not add it to your life list until you know without a doubt. This is pretty much the only rule birders have for life lists, but it is a really important one. The *Zoology 1 Notebooking Journal* has a page for you to begin your life list.

Project
Build a Bird Bath

You will need:

♦ Two terracotta, ceramic, or plastic saucers from large planters (You will use one in this project, but you will use both in the experiment below. Make sure they are exactly the same size, shape, color, etc.)

A water-filled saucer from a large planter makes an excellent bird bath.

When people are thirsty they can just run to the faucet, but birds have to search for the nearest puddle of water to get a drink. The birds that you have attracted to your yard with your bird feeder must drink many times each day, just like you. Making a bird bath will help keep the birds in your yard happy and healthy.

You can buy bird baths, but making one is simple and cheap. Saucers used under large plants make perfect bird baths, because most birds prefer their bird baths to be no deeper than 3 inches in the very deepest part.

To make a bird bath, just place the saucer outside and fill it with water. Ideally, your bird bath should be placed near a tree with overhanging branches so the birds will have a place to sit and preen after bathing. If cats are present, keep the bird bath away from dense shrubbery where cats can hide and surprise the birds. Different species will be attracted to the bath depending on the height and location. We will do an experiment to see which height the birds in your yard prefer.

Keep your bird bath filled with clean, fresh water at all times. Dump the water out and refill it every week or so. Use a brush to remove any algae that may have grown. Never use any chemicals to control algae. If you have a big problem with mosquitoes, you may want to purchase a small device called a water wiggler that keeps the water moving in your bird bath. This kind of device has the added benefit of making a trickling sound which birds love.

Now sit back and enjoy your bird bath. Once the birds have found this water source, they will visit it daily!

Experiment
The Best Bird Bath

Are birds attracted to baths that are on the ground or above the ground? Baths that are higher up are safer, because animals like cats are less likely to get the birds when they are higher up. Do the birds know this instinctively and stay away from the ground baths when a raised bath is available, or do birds instinctively fly to baths on the ground since that is where most puddles are found? These are the questions we want to answer with this experiment. Think about it, decide what you believe, and record your hypothesis on a Scientific Speculation Sheet.

Since we want to see how the height of a bird bath affects whether or not birds use it, the variable in this experiment will be the height at which the bird bath sits. You will need to keep everything else (the location, the color of the bird baths, etc.) the same. You will measure your results by counting the number of birds that visit each bird bath.

1. Choose a good location for your bird baths. They need to be in essentially the same place.
2. Set one bird bath on the ground.
3. Set the other on top of a pedestal, planter table, or some other high surface so that it is well above the ground.
4. Fill each bird bath with equal amounts of water, and check them from time to time to keep them filled and clean.
5. Make sure that the bird baths are identical except for the height at which they are placed. Remember, your experimental variable is height. Everything else must stay constant if you want your experiment to give you accurate results.

In this experiment, the height of each bird bath should be the only variable.

6. Choose one or two times each day to observe the bird baths. It is best to choose times during which the birds are active. Make sure you observe them at those times so that the time of day stays the same throughout the experiment.
7. As you observe the bird baths, count the number of birds that visit each and record those numbers on your Scientific Speculation Sheet.

After you have observed the bird feeders for a few days, look at your results. Do they agree with your hypothesis? Try to think of reasons for why the birds preferred the bird bath that they visited most often. Is there another experiment you could design to test those reasons?

Now that you have finished the experiment, fill out the rest of the Scientific Speculation Sheet, including the materials you used, the procedure, and your conclusions about why the birds might have preferred the bird bath that they visited most often.

Lesson 4
Flying Factuals

"Even the stork in the sky knows her seasons; And the turtledove and the swift and the thrush observe the time of their migration..." -Jeremiah 8:7

Now that you understand how God designed a bird's feather, it is time to take a closer look at the actual flying that birds do. Although feathers and wings are important instruments for flight, if you were able to suddenly sprout feathers and wings, you still wouldn't be able to fly. Why is that? Your bones are too thick and heavy for flight.

This hummingbird can fly because its bones are light and hollow.

God designed a bird's bones different from the bones of other creatures on earth. Bird bones are light and hollow, with very thin brackets running across the bones to make them extra strong. When we build a tall building, we put similar brackets in the building to make it sturdy. Well, this is how God designed the bones of a bird. He made them light and hollow but very, very strong.

Mammals and other vertebrates are quite a bit heavier than birds. If you found a turkey and a raccoon that were exactly the same size and picked them up, you would find the turkey to be much easier to lift. The main reason is that the turkey's bones are hollow and light, while the raccoon's bones are solid and heavy.

Try This!

Find a chicken bone. Break it in half and look at the structure of it. Do you see that it is hollow in the middle? Do you also see the brackets running sideways across the bones? Find a cow bone, such as a bone from a t-bone steak. Now compare it to the chicken bone. Which one is heavier? Can you weigh them with a scale? How many chicken bones would it take to weigh the same as a cow bone of the same size? If you don't have a scale, put one in each hand and close your eyes to feel which is heavier.

Mighty Muscles

The typical bird has a chest that is rounded and full. That's because of all the strong muscles in the chest. What do those muscles do? They help the bird flap its wings to develop the thrust it needs to fly. These muscles are called **flight muscles**, and they make up the breast of the bird. We often eat the breast meat of chickens and turkeys. When we do that, we are actually eating the flight muscles of the chicken or turkey!

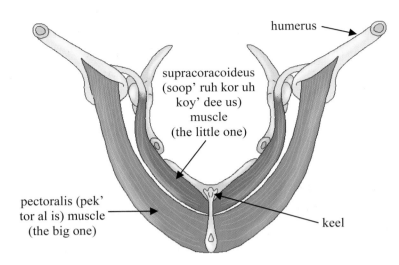

humerus

supracoracoideus
(soop' ruh kor uh
koy' dee us)
muscle
(the little one)

pectoralis (pek'
tor al is) muscle
(the big one)

keel

This is a diagram of the two major flight muscles in a bird.

Look at the drawing of a bird's flight muscles shown on the left. The muscles are attached to a bone in the bird's chest, called the **keel**. The other end of each muscle is attached to a wing bone called the **humerus** (hyoo' mer us). Every bird has two major flight muscles; a big one and a little one. The smaller muscle is used when the bird lifts its wings. This is called the **upstroke**. The bigger muscle is used to pull the wings down, which is called the **downstroke**.

Flap your arms like a bird. When your arms go up, that is the upstroke. When your arms go down, that is the downstroke. Why do you think the downstroke needs a bigger muscle? Well, the down stroke motion of the wing is how the bird gets the power in its flight. That muscle, then, has to be big so that the bird gets the power it needs.

Takeoff

To eat, a thrush pulls worms from the ground, while an eagle catches food that races along the ground or flies through the air. Which one do you think can get into the air more quickly, and which one do you think can fly faster once in the air? Well, a blackbird can get into the air more quickly because it needs to escape predators, while the eagle can fly faster because it needs to capture speedy prey. God gave each bird wings that are shaped especially for that bird's needs.

This thrush has its lunch – a tasty worm!

Do you remember that a bird must have the wind flowing over its wings in order to get lift? In fact, many birds turn to face the wind in order to take off. You might think it would be easier to fly in the same direction as the wind, but if you understand the science of flying, you can see that taking off against the wind can be better, because it allows for more air to flow over the wing, providing lift.

Large birds with big wings need to get the air moving faster over them before they can get the lift they need. They can't just jump into the air and fly off. They need to run a bit to get air flowing over their wings. If you watch large geese or swans on the water, you will notice they actually run along the water before they get up into the air. You won't often see a large hawk or eagle on the ground, because it prefers to land on a branch or cliff. That way, it can take off by jumping into the wind. Either way, the main thing to realize is that big birds need a lot of air flowing over their wings in order to be able to take off. Smaller birds need less lift because they are lighter. They can simply hop up and dart off. This is necessary for protection, since small birds are prey for many animals and therefore often have to make a quick escape to avoid being eaten!

Steering

How do birds steer while flying? Well, God designed the birds so that they could use various parts of their body to get the job done. In order to make a sharp turn while flying very fast, a bird must use its tail, which acts like a little rudder. Sometimes a bird will simply tilt one wing a bit higher than the other. That causes the bird to turn slowly in the direction of the wing that is lower. Other times, birds turn by flapping one wing faster than the other wing. This causes the bird to turn in the direction of the wing that is not flapping as quickly. Some birds use all these methods, and some only use one or two. Notice how the birds in your yard turn and try to figure out which method they use. Record that information in your notebook.

Flapping and Gliding

When birds fly through the sky, you will notice that they flap their wings for a while and then glide. To glide, they hold their wings straight out and sail through the air, like the glider you made in Lesson 1. Some birds can glide a long time, especially big birds with long wings. This helps them search for food or migrate while at the same time saving energy. After all, when a bird flaps its wings, it uses energy. If the bird can fly without flapping, the bird will not have to eat as much, because it will not be using as much energy. The smallest of birds, the hummingbird, has such tiny wings that it doesn't glide very much. Its wings flap almost continually while it is in the air. As a result, it eats *a lot* of food so that it has the energy it needs to fly.

Why does a bird flap its wings? Well, do you remember what I told you about drag? The air drags against a bird, slowing it down. When a bird flaps its wings, it is producing the thrust it needs to overcome drag and speed up. This makes more air flow over its wings, providing lift. When a bird has the speed it needs, it stretches out its wings and glides. Of course, while it glides, drag causes it to slow down, which reduces lift. This makes the bird drift downward. Eventually, the bird will have to flap its wings again to overcome the drag and get more lift. Most birds don't fly any higher than they need to, because climbing high into the sky takes a great deal of energy. There is also less air the higher you go, so it becomes more difficult for the bird to breathe the higher it flies.

When you see a bird traveling overhead, notice how often it flaps and glides. Does the bird tend to stay on a straight path, or does it go up and down? When a bird goes up and down, it is called **undulating flight**. Many finches use undulating flight.

The bird at the top of this drawing is using undulating flight.

Some bird species that look almost exactly alike can be told apart just by the way they fly.

Soaring

Soaring is very different from gliding. Have you ever seen a surfer? A surfer is someone that gets on a surf board and tries to "catch a wave." If he does it right, he can ride the wave all the way back to the beach. Well, in the air, there are heat waves called **thermals** that rise up from the ground. God has designed birds that soar to know where thermals are and how to jump on top of them for a ride.

When a bird is on a thermal, the rising air will lift the bird higher and higher. Sometimes the bird must soar in tight circles to stay on top of a thermal. Other times, the thermal is so large that the bird can go straight for many feet before it needs to turn to stay on top of the thermal.

This vulture is soaring on a thermal, looking for food.

Vultures (birds that eat dead animals) have wings perfect for soaring. Some people think that if a vulture is circling over an area, a dead animal is below. That isn't so. A vulture will fly down to stand near a dead or dying animal so that it can eat the animal. It doesn't circle above it. The bird is circling around to ride on thermals so that it can *look for* dead animals to eat. It's probably a lot of fun to ride on thermals!

Thermals rise as the sun heats up the ground. This makes the air right above the ground warmer than the air farther above the ground, and the warmer air begins to rise. Since the ground must be warmed to create a thermal, they are only created during the day. In the summer, it gets hot early in the morning, so that's when the thermals form. As a result, you'll see birds soaring early on summer mornings. In winter, however, the ground does not warm up until later on in the morning, so you won't see birds soaring until about 10 o'clock or so. Next time you are driving around town, check the sky for soaring birds! What time was it when you saw them?

Seabirds

Seabirds have thin, pointy wings which are stiffer than the wings of other birds. This is because the gusty winds of the ocean press hard against them. Seabird wings are designed to slice through the sea's gusty winds. A land bird with its wide, arched wings would get blown and tossed about by the ocean winds.

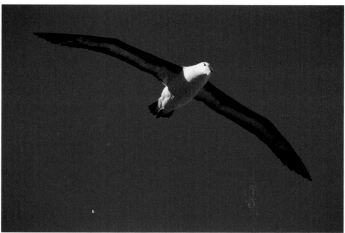

This albatross is riding a gust of wind above the ocean.

The ocean doesn't provide rising thermals of air like the land does, but seabirds are specially designed to ride on gusts of wind coming off the water. These gusts are small, however, so a seabird must be able to locate the next gust after the first gust is past.

An albatross, the bird with the longest wing span in the world (eleven feet!) can ride on the gusts of wind coming off the ocean for days at a time. It must do this to conserve energy since it spends most of its life out at sea, coming to shore or remote islands only briefly to lay eggs and raise its young.

Explain what you have learned about flight muscles and birds in flight.

Migration

For bird watchers, the fall and spring are wonderful and exciting seasons. This is especially true for birders that keep a life list. Do you remember what a life list is? Spring and fall allow birders to add unusual or rare birds to their life list. That's because in the fall, birds in the north fly south for the winter. In the spring, birds in the south fly north for the summer. In other words, birds **migrate** in the spring and fall. Migration is just part of being a bird. Most birds do it. Some will congregate in great flocks to migrate; some will fly alone. Amazingly, without being taught, each bird knows where to go and what to do. Twice a year, a bird prepares for its journey. It begins packing early, packing its body full of food, that is. Once packed, it leaves. Some birds take flight at night and sleep during the day. Some fly all day and rest each night. Some fly through the day and through the night, never stopping until they get there. They usually follow the same route every year.

As you learned in Lesson 2, birds that don't reside in your area but pass through are called migrants. Sometimes, they stop at your feeder for a bite to eat. They may even stay a day or two before moving on. If they really enjoy the food, they will probably come back year after year. What a wonderful way to enjoy a new species that you can add to your life list!

Why Do They Say Good-bye?

Why do some birds leave and some birds stay? Why do some birds come only for the summer and some birds only for winter? Where do they go when they leave? These are questions that have always fascinated ornithologists. Even today, scientists are trying to find the answers to these questions by experimenting with migrating birds, banding them, and studying their habits.

Why and how birds migrate has always fascinated scientists.

Ancient scientists, such as Aristotle, thought that perhaps the birds that disappeared in the winter dug holes in the mud, crawled in the holes, and **hibernated**. If you are not familiar with the word "hibernate," it means, "to sleep through the winter." That was Aristotle's hypothesis about what happened to the birds that left for the winter. Of course, we know today that Aristotle's hypothesis was wrong. Birds definitely do not dig holes in the ground and hibernate in them!

Why do birds migrate? The most accepted answer is they are programmed by God to instinctively go where food will be available. How do they know when and where to go? Is there something that happens to the environment that tells them it's time to prepare to leave? They certainly don't wait until food is scarce, and they leave before it even gets cold! How do birds know when to migrate? What triggers the instinct?

Many scientists think that the length of the day, which is called the **photoperiod** (foh' toh peer' ee uhd), tells a bird when it must migrate. When the days grow shorter in the fall, a bird's body produces chemicals called **hormones**. These hormones tell the bird to get ready for migration. It begins to load up on food, storing up vast amounts of fat to sustain itself on its long journey south for the winter. In the same way, when the days start growing longer in the spring, the bird's body once again produces hormones that tell it to prepare for the journey northward for the summer.

Once a bird knows that it's time to migrate, how does it know which way to go? How does it get to its destination every year without losing its way? Let's learn some of the answers to those questions.

Knowing Where to Go

Scientists who have studied bird migration have found that a bird will usually follow the same migration route year after year. In fact, some birds will stop in the same yard, at the same feeder, usually on the same day or week each year. If you see a strange bird in your yard during migration season, write down the date in your life list book. The next year, keep an eye out for that bird at the same time. See how close the bird gets to the same day as the year before.

Birds have an incredible sense of direction! Scientists experimented with certain terns, taking them from their home in the Gulf of Mexico and shipping them hundreds of miles away from their homes. They sent the birds places that they had never been before, over oceans and islands they had never seen. They then let the birds go, and, within a few days, the birds found their way back home, right back to their nest! Scientists also took a Manx Shearwater (*Puffinus puffinus*) from its home in Great Britain and took it to the United States. As soon as it was released, the bird flew 3,100 miles across the Atlantic Ocean (nonstop) back home to its nest in twelve days.

These Red-crowned Cranes (*Grus japonensis*) live in Manchuria and Siberia during the summer and migrate to South Korea and China for the winter. They never get lost going back and forth.

The ability for a bird to reach its destination without getting lost is called a **homing instinct**. What is even more amazing is that birds flying high up in the sky are continually blown off course by the wind, but they always get right back on course. How do they do this? If they get off course even a tiny bit, and they continue to head in the same direction, they will end up at the wrong place. The wind is strong and can easily cause birds to shift directions. Amazingly, these birds are designed with the ability to always adjust their direction to go the correct way.

Try This!

Stand at one end of a large room or yard. Pick a spot straight ahead to walk toward it. After you have taken a couple of steps, turn your body just slightly to the right. Continue walking straight ahead. You will now be heading to a different spot, and you will never reach the spot you originally picked unless you adjust your course correctly. Of course this is easy for you to do because you can see the spot you are heading toward. After all, you are only a few feet from the spot, not hundreds of miles away. God has designed birds with an incredible homing instinct. This gives them the ability to know which way to go even if they can't see where they are going.

Using Landmarks

So how do birds know where to go? Well, once a bird has migrated, it can use **landmarks** to help guide it to where it needs to go. Landmarks are usually large structures that don't move. They serve to help you know where you are. For example, when you are going on vacation, you may see a building or something along the side of the road that reminds you that you are going the right way. That is landmark. Can you think of any landmarks you use to know where you are?

Scientists believe that birds memorize the way things look during migration. They notice landmarks like large trees, mountains, houses, and other things they saw on the way last time. This may explain why a bird will return to the same feeder every year. It uses landmarks to remember where it found tasty food during its previous trip.

Sun and Stars

Landmarks might help a bird remember where to go, but what about the very first journey the bird makes? If a bird hasn't made the trip before, it hasn't had a chance to see landmarks. Scientists have learned that many birds actually navigate using the sun or the stars. Birds that fly during the day are led by the direction of the sun as it passes across the sky. Birds that fly at night tend to navigate by the pattern of stars in the sky. We call these patterns of stars **constellations** (kahn' stuh lay' shuns).

How do we know that birds navigate using constellations? Well, in experiments, scientists placed migrating birds in a large planetarium with stars reflected on the ceiling. The birds changed the direction they were flying when the researchers changed the constellations of the stars on the ceiling. Birds aren't the only ones that navigate by the sun and the constellations. Many years ago, people navigated in the same way. Sailors, for example, used an instrument called a **sextant** to measure the position of a particular star or the sun in the sky. That would tell them where they were on the ocean so that they would know where to steer their ships.

Sailors used a sextant like this to determine the position of a star (or the sun) in the sky, which helped them navigate.

Magnetic Fields

Some birds also navigate using the earth's magnetic field. The earth is a like a giant magnet, with a magnetic field that surrounds it. That is why a compass always points north. The needle of a compass is a little magnet, and it is attracted to the pull of other magnets, including the magnetic pull of the earth. This pull causes the compass needle to point north. Thus, no matter where you are, you always know which way north is by looking at a compass.

Studies show that some birds sense the earth's magnetic field so that they always know which way north is. This helps a bird navigate, because it tells the bird which way it should fly. If a bird is flying south for the winter, it knows that it must head *opposite* of north. As a result, if it gets turned around, it can always determine which way is north and then fly in the opposite direction.

Scientist have done experiments in which they have captured migrating birds and used machines that sent out a magnetic field that the birds thought was coming from the earth. By changing the magnetic field created by the machines, they were able to cause the birds to change direction. Scientists have found **magnetite** (a magnetic substance) in the heads of some birds. This, they believe is what helps birds sense the magnetic field of the earth.

Whether by landmarks, constellations, the sun, or magnetic fields, birds know when to go, where to go, and almost always make it to their destination right on time. The bird knows to do this because of the instinct it is given by God. Do you remember the Bible verse we looked at in the first lesson? God says to Job, "*Is it by your understanding that the hawk soars, stretching his wings toward the south?*" (Job 39:29). In this verse, God reveals to us that it is by *His* understanding that the hawk and all other birds know where, when, and how to migrate.

Enough Eating?

How do you suppose a bird gets the energy it needs to fly? The bird gets its energy the same way we do, from the food it eats! If it eats more food than it needs, the excess energy is stored as fat, which can be used at a later time. So birds fatten before they start their migration. You'll notice birds getting nice and chunky right before they leave, because they are eating a lot more than normal, storing the excess food as fat.

This Pacific Golden-Plover (*Pluvialis fulva*) makes a 2,500 mile trip without stopping.

Some birds travel very long distances without ever stopping for food or water. The Pacific Golden-Plover, for example, travels nonstop for about 2,500 miles when it migrates! Can you imagine making such a trip? It usually takes the Pacific Golden-Plover just under 4 days to make the flight, and it never stops for food or water, because much of the trip is over the open sea, and the Pacific Golden-Plover cannot swim! It can make the trip because it eats so much that by the time it starts, it has added more than half of its normal weight in fat! That fat provides the energy the bird needs, and it also supplies the bird with water, because as the fat is burned for energy, water is made. The bird uses that water so it doesn't have to stop for a drink.

Are We There Yet?

This toucan doesn't need to migrate, because it lives in the warm rain forests of South America.

Some birds migrate a thousand miles or more, but some may migrate a shorter distance, such as from a high mountain to the valley below, where it is a bit warmer. Birds like the Black Rosy-Finch and the Mountain Quail breed high up in the mountains and move down the mountain into the warmer valleys for the winter. Of course, some birds don't migrate at all because they live in a warm tropical environment and eat the fruit and other tropical food that grows there all year long. Many hummingbirds, toucans, and parrots that live in Central and South America, for example, never leave the warm tropical forests in which they live.

Some birds don't migrate because they can survive on the food available in the cold season: seeds, tree buds, and dry berries. Because insects aren't available to birds during cold winters, insect-eating birds usually migrate, but others (chickadees, nuthatches, titmice, and woodpeckers, for example) change their diet in the winter. Instead of eating insects, they will eat insect eggs, cocoons, seeds and, of course, the suet you make for them.

Migrating birds usually stop along the way to rest and refuel. Others, like the Pacific Golden-Plover, fly the entire way without stopping. If a bird migrates long distances without stopping, it must be careful to eat just the right amount of food for the journey. If a bird eats too much, it will be too heavy for the journey, and it will use up more energy than it should flying with all that extra weight. Have you ever carried something heavy a long way? Perhaps you had to carry a backpack up a mountain or through the airport. Maybe you had to carry a heavy sack of groceries from the car to the kitchen. Carrying extra weight uses up a lot of energy. You were probably tired after you did that work. A bird needs to make sure it doesn't have too much weight, or it will be too tired to complete the journey.

At the same time, however, if a bird doesn't eat enough, it won't be able to complete the journey. Have you ever started school on an empty stomach? You felt tired and not interested in what you were learning because you didn't get enough of the right food in your body. Imagine how a bird would feel if it was trying to fly to Mexico without enough food. It would run out of energy. A bird needs to eat exactly the right amount of food so that it will not get too fat or be too hungry to make it the whole way.

In addition to eating just the right amount, a bird needs to fly at just the right speed on its journey. Do you know anyone who runs in marathon races? A marathon is a long distance race that covers just over 26 miles. In order to finish the race, a marathon runner needs to find just the right speed to run in order to make it the whole way. He can't run too quickly, or he will get tired out, but he can't run too slowly, or he will take too long and finish last.

Migrating birds have the same difficulty as marathon runners. They can't fly too fast and use up their energy too quickly, yet they can't fly too slowly or they will also run out of energy before they finish the journey. Because God gives birds the understanding they need, birds know the exact speed at which they need to fly and how much food is necessary to make the trip!

Champion Migrator

The champion of all migrating birds is the Arctic Tern. This tern isn't such a big bird (about a foot long), but it flies more than 20,000 miles each year, from the Arctic Circle to the Antarctic and back again. Can you trace your finger on a globe from the North Pole to the South Pole? That's the Arctic Circle to the Antarctic. Both places are the coldest regions in the world.

This Arctic Tern (*Sterna paradisaea*) has dinner in its mouth.

It takes the Arctic Tern four months to go one way and four months more to go back the other way. That's eight months of traveling, which means this little bird spends most of its life migrating. Why do these birds fly from one cold location like the Arctic to another cold location like the Antarctic? We are not really sure. Most scientists believe that Arctic Terns like cold weather, but they also like a lot of sunlight. During the summer, they are in the Artic Circle, where the days are long. However, as winter approaches in the Arctic Circle, the days get shorter, so they fly to the Antarctic. When they get there, it is winter in the Arctic Circle, but it is *summer* in the Antarctic. As a result, the days are once again long. The Arctic tern's migration, therefore, allows it to see more daylight than any other bird in creation.

Perils on the Path

Migrating birds face many dangers. Storms can come suddenly, and because the bird doesn't know the region, it doesn't know a safe place to find cover. Hawks, owls, and eagles prey on other birds. Hunters are another threat to migrating birds, because hunters set themselves up along a well-known migration path, waiting for the birds that will fly along it.

Despite their excellent means of determining where to fly, birds can occasionally get off course and end up somewhere a long, long way from their destination. Perhaps they got caught in a wind storm and got off track. Maybe they got sick or hungry and couldn't get back on the path. Maybe they were injured and lost their ability to stay the course. Whatever the reason, some birds end up where they have never been before. These birds are called **vagrants** (vay' gruhnts). Vagrants are exciting for birders, because they get to take a look at a bird that they would not normally get to see. When a vagrant bird is spotted, many birders will drive hundreds of miles to look at it. There are even email lists where people can find out if there are vagrant birds anywhere near them.

How High Can You Go?

Migrating birds usually fly about 3,000 to 6,000 feet above the ground, but some birds have been found flying at levels that no other animal could survive. Did you know that people who climb mountains are not supposed to climb above 25,000 feet? The area of a mountain above that height is called the "death zone," because people cannot survive high up in the atmosphere. This is because the amount of air gets lower as you go higher, which make it difficult to breathe. When a mountain climber begins to get high up a mountain, even as low as a few thousand feet, he begins to breathe faster, panting because he has a hard time getting the oxygen he needs. As he climbs higher and higher, his heart rate also begins to beat incredibly fast. If he reaches the death zone, his body functions quickly deteriorate, and if he stays too long, he could die.

Even though people and most animals cannot survive at such elevations, Bar-headed Geese fly over Mount Everest (which is more than 29,000 feet high) in their spring migration every year. A

pilot reported running into a Griffin Vulture flying 37,000 feet above the ground. How can some birds do this? Well, God designed birds with a special breathing system. You see, when people (or animals) breathe, our lungs fill with air. Some of the oxygen in the air is transferred to our blood, but not all of it. In fact, when we breathe out, we get rid of a waste product called carbon dioxide as well as more than half the oxygen we just breathed in. In other words, we don't use all of the oxygen that we breathe in. Birds are able to use a lot more of the oxygen in the air, because the air they breathe passes through their lungs *twice*. As a result, they can get a lot more oxygen from the air than we can!

These Bar-headed Geese (*Anser indicus*) can survive at altitudes that would kill most animals.

Flocks or Loners

Some birds flock together and make the journey in huge numbers. Do you remember the story of the now extinct Passenger Pigeon? During migration, flocks of Passenger Pigeons covered the sky like a dark cloud.

This flock of Snow Geese has just arrived at its winter home in New Mexico. They spent the summer in the high Arctic tundra.

Flying in flocks makes traveling safer for many birds. There is safety in numbers, and there are many predators they will face during their travels. This might be the reason that some smaller birds migrate only at night and find a thicket in which to sleep during the day. Larger birds like geese are often too big for birds of prey. They migrate during the day or night and find a nice water hole or marsh in which to rest.

Many small birds that fly in flocks simply flitter up and down like a wave through the sky, but some birds are given special instincts that enable them to fly in formation. The tell-tale "V" pattern

This is a photo of Canada Geese flying in formation.

you see in the photo on the left allows the birds to fly faster and save energy. The bird in front works hard as he breaks the wind current, and that makes it easier for the birds behind to fly. When he gets tired, he falls back and a new bird takes the lead. This happens over and over again, saving energy for all the birds in their journey. Do you know which birds fly in formation? Geese, ducks, gulls, and some waterfowl often do this.

In Exodus, chapter 16, we read that the Israelites, God's chosen people, had been traveling in the desert in search of the Promised Land. They began complaining that they would starve to death, but the Bible says God sent quail that "covered the camp" in the evening. The Israelites ate the quail meat, and after that, God sent bread down every morning (except for the Sabbath morning). Although we cannot be certain, it is thought that God caused Coturnix Quail to stop their migration so that they would land in the midst of the Israelite camp. Descendants of these same quail still travel between their winter quarters in Africa and their breeding grounds in West Asia and Eastern Europe.

Not all birds seek out their own kind when migrating. Some birds actually travel in mixed flocks. Sometimes swallows, sparrows, blackbirds, and some of the shorebirds can be found in flocks made up of several different species.

Some birds, like eagles and many other birds of prey, travel all alone. Since they are not prey for other birds, they don't need the protection that large flocks afford.

Left Alone

Some birds do the unthinkable and abandon their young chicks, flying south without them. The Bristle-thighed Curlew and the Short-tailed Shearwater actually leave the poor chicks before they have ever flown from their nest. They just up and leave, flying to a distant country thousands of miles away. They leave no directions for their little ones to follow. Yet, as is common with God's magnificent creatures, the little chicks are very resourceful. They jump from their nests, learn to find their own food, fatten up for their flight, and flock together with other abandoned chicks to fly to the very spot where their parents are. They fly 5,000 miles *without ever stopping.* How do the little chicks do it? How do they know where to go? How do they know not to stop? Remember, these little chicks have never been there before, and they

This Bristle-thighed Curlew (*Numenius tahitiensis*) leaves its young to fend for themselves.

have no parents to guide them on their journey. The incredible flights of these and other migratory birds point unmistakably to God, who designed His creation to do those things that would bring Him glory and honor!

Tell in your own words what you can remember about bird migration.

What Do You Remember?

How are bird bones different from the bones of other animals? Where are a bird's flight muscles located? Tell about the different kinds of flying birds do. What does a bird use its tail for when flying? What causes a bird to migrate? How does a bird find its way while migrating? Why do some birds flock together while migrating? Why do others migrate alone? What is the benefit of flying in formation? Which birds abandon their young when they migrate?

Nature Points

You will have a lot of short-term visitors at your feeder during migration season. During these times, make sure your feeder is equipped with the best food available so that your yard will become a regular landmark for migrating birds that pass over your area.

If you have kept good records of the birds you see in your yard, look back through your bird book and take note of birds you recorded that you are not seeing anymore. Where did they go? Try to find out.

Often, when flying to their breeding grounds, male birds arrive first and begin preparing a nest for the arrival of the females. In spring, watch your yard carefully to see which migrating birds arrive first.

Notebook Activity

Write down all that you can remember from this lesson in your notebook. Be sure to include the information you learned about flying and migration. If you have the *Zoology 1 Notebooking Journal*, use the Fascinating Facts pages to record your learning.

Younger Students:

Choose one species of migrating bird, and using a map of the world or of the area of migration, trace its route of travel from its winter home to its summer home. Place your map in your notebook. Write a paragraph about this bird's habits and draw or cut out and paste a picture of this bird on a piece of paper for your notebook. If you have the *Zoology 1 Notebooking Journal*, a template for this activity is provided, including a map.

Older Students:

Research where the birds in your town go during the winter and where the wintering birds go during the summer. Also make a list of all the non-migrating birds in your area. Write down all that you learn. If you are making a field guide, be certain to include this information about each species. Birds that stay in your area only during the summer are called "summer residents." Birds that only come in the winter are called "winter residents." Birds that stay year round are called "permanent residents." Migrants are those birds that simply pass through. Do you remember the name of lost birds? They are called "vagrants." A template for this activity is included in the *Zoology 1 Notebooking Journal*.

Experiment
Which color do birds prefer?

During the migration period, you can attract hummingbirds to your house with red colors and red hummingbird feeders filled with sugar water. Hummingbirds are greatly attracted to the color red and will pause from their long migration to stop by and get refueled for the rest of their journey. Do other birds like the color red? What other color might attract birds to stop by during their migration flight? Let's do an experiment to test whether or not other birds prefer red or some other color.

You will need:

♦ Two bird feeders that are exactly the same and can be painted (We used wooden tangerine crates to make our feeders, but you can use any kind of feeder, even a soda pop bottle feeder like the one you made in Lesson 2.)
♦ A scale to measure the weights of the feeders and seed each day.
♦ Spray or acrylic paint: red and green (You can use a color besides green, but be sure that one of the colors you use is red, because we are testing whether or not other birds like that color.)
♦ Bird food

1. Use a Scientific Speculation Sheet to write down your hypothesis of which color the birds will prefer. They may also not prefer either, so that could be your hypothesis.
2. Paint one bird feeder green and the other one red. Let them dry.
3. Fill the feeders with the same kind of bird food. Weigh each of them. Make sure they are the same weight when you put them outside.

4. Remember, you need everything about the two feeders (except the color) to be exactly the same. Find a place where you can set both feeders so that they are in the same location and at the same height.
5. At the same time each day, weigh each feeder and write down the weight.
6. If you need to refill one feeder, refill both of them until they weigh exactly the same amount. This way you begin again and are able to tell which one continually ends up lighter at the end of each day.

7. Be certain squirrels are not removing the seeds from your feeders. This will skew the results.
8. If one of the feeders consistently weighs less than the other, that is the color the birds prefer.
9. Fill out the rest of the Scientific Speculation Sheet. Was your hypothesis correct?

Lesson 5
Nesting

"The bird also has found a house, and the swallow a nest for herself, where she may lay her young, even Your altars, O LORD of hosts, my King and my God." -Psalm 84:3

A rabbit lives in a hole. A bear often makes its home in a cave. You and I have a safe home to live in every day. But – this may surprise you – nests are *not* bird homes. Usually, a bird will use its nest only to raise its young. It's not where a bird lives year round. Once a baby bird is grown, it doesn't return to its nest, and once a bird is done raising all its young for a season, it usually doesn't need the nest any longer. It only sleeps in the nest when it is incubating eggs (keeping them warm) or caring for its young.

This Field Sparrow is caring for its young in the nest. Once the young are gone, the bird will no longer use the nest.

I bet you are wondering where a bird sleeps since it doesn't live in its nest. Well, if a bird prefers to make its nest in a tree hole, it will likely find a hole in which to sleep for the night; but it won't use a nest. Most owls will sleep the day away hidden in a forest tree that is thickly covered with leaves. Ground birds, like quail and pheasants, will spend the night sleeping on the ground under a bush. Sparrows, hummingbirds, and cardinals will find a thick bush in which to roost for the night. If you are not familiar with the term "roost," it simply means "to rest or sleep." The thicker the bush, the dryer they stay on a rainy night. Do you have any thick bushes in your yard that could provide a safe roosting place for a bird?

Very few birds use their nests after they are done raising their young. However, some species (especially those that live in desert areas) use their nests all year round as protection. During the day, the nests protect the birds from the hot desert sun, and during the night, they protect the birds from the cold. They also protect the birds during sandstorms.

A nest that hasn't had a bird visit it in several days has usually been abandoned and will probably not be used again. The next year, some species go back to the same nest, but most can't help themselves from building a whole new one. It just comes naturally. But remember this: It's against the law to keep a bird's nest. This is the government's way of keeping the birds safe from those who might sell nests and collect them with eggs still in them.

Home Builders

For most birds in North America, nesting season begins in the spring around March. The warming weather and the lengthening day set off an instinct that tells birds to begin constructing nests. By the end of August, nesting season ends. In very warm tropical climates, where the weather is always just right for baby birds, nesting season can last for up to eight months.

This stork is gathering hay to make its nest.

In the spring, many birds can be seen pulling at moss, yanking at dead strands of grass, and poking around in bushes looking for materials that they will use for nest building. Some will pick up yarn, hair, string, or dryer lint to add to the nest. Hummingbirds can be found pulling lichen off trees and snatching bits of cobweb which they use to attach their tiny nest to a tree. Usually, the female builds the nest, and the male assists her. In some species, the male does nothing, and in others, the male builds the nest and the female does nothing.

Many birds "glue" their nests together with items like cobwebs, caterpillar silk, mud, and even their own saliva (spit). Most nest builders like to put soft material in the part of the nest that will hold their eggs and young. Some birds even put herbs and spices in their nests. Researchers believe that these herbs help fight off bacteria or help in some other way that we don't completely understand.

A few bird species decorate their nests with strange things! They might choose bright, shiny objects like money, tin foil, gold buttons, or other metal objects. Bowerbirds decorate their nests with colorful objects such as glass, insect wings, pebbles, and flowers. Every once in a while you might see a bird carrying an odd item in its bill, like the bowerbird bird on the right. Most likely, the bird will use the item as a decoration for its nest!

This bird will use the bottle cap in its mouth to decorate its nest.

A bird's nest building improves over the years. New nest builders don't build as well as more experienced nest builders, but all birds know how and where to build their nests. Even birds raised in captivity without a nest will build a nest during the proper season, if they are given a chance.

Types of Nests

This is a cup nest, as it is shaped like a cup.

When you think of a bird's nest, what do you imagine it looks like? I generally think of a **cup nest**, such as the one pictured on the left. A cup nest, however, is really only one kind of nest. There are so many different ways that birds nest, from digging holes in the ground to even sticking some twigs and leaves inside the "o" of a McDonald's sign. If a bird simply scrapes a little depression in the ground and lays its eggs there, we say this is its nest, and we also say that this is where it nests. So the word nest can be a noun or a verb. A bird nests in a nest!

You will be surprised how many different nesting habits birds have. Some are strange and unusual, but all of them are a result of God's special design for each bird. Some nests can be as large and weigh as much as a car, like an old eagle's nest. Some nests can be as small as a thimble, like the nest of a Bee Hummingbird. Let's explore some interesting nests now!

Unusual Nests

The tailorbirds, a kind of warbler, makes a little cradle for its eggs by weaving two leaves together with plant fibers and spider webs. That's an interesting and unusual nest.

The bowerbird builds a **bower** (a little gazebolike structure made of dried leaves, straw, and twigs) right on the ground. Then, it decorates its bower with baubles such as shells, rocks, and feathers. The Satin Bowerbird [its scientific name is *Ptilonorhyncus* (til' uh nor ink' us) *violaceus* (vye uh lay' see us)] will use anything it can find, as long as it's blue. It will use blue straws, blue lids, blue ribbon, or any other blue thing it can find. Why does this bird build such a structure? Well, the only reason is to impress the females. You see, only the male bowerbird builds a bower. When it is done, it will call over the females and show off its great work of art with loud calls, strutting around as if to say, "See what I did!" If a female likes the nest, they become partners. The funny thing is, after all his hard work, she runs off and builds a nest in a nearby tree for their young!

This Satin Bowerbird has almost completed its elaborate bower. Notice all of the blue decorations.

Weavers

This weaver is putting the finishing touches on its nest. Notice the other weaver nests in the photo. They are already finished.

Weavers are amazing birds that can actually weave a hanging, basketlike nest using only their feet and beaks. They spend days working on their creations, which can be used for shelter from predators or the outdoor elements even when they are done raising their young.

Do you think you could weave a nest from grass or pine straw that was strong enough to hold eggs and baby birds using just your fingers?

Social weavers are birds that join other birds to weave a huge apartment complex, where every bird has a compartment of its own in which to lay its eggs. In other words, such weavers all live in one huge woven home, but they all have their own separate rooms.

No Nests

Some birds build no nests. Actually, anywhere a bird lays its egg is a nest, so even birds that don't *build* nests still *have* nests. The most famous bird that doesn't build a nest is the Emperor Penguin. The female lays her egg and rolls it onto the male's feet, and the male keeps the egg warm by covering it with a thick roll of skin and feathers (called a **brood pouch**) that exists between its feet and stomach. He holds the egg like that for *nine weeks*, waiting for it to hatch.

Other **no nesters** will find a nice spot on the ground and, without so much as moving over a leaf or stone, they will lay their eggs right there. The Short-eared Owl, for example, might find some trampled down leaves and lay its eggs there without doing anything else.

This White Tern (*Gygis alba*) lays its egg on a tree branch without building a nest for it.

One no nester, the White Tern, finds a nice tree branch and lays its one single egg right on the branch with no nest to keep it cradled! It spends the day like an acrobat, sitting on the egg, carefully

in the cavity of a large tree. The male then stands outside the cavity while the female sits on the eggs, and they both work together to *build a wall that covers the opening of the cavity*. This wall has a tiny slit through which the male can provide food for the female as she sits on the eggs, keeping them warm. The female stays shut up in the cavity, completely hidden from predators and dependent on the male while she cares for the eggs and the young that hatch.

Platform Nesters

A **platform nest** is a bunch of twigs and foliage that, when put together, look mostly flat. Raptors (birds of prey like hawks and eagles) and other large birds build huge platform nests on the sides of cliffs or high up in a large tree. They can spend months working on their nests, adding branch after branch for weeks on end. They often return to the same nest year after year and continue building it up. Even after the nestlings have hatched and flown away, some platform nesters might add a branch or two to their nest now and then. They must really enjoy nest building!

This is a photo of Bald Eagles and their platform nest.

Because some platform nesters return to the same nest every year and continually add to it, their nests can get *huge*. A Bald Eagle's nest, for example, can weigh as much as *a ton* (that's how much a small car weighs)! It is often built in a tree, and it can become so heavy that it damages the tree it is in. Some eagles build their nests on cliffs. This is much safer, because the eagles don't have to worry about a cliff being damaged by the weight of the nest! Do you remember that eagle's nests are protected by the government? If you have one on your property, you are not allowed to build anything near it, and you can't cut the tree down that supports it.

A few water birds (like grebes and loons) build platform nests right on the water, where they actually float. The nests don't move, however, because they are anchored to plants that are attached to the bottom of the body of water. These birds build nests on the water because they don't walk well on land.

This is a photo of a Horned Grebe at its floating platform nest.

Their legs are not designed for life out of the water. So, they find a nice shallow part of the water in which to build their nests. That way, they don't need to walk to their nests; they can just swim to them! When the babies are ready, they can simply hop right into the water and begin their aquatic life.

Cup Nesters

The **cup nest** is probably the most common of all bird nests. Its name tells you that a cup nest is shaped like a cup or a bowl. Many songbirds (remember, they are called passerines) build cup nests. These nests can be built in the limbs of a tree or even on the eaves of a house. Usually they are built in a crook where one limb meets another limb; however, some birds are masters at simply securing the nest right onto the limb of a tree. They'll use a lot of materials that act like glue: mud, rotten wood, dung, spider webs, and caterpillar silk. They may even use their own saliva mixed with food to secure the nest to the branch.

This Chipping Sparrow nest has been built in a crook where three tree limbs meet.

Cup nesters use all kinds of materials to build a nest: twigs, grass, lichen, moss and leaves; and they use all kinds of materials to hold it together. Most cup nesters use coarse material for the outside of the nest. This provides protection and camouflages the nest. They then line the inside of the nest with soft, cozy material like moss, fur, down, and cotton.

This hummingbird's cup nest is "glued" right to the tree limb.

Many cup nesters prefer to nest extremely close to the ground in low bushes and thickets. Sometimes they will even nest in a potted plant on your porch! Would you believe that a few cup nesters actually build their nests on the ground? Sparrows, cardinals, and many other song birds prefer to nest in bushes or near the ground, far away from owls, hawks, and Blue Jays that may eat their young. If you have a lot of bushes in your yard, it will be a popular place for cup nesters.

There are several kinds of cup nests that are more elaborate than the little cup nestled in a tree. A **suspended cup nest** is attached to the branch at the top and sides but then drops down below. The bird weaves an intricate and very tight vase-like nest for her eggs with a little opening in the top. The eggs are laid inside, and the bird is almost hidden from view when she incubates them. The mother bird can sit on the branch above the nest and bend down to feed her little hatchlings, which are cuddled safely inside the suspended cup. The Red-eyed Vireo makes a suspended cup nest.

A **pendulous** (pen' joo lus) **cup nest** is much like a suspended nest because it also hangs down below the branch and has a small opening at the top, but it is very soft and flexible. Orioles are the most popular builders of pendulous nests, weaving amazing long bags that hang far below the branch.

This pendulous nest was built by an Audubon Oriole.

The smallest cup nests are made by hummingbirds. They can be as small as a thimble, which is the case for the Bee Hummingbird's nest. That tiny nest holds eggs the size of peas. The largest cup nest probably belongs to the stork, whose nest can be nine feet deep and six feet wide. The stork's nest is so grand that many smaller birds make their nests in its slits, holes, and branches!

Try This!

Building a cup nest may seem like a simple chore, but let's see if you can do it as well as a bird. You will need mud, twigs, grass, string, cotton, leaves, and anything else you might like to use to build a nest. Try to build a nest that stays together and could be placed in a tree. Use mud as the foundation and then begin weaving other materials into your nest. Be sure to add some soft items in the cup to cushion the eggs.

Adherent Nests

Adherent (ad heer' unt) **nests** adhere (that means "stick") to the side of a building, tree, cliff, or other vertical structure. Birds that use these nests essentially build their own cavities with mud or other materials for nesting. Swifts and swallows are the most common adherent nesters. Swallows can build an almost perfectly round nest out of mud. Some species make cup-shaped nests, while others make jug-like nests with little holes in the sides. They take little mud pellets in their mouth and mix them with their saliva, making a special putty or clay. As it dries, it becomes hard, like plaster or adobe (a brick-like substance made from clay and straw). Perhaps the Pueblo Indians got the idea for their adobe homes from these smart little birds.

Notice how this swallow's nest sticks to the wall of this building.

The process of building these homes takes a long time. Early in the morning, the birds make the putty and then add it to the nest. They then allow it to dry through the afternoon. Each day a little more is added to the nest. Once it is complete, they line the inside with soft material like feathers and grass. What a cozy, secure place for the birds to raise their young!

As it turns out, bird saliva is great for making glue. In fact, certain species of swiftlets make their entire nest out of saliva with nothing added to it. The male regurgitates (throws up) a long, thin strand of saliva from glands under its tongue. The saliva is then wound into a half-cup nest which bonds like quick-drying cement to a cave wall. These swiftlets choose nesting sites high up on the walls of dark caves. Flying through dark caves is easy for these birds because they send out clicking sounds that bounce back to them if the sounds hit anything. The birds can hear the sounds that bounce back, which tells them if there is something in front of them. This is called **echolocation** (ek' oh loh kay' shun). Bats use this method to find their way in the dark as well, so we'll learn more about echolocation when we study bats.

If you think it odd that a bird builds a nest from saliva alone, you will think it even odder that this saliva nest is considered a delicacy (something yummy to eat) in China. The Chinese put the entire saliva nest into a soup called Bird's Nest Soup. It is a highly prized dish and quite expensive, since obtaining the nests is dangerous work. Would you like some Bird's Nest Soup?

Egg Color

Most birds that lay their eggs in holes or cavities have white eggs. A few birds that lay their nests on the ground will lay white eggs, but they quickly become the same color as the dirt and mud with which they come into contact. This helps the eggs to be camouflaged. Eggs laid in trees are often speckled with blues or greens. This helps them to blend in with the leaves of the tree. The robin is famous for its beautiful blue eggs.

What Do You Remember?

Name a few birds that don't build nests. What is a mound nest? What is the difference between an earth-hole nest and a cavity nest? How long is the tunnel in which a puffin builds its nest? Where does a Red-headed Woodpecker like to nest? Where does a cardinal like to nest? Which birds build platform nests? Which is the most common type of nest?

Nature Points

On your next nature walk, or even on a drive through the country, look for old dead trees or even living trees with a dead branch or two. See if you can identify any small or large holes in the dead tree. What kind of bird or animal might live there? How high is it? How wide is the hole?

The best time to find abandoned bird's nests is in the winter when they are easily seen in the leafless trees. As you drive around or go on nature walks, keep an eye out for the nests on the limbs of trees.

Notebook Activities

Draw a picture of each kind of nest and note at least one bird that creates that kind of nest. The *Zoology 1 Notebooking Journal* has templates for this activity.

Older Students: Find out which kinds of nests the birds that visit your feeders prefer. You can research with books at the library, on the Internet, or in an encyclopedia. You can record what you learned in your notebook. The *Zoology 1 Notebooking Journal* provides a template for this activity.

Make an Advertisement

You will need:
♦ Real estate advertisements from the newspaper
♦ Paper or the template on page 69 of your *Zoology 1 Notebooking Journal*
♦ Colored pencils

Knowing what you know about nests and the nesting materials that birds prefer, design a real estate advertisement that would entice a specific kind of bird to purchase a nest. Read an assortment of real estate ads from the paper. Notice the words and descriptions used to make the house appealing. Write up and illustrate a real estate ad to sell your nest to the particular birds that prefer that kind of nest. Make sure to advertise the qualities of the nest that would be attractive to the bird, like where it is located, how high off the ground it is, and what materials were used to build it.

Project
Build a Birdhouse

Many years ago, the place where you live probably had a lot more trees, but they have been taken down for farming, houses, or businesses. It used to be easy for a cavity-dwelling bird to find a dead tree trunk in which to nest, but now it is much harder. Most trees that die are cut down or fall down because they are not protected by other trees around them. Long ago, if a tree died in the forest, it took many, many years for it to actually fall to the ground because it was protected from the wind by all the other trees in the forest. This enabled many birds to easily find a good home.

Today, you are going to help out a cavity-dwelling bird by building a house in which it can build its nest. Your birdhouse will require adult supervision and help to build. If you really enjoy this project, make several birdhouses. If you get really good at it, you can start a birdhouse building business! If you want to make more elaborate birdhouses, check the course website I discussed in the introduction to this book. It has links to instructions for building other types of birdhouses.

You will need:
- A 1-in x 6-in piece of lumber at least 5 feet long. Use cedar if you can find it. (Many lumber stores will cut the board for you. If they do you will need four pieces 9 inches long, one piece 8¾ inches long, and one piece 7 inches long).

- Outdoor nails or wood screws that won't rust
- Screwdriver and hammer if you are using nails
- Drill
- Drill bits: one ¼-in and one ⁷⁄₆₄-in. They don't have to be exactly this size, but something close.
- Hole saw attachment for drill (1½ inches for a birdhouse this size)
- Two 1½-in x 1-in middle hinges (should come with screws to attach the hinges)
- 1 gate hook and eye assembly (1-in assembly)
- Tape measure (or ruler)
- Two outdoor wood screws that will not rust, 2 inches long

1. If the lumber store did not cut the board for you, have an adult cut it into six pieces: four that are 9 inches, one that is 8¾ inches, and one that is 7 inches.
2. The piece that is 8¾ inches long will be the front of the bird house. Have an adult use the 1½-in hole saw on a drill to drill a hole that is centered on the board, about 6 inches from the bottom.
3. Choose one of the 9-in pieces that will be the back of the birdhouse. Have an adult drill two ⁷⁄₆₄-in holes about 2 inches from the top and 2 inches apart. Later, you will use the two outdoor 2-in

wood screws to fasten the bird house to a post, fence, or tree. These holes will make it easier to get the screws started.

4. Choose two of the 9-in pieces to be the sides. On both boards, have an adult drill three ¼-in holes 1½ inches from the top. These holes will be for ventilation, so that the birds will have some fresh air.

5. The 7-in piece of wood will be the bottom of your bird house. Have an adult drill five ¼"-in holes spaced far apart, roughly in the same pattern as the five dots found on dice. These holes will be used for drainage should water enter the bird house.

6. Now it is time to assemble your birdhouse. There may be a rough side and a smooth side to the board. If possible, put the rough side toward the inside of the house. This helps the parents and the young birds climb in and out of the house.

7. Place the back piece on top of the bottom piece and fasten the pieces together with screws or nails. If you choose to use screws, have an adult drill a ⁷⁄₆₄-in hole wherever you want to use a screw. It will make putting the screw in easier.

8. Place one of the side pieces on the bottom board with the ventilation holes on top, and nail it or screw it to the bottom piece. Then nail or screw it to the back piece.

9. Repeat Step #8 with the other side piece.

10. Place the 9-in piece that has no holes on top. It should be even with the back piece, so there is no overhang in the back. There will be an overhang on the front to keep rain out of the entrance hole. Nail or fasten the top piece to the back and side pieces.

11. Have an adult help you attach the front piece to a side piece with hinges so that it will open like a door. The hole in the front piece should be closer to the top of the bird house. Make sure before putting on the hinges that there is a little bit of room above and below the front board so that it will not rub on the bottom or top when you open and close it. Do not put a perch on the front; it will attract predators.

12. On the other side, attach the gate hook and eye to keep the front closed when latched.

13. You have finished your birdhouse! You can paint or stain the outside, but don't paint or stain the inside. The birds like it to be natural wood. You can use any color, but shades of brown or other earth tones seem to work best.

14. Open the front and use the two 2-in outdoor wood screws (and the holes you drilled for them) to attach your birdhouse to a tree, post, or fence. It is best to have the house facing an open area not obstructed by branches or twigs. Once you have hung your birdhouse, close the front and latch it.

Here is a list of birds that commonly use this kind of birdhouse. Try to place your birdhouse according to the directions given in the list if you want to attract the kind of bird that is listed. You should also check your field guide or the internet to make sure the birds you are trying to attract are in your area.

Bluebirds – 3 to 5 feet above ground, in an open area facing a field or an open yard
House Wrens – 4 to 10 feet above ground, in a partly shaded area (about 60% sun)
Chickadee – 4 to 8 feet above ground, in a partly shaded area (40% to 60% sun) near large hardwoods
Titmouse – 4 to 10 feet above ground, near a wooded area
Prothonotary Warbler – 3 to 6 feet above ground, over water or near a marsh, stream, or pond.

Experiment
Which Nest Material Does a Bird Use?
(An early spring experiment)

In the spring, if you watch carefully, you will notice birds searching for nesting material. You might see a bird flying by with a long strip of hay or pine straw in its mouth. If you look closely, you will probably notice a faint hustle and bustle in bushes and trees as nests are being built.

In this experiment, you will provide nesting material for birds. Design an experiment that tests which materials the birds will like the best. The constants will be where you place the material (make sure it is somewhere that will not get blown away) and how much material you place there. Your variable will be the types of materials you place out there. You could test anything you think birds may use. A list of possible nesting materials is below. You could even test one type of yarn in three different colors, guessing which colors the birds will prefer the most. Begin with a hypothesis and use a Scientific Speculation Sheet to record your experiment. Below is a list of potential materials.

Natural Items:

Dead leaves
Dead twigs
Wood shavings
Dried grass, hay, or straw
Pine needles
Bark strips
Common moss, peat moss, or Spanish moss
Plant fluff (like dandelion parachutes)
Feathers (down feathers work best)
Human hair
Animal hair (especially horse hair)

Manmade Items:

Shredded paper
Thin strips of cloth (about 1" x 6")
Thread, string, or yarn
Raveled rope
Raveled burlap
Dental floss
Bristles from an old paint brush
Furniture stuffing
Cotton batting or other stuffing material
(You could place in a suet feeder so that it doesn't blow away.)

Lesson 6
Matching and Hatching

"Like an eagle that stirs up its nest, that hovers over its young, He spread His wings and caught them, He carried them on His pinions." – Deut 32:11

Of course, all the nest building you learned about in the previous lesson would not make sense if there weren't baby birds to fill the nest. In spring, birds begin searching around for a partner with whom they will have young. A match is made when two birds decide to raise young together. This is called **mating**. Often, the early spring is filled with chirping, flirting birds trying to attract or choose a mate. Male hummingbirds, grouse, and turkeys try to mate with as many females as possible; whereas other birds, like eagles, mate with one another for life.

As I said in the previous lesson, nest building usually begins in the spring. A bird generally seeks a companion before it builds a nest. Both male and female birds are looking for a mate, but it's usually the male birds that do all the showing off in order to attract a mate. They showcase themselves to the female birds, saying "Look at me! Pick me! Pick me!"

This is called **courtship**. The male courts the female, trying to prove he is the best choice for her. The female sits back and watches the displays of male birds until she determines which one has earned the right to be her mate and the father of her young.

Showcase

How does a male bird show off his fitness for fatherhood? Well, each has its own ways. A male songbird sings loudly and clearly with lots of songs. He may even bring a twig as a gift to a female, showing how well he can pick nesting material. He also flashes and prances around, flying about in big fluttering acts to show off his beautiful breeding plumage. The Blue-footed Booby sports fancy bright blue feet, and the male holds up one then the other in a sort of dance to show the female bird how utterly special he is with his bright, blue feet! In fact, many male birds have special, colorful feathers that grow in for mating season. It's as if the males are getting new clothes for courtship. Some model fancy colored bills, like the puffin, which sports a new colorful beak, quite different from the dull gray beak it has for the rest of the year. Others, like the Purple Finch, have bright, colorful feathers that attract females.

The more brightly colored male Purple Finch (right) uses its colors to attract a female mate (left).

To attract and impress female birds, the males can often be found doing such things as raising their beaks in the air, flapping their wings, jumping up high into the air, fluffing up their tail feathers, or rocking back and forth. Some male cranes can leap seven feet into the air to show off their stuff.

This male Magnificent Frigatebird is inflating its red throat pouch in hopes of attracting a female.

Some birds have even more complicated displays. One kind of pheasant raises the crest on its head, spreads it tail feathers over its head, and jumps about in front of the female making whistling sounds. Several birds like the turkey and the peacock fan out their showy tail feathers to attract their mate. The Magnificent Frigatebird has a red throat pouch during the mating season. When he sees a female, he inflates the red pouch on his throat into a big red balloon. A few other birds also have colorful throat pouches that expand into a large balloon when they are trying to find mates.

One interesting courtship activity is performed by the Greater Bird-of-paradise. Have you ever played freeze tag? It's a game where you freeze in place when someone tags you. These birds actually freeze in place. The males all flock together in one area, spreading their wings and quivering their tail feathers to attract the ladies. When a female approaches a male, he freezes in place so that the female can "inspect" him. The female flies and hops around, looking at each male trying to decide which one she will choose. Once a choice is made, off they go.

As I mentioned in the previous lesson, a male bowerbird will build a bower and decorate it with bright, shiny objects and flowers. He then calls to the females with lots of loud noises to come and see his creation. Other birds also build nests to attract mates. The House Wren will build several nests. When the female arrives, if she thinks he did a good job, she chooses one of the nests and adds some soft nesting material to it, indicating that it is the one she prefers and that he is her mate. The other nests built by the House Wren aren't used.

Some hawks attract a mate by flying around doing amazing acrobatics in the air. Courting eagles have been seen flying toward one another at top speed, clasping their talons together in mid air, falling hundreds of feet towards the ground, and then letting go and flying up again before they actually hit ground. Now that's an interesting way to make friends! Some birds are a bit more delicate in their courtship rituals. A male Superb Fairywren chooses a nice, yellow flower petal and brings it to the female as a gift. He will only use yellow petals! Don't you wonder why the color yellow is used? Does the bird with the best looking petal win? No one knows for sure. One very strange bird, the

Palm Cockatoo takes a stick (or other hard object) in its foot and becomes a drummer, drumming it against a tree until the female picks him. There are many other courtship rituals performed by birds. In the spring, keep your eye out for strange behavior. It's probably a male bird trying to attract a mate.

In many species, once a female has her eye on a certain male to be her partner, she will allow him to bring food to her. He will actually catch fish, insects, mice, or whatever it is the bird happens to eat, and bring it to the female, placing it directly into her mouth. The female will sometimes sit in a tree or in the hole they have chosen for their nest and clack loudly for food. She will be very demanding about being fed by her mate. This happens even before she lays her eggs.

Remember the hornbill we learned about in the previous lesson? The male feeds the female through a hole as she is closed up inside the tree. That's a big job for the father bird to do! Many other birds feed the female while she incubates the eggs, so bringing her food during courtship is a way to show her what a good provider he will be.

These Swallow-tailed Gulls are performing a feeding ritual in which the male regurgitates food into the female's mouth.

Have you ever heard two people sing a duet? They sing a song together, and they each usually have their own part. Well, some birds also sing duets. After the match is finally made, the male and female will sing together; this is called **duetting** (doo et' ing). It occurs especially after they have secured their nesting territory and is their way of telling other birds to stay away from their home.

Can you tell someone what you remember about the courtship rituals of birds?

Helpful Mates

A few birds (like some species of owls, eagles, geese, and puffins) mate for life. That is, they stay together for their entire lives. Of the birds that don't mate for life, most birds stay together at least until their young leave the nest. Most of the time, both the male and female are responsible for the parenting duties. This is a full time job, and it works best with both parents on duty. Some parents even get help with the job from other birds.

Do you have younger brothers and sisters? Do you help take care of them? What do you do to help out your parents? If you don't have younger siblings, you probably know others who do. Do they help their parents out with their younger brothers and sisters? If so, they are good older brothers and sisters and good children to their parents. Some birds have children that are helpful in the same way! In several species, like the Australian Kookaburra, kingfishers, Acorn Woodpecker, Florida Scrub-Jay, and Red-cockaded Woodpeckers, young birds that have not yet mated and started their own families will help their parents raise the next clutch of eggs. This is called **cooperative breeding**. They may even help incubate the eggs, and they will often help find food for the young. Those birds are good brothers and sisters!

Usually the male's job is to protect the nest while the female incubates the eggs. A male will sit in the trees near the nest and sing loudly with many songs, letting other birds know this is his territory, so stay away. Often, he will bring the female food while she sits on the eggs. When the young hatch, he will help feed them. Some males also share the incubation duty. If the male and female birds are colored the same, they may both sit on the eggs. Usually that color is brown or gray, to keep them hidden while on the nest.

In this Ostrich family, the male is black and the female is brown. These colorings allow the male to stay camouflaged while incubating the eggs at night and the female to stay camouflaged while incubating the eggs during the day.

Although they are colored differently from the females, male Ostriches share the task of egg incubation. In this case, the fact that they are colored differently helps them tremendously. You see, the male (colored black) will sit on the eggs in the black of night, while the female (colored brown) will sit on the eggs in the day where she is camouflaged against the brown grass. Both hunch down on their ground nest and try to blend in with the environment. They don't really put their head under the ground, as legend has it, but they do lay their head down as close to the ground as possible so as to blend right in when sitting on their eggs.

Single Parents

Not all birds share the parenting duties. Some will not even stay together after the eggs are laid. Instead, either the male or the female is left to do all the work. This is true for hummingbirds, where the male doesn't even know where the nest is that houses his young. In fact, he may have several mates and several clutches of eggs around the city. Thankfully, hummingbirds usually lay only two eggs at a time, so the female's job isn't quite so hard. Unbelievably, there are some female birds that lay their eggs and then leave, letting the male do everything else. The male cassowary does all the child rearing, sitting on the eggs and caring for the young once they hatch.

The Mallefowl (*Leipoa* [lye poh' uh] *ocellata* [ah suh lah' tuh]), sometimes called the thermometer bird, is another species in which the male takes care of the eggs. Its eggs can't hatch unless they are kept at a constant 91-92 degrees Fahrenheit. The male controls the temperature of the eggs by building a mound nest out of twigs and dead plants. As the dead plants begin to rot, the nest begins to warm. The female lays her eggs in the nest when it reaches the right temperature, and the male then covers them with sand and sometimes more rotting plants. As the plants continue to rot, they continue to release heat. This warms the eggs. That's not the end of the story, however.

Amazingly, God equipped this bird with a built-in thermometer on its tongue. If the male's thermometer tongue tells him that the mound is a bit warmer than normal, he frantically throws off some of the sand that covers the eggs. This cools the eggs a bit. If the temperature is not as high as he knows it should be, he covers it with more rotting plants, which warms the eggs. All day long he works and works on the pile for seven weeks. If he misses work one day, the chicks may die because the eggs got too hot or too cool.

This Mallefowl must have sensed the temperature of the eggs rising, because it is scratching sand off the nest.

Once the chicks hatch, it's their turn to do some hard work. It takes them about 15 hours to dig their way out of the mound that kept them warm. How do the chicks know that they must do this? Once they dig their way out of the mound, they are already able to walk, fly, and find food.

The Mallefowl provides incredible testimony to God's handiwork. Here is a bird that knows exactly how to care for its eggs, right down to the exact temperature at which they need to be kept. It has an amazing tongue that is able to precisely read the temperature of the nest, and it knows what to do if it gets too hot or too cold. God's design of the Thermometer Bird is nothing short of astounding!

Exceptional Eggs

If you have never touched a bird, I bet you have at least touched a bird's egg! We have come to be very dependent on the little hen in our culture. Her eggs have become a well known part of breakfast and a main ingredient in cakes and cookies!

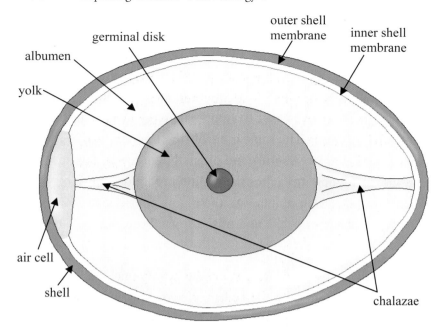

albumen
germinal disk
outer shell membrane
inner shell membrane
yolk
air cell
shell
chalazae

Have you ever looked at a cracked egg very carefully? As shown in the drawing on the left, one simple egg has many different parts. Surrounding the outside of the egg shell is the **cuticle** (kyoo' tih kul). The cuticle is a thin layer of a dried protein that helps keep bacteria from going inside the egg. The cuticle is washed off the eggs you get from the grocery store. Once the cuticle is gone, the egg has less protection, so it must be eaten within a month or so, or it will rot.

The **shell** protects the chick (called an **embryo** [em bree' oh] while it is in the egg) developing inside. Each shell, though it looks solid, actually contains thousands and thousands of little tiny holes, called **pores**. These pores allow air into the egg, and gases also exit the egg through these pores. We will do an experiment later on to help us understand and remember that egg shells are porous. Inside the shell there are two thin coverings called the **inner shell membrane** and **outer shell membrane**.

Another important part of the egg is the **albumen** (al byoo' men), which is usually called the **egg white**. The albumen is made up of water, protein, and many other chemicals. The water in the albumen keeps the egg from drying out, and the proteins help feed the embryo. The albumen also acts as a "shock absorber," protecting the embryo from hitting against the inside wall of the egg if it is moved. The albumen also protects the embryo from bacteria, because many of the chemicals in it are harmful to bacteria. If bacteria get into the egg through the pores, these chemicals stop them before they can harm the embryo.

An egg also contains a **yolk**. Often, people confuse the yolk with the embryo, but they are completely different from one another. The yolk is filled with energy rich foods for the growing embryo to eat. In other words, the yolk is the embryo's primary food supply as it develops in the egg.

When you crack open an egg, you will also find the **chalazae** (kuh lay' zee). These are ropey strands that anchor the yolk in place. If the chalazae are particularly prominent in your breakfast eggs, it means they are exceptionally fresh.

At the top (the wider end) of every egg is a small pocket of air between the inner and outer shell membranes. It is called the **air cell**, and it grows as the egg gets older. When the chick is almost ready to hatch, it pokes its beak through the inner shell membrane and into the air cell. It then starts breathing the air in that air cell.

With all of this talk about the embryo, you might wonder where it is in the drawing. Well, at first, the embryo is a tiny little circle called the **germinal disk**. As the embryo develops, however, it gets bigger and bigger, taking up more and more of the egg. This works out, of course, because as the embryo develops, it eats the yolk, which gets smaller and smaller. The albumen also gets smaller, as it transfers water and nutrients to the yolk. Now please understand that the eggs you get at the store do not have embryos in them. In order for an egg to have an embryo in it, the hen that laid the egg must have mated with a male chicken (called a rooster). If the hen doesn't mate, it still lays eggs, but because there was no male involved, the egg has no embryo and is called an **unfertilized egg**.

Try This!

You can see the air cell in a cracked chicken egg. Crack the egg on the pointy end, and open up a quarter-sized hole in it. Dump the inside of the egg out into the sink, and rinse it out with water. Now you should be able to see and feel the pocket of air on the other side of the egg. Try to peel the inner membrane from the inside of the egg. Be certain to wash your hands with soap and warm water when you are finished.

Clutch

Do you remember that all the eggs in a nest are called a clutch? Songbirds usually lay one egg per day until the clutch is complete. It usually takes an hour or so for the egg to come out. The female does not start incubating the eggs until the clutch is complete. A clutch may be one egg or many eggs, depending on the bird. The now extinct Passenger Pigeon laid only one egg in each clutch. This was one of the problems that led to its extinction. Other birds that only lay one egg include albatrosses, petrels, some species of penguins, and pigeons. Gulls and terns usually lay two eggs, hawks and songbirds lay two to five eggs, and ducks lay about ten eggs.

This Pied-billed Grebe is caring for her clutch of four eggs. This species tends to lay four to seven eggs per clutch.

Generally, the older the bird, the more eggs it will lay in its clutch. Birds that live in colder regions tend to lay larger clutches than birds that live in tropical climates. In addition, birds that nest alone have larger clutches than those that nest in large colonies. Finally, birds that are smaller generally tend to have larger clutches than the bigger birds. There are exceptions to all of these rules, of course, but at least they give you a general idea.

Incubation

Why do you think a bird sits on its eggs? To keep them warm, of course. This might sound like an easy job, but it is not! You see, a bird's feathers are designed to insulate the bird. That means the bird's body heat stays in the bird. When it is time to incubate, however, the bird's body heat needs to *leave* the bird and go to the eggs. How does this happen? God designed birds to do a wonderful thing when its time to incubate their eggs. They lose feathers on their belly where they sit on the eggs. This little patch of exposed skin is called a **brood patch**, and it allows the bird's body heat to leave the bird and warm the eggs. When the eggs are warm enough, the bird can fly off and gather food for a short time, knowing that the eggs will not cool off too much before it gets back. Some birds, such as geese, will actually pluck off their feathers in anticipation of the eggs they will lay. In other words, they make their own brood patch.

Why do bird eggs not break when the mother sits on them? Eggs are designed to withstand a lot of weight, if the weight is distributed evenly over the whole egg. A bird knows exactly how to sit on her eggs without breaking them. When coming to the nest, she will place both feet on either side of the clutch, arrange the eggs with her beak, and snuggle down on them, wiggling until she gets them right next to her brood patch. She will then settle down for a long day or night of incubating.

During incubation the eggs have to be turned regularly so that they will be heated evenly. Some birds do this with their feet, and others do this with their beak.

Try This!

Did you know that eggs are amazingly strong, even though everyone thinks they are so fragile? If you squeeze an egg with your bare hand, it will not break!

Place an egg in the palm of your hand (make certain you are not wearing a ring). Close your hand so that your fingers are completely wrapped around the egg. Squeeze the egg by applying even pressure all around the shell. The egg will not break. Hold the egg over the sink while you squeeze it if you're worried. The reason this works is because the rounded form of the shell distributes pressure evenly all over the shell. By completely surrounding the egg with your hand, the pressure you apply by squeezing is distributed evenly all over the egg. The egg won't break if it has even pressure all the way around it. At the same time, however, eggs aren't as tolerant to *uneven* forces. This is why they crack easily on the side of a bowl.

Development in the Egg

As the baby bird develops, the yolk and albumen begin to be used up until there is nothing but a baby bird inside along with a bit of wet, sticky albumen. Incubation can be as short as ten days for songbirds and as long as three months for the albatross or the kiwi. Usually, the larger the bird, the longer incubation takes. The cowbird, which lays its eggs in the nests of other birds, has an extremely short incubation period: ten days. This ensures that the cowbird chick gets fed first and most often.

If you would like to really learn about incubation, the course website that I mentioned in the introduction to this book has links to places where you can purchase an incubator and eggs so that you can watch the entire process yourself. It is a truly wonderful thing to see, and I encourage you to take the time do it, if you can afford to purchase the necessary equipment and have the time to raise the chicks.

Egg Tooth

So how does the hatchling get out of the egg once it's ready? When a baby bird inside an egg is almost fully developed, it needs more air than it is getting through the egg. To get more air, the tiny bird will puncture the inner membrane and stick its beak into the air cell that I told you about before. Conveniently, the shell is also a bit more fragile at this exact spot.

To help the chick break the egg shell when it is time to hatch, God placed a sharp notch (called an **egg tooth**) on the top of the baby bird's beak. As the bird begins to need more air and nutrients, the discomfort causes

This Red-legged Partridge chick has just broken out of its egg.

the bird to wiggle and move until the egg tooth breaks open the egg. This usually happens at the place where the air pocket is located, since this is where it is getting air. The egg tooth is lost as the chick grows because the chick doesn't need it once it is out of the egg.

Baby Birds

"He provides food for the cattle and for the young ravens when they call." – Psalm 147:9

Most hatchlings are blind, featherless, and unable to stand. Since they are featherless, the parents will have to continue to keep these newly hatched birds warm. This is called **brooding**. Once the babies get some feathers, they will not need to be kept warm except maybe at night. At first, the most these little critters can do is lay their heads back, open their mouths wide, and squeak. These birds are called **altricial** (al trish' uhl) which means they require special care after they hatch. All passerines are altricial. Pelicans, hummingbirds, woodpeckers, and swifts are also altricial.

Parents of altricial chicks begin by feeding them regurgitated food, and as they get older they simply give them insects and worms found on the ground. Have you ever heard the phrase "the squeaky wheel gets the grease?" It's a phrase that means the person who has the most to say about something usually gets what he wants. Well, scientists have learned that parent birds feed the chick that hollers the loudest. The assumption must be that the loudest bird is the hungriest. This can be a problem if the loudest bird is a brood parasite, because the parent will continue to feed it, letting the other chicks get weaker and weaker, unable to yell loudly enough to be heard. Usually,

Every nestling in this cardinal's brood wants to eat.

however, this system works. All birds open their mouths wide, and the one that didn't get fed last time is more anxious for the food, squeaking a bit louder, reaching up higher with its mouth above the rest. The other chicks aren't as hungry, so they don't holler as loud. That way, everyone gets enough food.

All birds have a sac in their body (called a **crop**) that stores and softens food. Some birds (like penguins, pigeons, and flamingos) also use their crops to make **crop milk**, a fluid that the birds regurgitate into the mouths of their young. For some of these birds, crop milk is the only food that the young get for several days.

Little by little, these fragile birds are able to do more than just squawk with open mouths. They will see, grow feathers, and move around a bit in the nest. At this point they are called **nestlings**. After a few weeks, they begin to stand at the edge of the nest and stretch their wings. At that point, they are almost ready to begin their first flight out of the nest. In time, they start to make short, clumsy flights and are called **fledglings** (flej' lingz). When a baby bird flies from its nest, it is said to have **fledged**. Rather than being taught by its parents, a baby bird simply jumps from the nest and flaps its wings, teaching itself to fly. Young birds are soft boned and will not get badly injured if they fall from the nest to the ground. After weeks of practice, the bird will become a good flyer. Sometimes, birds will stay near their parents and beg for food long after they have fledged. Some birds have to ignore their young to encourage them to start taking care of themselves.

Once the young have learned to fly and find food, the parents are done. If it is early in the season, some birds will have a second brood. If time allows, a few will have even a third brood, but many birds have only one brood per season.

Precocial Birds

Have you ever heard the word **precocious** (prih koh' shus)? The word is often used to describe really young children who act a lot older than their age. Well, some birds are precocious as well. The moment they hatch, these baby birds have feathers (down), can see, and have strong legs that they begin to use almost immediately. If they are swimming birds, they can swim right away. These hatchlings are called **precocial** (prih koh' shul), which sounds a lot like "precocious."

Chickens, ducks, geese, ostriches, turkeys, and swans all hatch precocial. Some precocial hatchlings are quite independent. They follow along behind their parents and are shown where the food is. Others require their parents to pick up the food and feed them. Whichever feeding method they use, most precocial young stay near their parents for protection. A swan will even carry its young around under its wings or on its back for a while. Parent birds with young nearby can be very aggressive towards any animal or human that comes near their young. Swans and geese will hiss and even chase and bite strangers in their midst.

A young swan (called a cygnet) rides on its parent's back.

The one thing most precocial birds cannot do is fly. The megapode is an exception, as it can fly within one or two days after hatching. Can you guess why God made the megapode able to fly so early in its life? It is because megapode parents do not care for their young at all once they are hatched. As a result, a young megapode must take care of itself very quickly, or it will die.

Interestingly, most birds that are precocial are hatched from nests on the ground. Being precocial is helpful to these birds because many predators could get them if they were helpless on the ground. Eggs from birds that have precocial young take longer to incubate than eggs from birds that have altricial young. Can you guess why they needed longer to incubate? This gives them more time to develop inside the egg.

Mother birds often gather their young under their wings. Jesus described this when He was lamenting over His people who would not believe in Him: "O Jerusalem, Jerusalem, you who kill the prophets and stone those sent to you, how often I have longed to gather your children together, as a hen gathers her chicks under her wings, but you were not willing." (Matthew 23:37). The way a mother hen loves and cares for her chicks is a picture of how Jesus longs to love and care for you.

What Do You Remember?

Which is usually more colorful, a male or female bird? What do you call a group of eggs in a nest? What is it called when a mother bird sits on her eggs? What are the patches of featherless skin called that a bird develops when incubating its eggs, and what is their purpose? Can you name the parts of an egg? What is the name of the bump on the bird's beak that helps it break out of the shell? If a bird is completely dependent on its parents, what is it called? If a bird is born with feathers and the ability to see and walk around, what is it called?

Nature Points

If you have young birds in your birdhouses or you happen upon a clutch of eggs or baby birds, be certain not to touch them or disturb the nest area. Some birds will not come back to eggs or young that have been disturbed by humans. You can look at them, but don't handle them at all. The parents will watch closely from a hidden spot while you check on them. If they are very upset about it, they may attempt to move the young to a safer place. They may also abandon them, so be careful!

If you find a baby bird or eggs on the ground, call a local wildlife expert to find out what you should do. Don't attempt to put eggs or a baby bird back into the nest until you have heard from an expert. If the bird is a fledgling but is having trouble flying, it may have just fledged. It is best to leave this bird where it is, because the parents know where it is and are still taking care of it.

Notebook Activities

Write down all the fascinating facts you remember from the lesson. Include information about courtship rituals, eggs, hatchlings, and fledglings. The *Zoology 1 Notebooking Journal* provides templates for you to record your learning.

Make a comic strip

Make a comic strip telling the story of a chick from the beginning inside the egg to finding a mate and incubating its own eggs. Try to add entertainment to your comic by including information that is interesting. You could even do yours about brood parasites like the cowbird or the European Cuckoo, or strange birds such as the megapodes of Australia. Whichever bird you choose, tell the story in a way that reflects human thoughts about their lives, even though they don't have such thoughts. For example, when a cowbird first looks at the bird that is taking care of it, the cowbird could say, "Gee, that doesn't look like my mom."

Let's make a comic

Your comic strip will be inside small boxes, with each box telling the next part of the story. If you have the *Zoology 1 Notebooking Journal,* a template is provided for this activity.

You can have words under the box telling what is happening, as well as call-out balloons (like the one in the clown drawing on the previous page) that tell the reader what the bird or anything else in the comic is saying. The boxes in your comic strip should look something like the boxes below, although your strip might have a lot more than just four boxes:

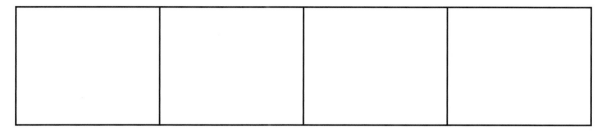

Experiment
Candling

In this experiment, you will make guesses about what kinds of changes you will see in eggs that are left out over several days or weeks. You will candle them to observe and evaluate the differences you notice. The changes will be most obvious at the tip of the egg, involving the size of the air cell.

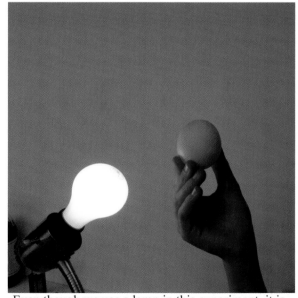

Candling eggs is used by poultry farmers to determine how fresh the eggs are and what grade to give them. It is also used to determine whether an egg has a chick growing inside. Your eggs will probably not have chicks in them if you bought them. Every egg, before it leaves the poultry farm and ends up on the grocery store shelf, is graded by candling. Grade A eggs are only a few days old and in good condition. How do they tell if an egg is in good condition? When the grader is looking at the egg being candled, the egg must have a thick, well centered yolk, a very small air cell, and a clean, sound shell.

Even though we use a lamp in this experiment, it is still called "candling," because the technique was first done using a candle as the light source.

Your hypothesis will be to decide what you think will happen to the egg as it gets old. Does the center of the egg look different? Does the air sac get larger? Does the white of the egg begin to darken? If you leave your eggs out, how long will it take them to spoil? Record your hypotheses on a Scientific Speculation Sheet.

You will need:

♦ A bright lamp with the shade removed
♦ A large box or low table
♦ A raw white egg (You will need a second one at the very end of the experiment.)
♦ A darkened room
♦ A pencil
♦ A bowl (It should be deeper than the height of an egg on its side.)
♦ Water

1. In the darkened room, set the lamp on a box or table a couple of feet above the floor, but not directly in front of your face. You don't want the light to shine in your eyes.
2. Grab the egg by the small end, and with your thumb and fingers, move it quickly back and forth several times. This moves the yolk nearer to the shell.
3. Hold the egg with the larger end near the light at a slanted position. Can you see the yolk in the center? If you cannot, play with the orientation of the egg until you can see the yolk.
4. Record how it looks and draw an illustration of it. You will want to make a new drawing each time you observe the egg.
5. Can you see the air cell? It should be a thin line running around the larger edge of the egg. Trace around the air cell with a pencil to keep a measure of its size.
6. Run your experiment for two to four weeks, candling every few days to every week. Don't put the egg back in the refrigerator. Leave it out, but put it in a safe place. The differences will be more dramatic if you wait a week between candling, but you may wish to do it more often. Record everything on the Scientific Speculation Sheet you used to write your hypotheses.
7. Once you are done with your experiment, fill the bowl with water.
8. Place the old egg and a brand new fresh egg into the bowl that is now full of water. What happens?
9. Try to come up with an explanation for what you saw. The proper explanation is given with the answers to the narrative questions in the back of the book.

Optional Experiment
Do Eggs Absorb Water?

Remember that eggs are porous, with little pores that let air in and out. What else can penetrate the egg? Can water penetrate an egg? I want you to design an experiment that will answer this question.

How will you design this experiment? What will be your constants? What will be your variables? Design and perform your experiment, using a Scientific Speculation Sheet to record your hypothesis, the materials and methods you used, your results, and your conclusions. You can check the course website I discussed in the introduction to this book to see if your conclusions were correct.

Lesson 7
Bats

I hope you enjoyed your study of birds. As I mentioned in the first lesson, however, birds aren't the only flying creatures in creation. So let's move on and talk about some of God's other incredible flying creatures. When you're washing up and getting ready for bed, a bat somewhere, possibly very nearby, is rubbing the sleep from its eyes and looking forward to a long night of fun, frolic, and food. And just before you begin to rub the sleep from your own eyes, the bats in your area are bathing their babies, washing themselves, and getting ready for a long day of sleep. As you probably know, bats are **nocturnal** (nok turn' uhl), which means they are most active at night.

To some people, bats seem creepy and unpleasant, but this is only because bats come out at night. Because of this, people tend to draw pictures of bats with unlikable things. Therefore, because an unlikable thing is drawn with a bat, people think of bats in a negative way. This is unfortunate, because these little creatures that God made are actually more helpful to you than cats and dogs. Try to guess right now why this is true. A little later on, you will find out. What most people don't realize is that bats are among the gentlest and kindest of all God's creatures. They may look fearsome in photographs, but they are

Most bats are no bigger than this boy's hands.

actually gentle, shy, and usually very small. Believe it or not, most bats are no bigger than the size of your thumb, with wings that are as long as both of your hands spread out with your wrists together.

Unfortunately, people in many cultures, including ours, consider bats nothing more than flying mice or rats. In Germany, the word for bat, Fledermaus, means "flying mouse." The French word for bat, *chauve-souris,* means "bald mouse." In Mexico, bats were believed to be rodents that had gotten so old they sprouted wings. They were given the name "Rata Vieja," which means "old rat."

Contrary to popular belief, a bat is completely different from a rodent, both inside and out. The only thing bats and rodents have in common is that they are both **mammals**, which means they have fur, give birth to babies, and nurse their babies with mother's milk. Bats have wings, but rodents do not. Bats are much cleaner than rodents. Bats usually give birth to only one **pup** (that's what we call a baby bat) per year, while rats can give birth to sixty young rats per year! A bat lives for about thirty years, while rodents live only about three years.

There are many myths about bats that are not true. Some people have said that all bats carry rabies. That's not true. If a bat contracts rabies, it will get sick and die within a week. Bats can get rabies, just like dogs, cats, raccoons, and any other animal that spends time outside. However, when a dog gets rabies, it becomes aggressive and wants to bite people. When a bat gets rabies, it is not aggressive. It will only bite if it feels threatened. It gets very sick, however, so if you ever see a bat on the ground, it might be dying of rabies. A bat on the ground is almost certainly sick, so you shouldn't pick it up! You should always call a wildlife expert if you see an injured or sick wild animal.

Scientists have kept records of bites from rabid bats (bats with rabies) for more than 40 years. And in all that time, it is recorded that only one person per year has gotten rabies from a bat bite. There are usually millions of bats residing near people, but in those last forty years, only 40 people got rabies from bats. More than 40,000 people have been injured by dogs, but people don't fear dogs the way they fear bats. Do you know why? It's because dogs are called "man's best friend," but people connect bats with scary things like Halloween. The connection of bats with scary things and the myths about bats cause people to fear them.

Believe it or not, there is one place in the world that never developed negative attitudes towards bats. The Chinese word for bat sounds the same as the Chinese word for happiness. China is the only nation that doesn't have a widespread dislike for bats. In fact, pictures of bats decorate homes and buildings all over China.

Keystone Bats

This fruit bat (*Pteropus seychellensis*) helps various plants reproduce.

Many species of bats are **keystone species**. Do you know what that means? A keystone species is important to the survival of many other species. There are two kinds of bats: **fruit eaters** and **animal eaters**, and both are keystone species. Without fruit-eating bats, hundreds of kinds of important fruit trees would disappear. They both pollinate them (help them to reproduce) and they spread the seeds to new places to grow new trees. We would have a hard time finding avocados, bananas, mangoes, figs, cashews, and balsa wood if it weren't for fruit bats.

Most animal-eating bats eat insects, which keeps the insect population under control. Some animal-eating bats can eat more than 600 insects in one hour and will eat like that for about 10 hours each night! Can you tell me how many insects that bat would eat in one night? That's a whole lot fewer annoying insects each night!

Bat Anatomy

What do you think you would look like if your hands, just your hands, were as long as your entire body? What if your hands were twice as long as your body? Imagine that for a moment. Now imagine your hands as wings! One of the most bizarre features of bats is that they fly with their hands. In fact, the order in which we place bats, **Chiroptera** (kye rop' tur uh), means "hand-wings" in Latin.

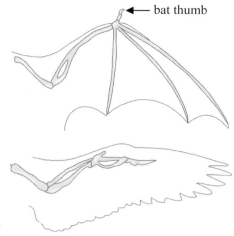

← bat thumb

Bats and birds have very different wings.

The drawing to the left shows the different bone structures of a bat's wing and a bird's wing. Do you see how very different they are? Birds don't have the long finger-like bones in their wings that bats have. While a bird can't move its fingers individually, a bat can. This allows a bat to change direction in flight or to fly in any pattern it needs so that it can catch a nice juicy moth for dinner. A bat flies like it is "swimming" through the air – pushing both wings down and backward. Most bats then fold their wings to bring them back up so that they can do it again. You try it! Pretend that you are swimming through the water. That's how a bat flies.

A bird's wing is made up of feathers, while a bat's wing is made of stretchy, thin skin called a **patagium** (puh tay' jee uhm). This thin membrane of skin stretches between each finger bone, connects to the bat's ankles, and usually connects to its tail, if it has one. When a bat folds its wings next to its body, the skin puckers up almost as if it is shrinking. Stretch your thumb and pointer finger out. Notice the skin between them is nice and tight. Now, slowly move those two fingers together. The skin puckers and wrinkles. That is what a bat's wings look like when they are not stretched out.

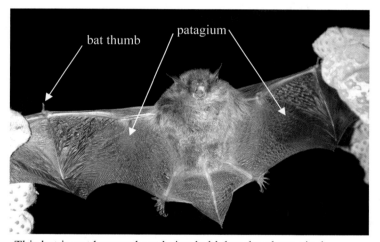

bat thumb   patagium

This bat is not happy about being held, but the photo nicely shows how the patagium connects the arms, legs, and tail.

Bats have one claw, sometimes called a **bat thumb**, that sticks out the top of the wing. They use their "thumb" to climb and crawl, hooking it into the ground (or the bark of a tree) and then pulling themselves in the direction they want to go. Interestingly enough, a bat will also use its thumbs to clean out its ears, much like you might use a cotton swab.

When a bat wants to fly, it will simply let go of its roost and begin flapping its wings. Bats that land on the ground will often need to jump up into the air or climb up a tree to get the lift needed to fly. That's because a bat's wing has great maneuverability (more than that of a bird), but not a lot of lift. While most birds can take off easily from the ground, most bats cannot.

Echolocation

Another interesting thing about bats is that even though they can see with their eyes, they also use their ears to help them "see" in the dark. Because of this, they are able to fly in the deepest, darkest cave and the darkest, moonless night where no eye could see. This way of "seeing" is called **echolocation** (ek' oh loh kay' shun). Basically, that means they use "echoes" to "locate" where everything is.

Echolocation is a lot like the sonar that submarines and ships use to locate things underwater. Here is how it works: When a bat takes off in flight, it starts making sounds. Can you click your tongue against the roof of your mouth? Can you whistle? Attempt to snort noises through your nose. You can hear the sounds you are making, right? Well, a bat can hear the sounds it is making in echolocation, but *we* can't hear them. Scientists have instruments that can measure them, but they are too high pitched for our ears.

When a bat makes its noises, the sound waves move away from the bat. If they hit something, they bounce back to the bat. That bounce is called an **echo**. If nothing bounces back, the bat knows there is empty space in front of it and it can fly forward. It's sort of like throwing a ball with your eyes closed. If it hits a wall and comes back, you know there is a wall in front of you. In fact, you might be able to "bouncelocate" if you had a bag of balls. You could walk around blindfolded and perhaps never run into anything if you simply threw balls as you walked. If a ball came back to you immediately after you threw it, you would know the object it hit was really close. If it came back after a slight pause, you would know that the object is further ahead. If it never came back, you have freedom to move forward without hitting anything.

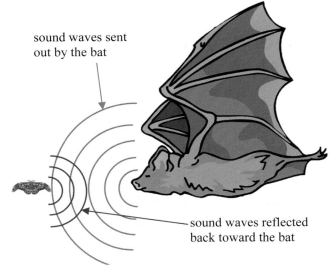

sound waves sent out by the bat

sound waves reflected back toward the bat

In echolocation, a bat sends out sound waves that bounce off things (like insects) and return to the bat. This allows the bat to "see" the insect, even in the dark.

This is exactly how a bat uses echolocation, except it's much more sophisticated because God made it, and God always makes things really well.

Have you ever tried to catch a butterfly or a dragonfly that was flying by? It's a difficult thing to do, isn't it? It's not at all difficult for a bat, however, because it uses echolocation to find and catch its prey. When a bat begins its nightly exploration, it sends out about 10 calls per second, but as soon as it picks up an echo from something good to eat, the calls increase up to 200 per second. This increase in the number of sounds is called a **feeding buzz**, which is necessary so the bat can pick up all the erratic and quick moves of the flying insect it is trying to catch. When the bat is following its prey and the echoes suddenly stop returning, this tells the bat the insect has headed in a different direction. The bat then turns its head and sends out sounds in every direction to locate the insect. Once it starts getting echoes again, it heads right for the insect. Can you imagine trying to catch a tiny little gnat on a dark night? Because of its incredible echolocation, catching a gnat at night is no problem for a bat!

The echolocation calls, which are silent to us, are very loud and piercing for a bat. In fact, they are so loud that some bats could be made deaf by their own calls. God took care of that by designing these bats' ears in a special way. There is a little muscle God placed in the ear that squeezes the middle ear shut as the bat calls. This protects the bats from being deafened by their own call. As soon as the call ends, the muscles loosen and the bat is ready to listen for its echo, which is much fainter.

Hearing and understanding the echoes that return to the bat requires a huge amount of complex structures to be present in the bat's brain. Because of this, bats are the subject of many, many important studies done by biologists, medical doctors, and even the U.S. military. The military actually spends hundreds of thousands of dollars each year to study echolocation in bats.

Bats also have good eyesight and are able to see their prey and where they are flying if it's not too dark outside. A bat can see in the dark better than you and me, so if someone says you are as blind as a bat, tell them, "Thank you! I do see rather well."

Creation Confirmation

Echolocation provides us with a great example of God's design in nature. The navy uses **sonar** in its ships and submarines as a way of being able to "see" underwater. Naval sonar works much like bat echolocation: a device on the ship sends out sounds, and when those sounds bounce off something, a receiver on the ship analyzes the echoes. This allows the crew to determine what's up ahead underwater. The brilliant scientists that have been employed by the navy, however, can't produce a sonar system that is anything close to that of a bat. This is why the U.S. military spends so much money researching

The sonar system on this ship was clearly designed, but it is crude in comparison to what a bat has!

bats. The military wants to use the information it learns from bats to improve its sonar systems. The sonar system pictured above is clearly the result of hard work done by intelligent designers. Since the bat's echolocation system is much more sophisticated, it should be obvious that bats are the result of an amazingly Intelligent Designer, whom we call God.

Explain what you have learned about bats so far in this lesson.

Microbats

Most bats that eat animals and insects are surprisingly small. These small bats are called **microchiropterans** (my' kroh kye rop' tur uhnz), or **microbats** for short. Microbats have small, sharp teeth for chewing their food. They are carnivores, eating mostly insects. There are some species, however, that eat frogs, salamanders, fish, and even blood.

Try This!

To give you an idea of just how important bats are to us, let's do some math. A little brown bat, the most common bat in North America, can catch 600 mosquitoes in one hour. Let's pretend that mosquitoes are all it wants to eat (it loves mosquitoes but will also eat other insects). A little brown bat usually feeds for 10 hours every night. How many mosquitoes can the bat eat in one week? How many can a colony of 100 bats eat in one week?

The little brown bat (*Myotis lucifugus*) eats a *lot* of mosquitoes!

Now imagine that your city is home to 50,000 little brown bats. How many mosquitoes would these 50,000 bats eat in one night? How many would they eat in one week? Now imagine that some people who didn't know much about bats started a bat reduction program in which everyone was told to kill off the bats because they carry rabies (even though you and I know that this is rare). How many more mosquitoes would you have in your city once the bats had all been dead for a year?

Although most bats eat insects, a few bats eat things like small frogs, scorpions, and animals that creep along the ground. Some microbats are even incredible fishermen, with sharp claws that they use to snatch their prey. Fishing bats mostly live in tropical areas near lakes and rivers. They also use echolocation as they are gliding close to the surface of the water. Their echolocation so amazingly specialized that it can detect a minnow's fin even if a part as small as a strand of hair is touching the surface of the water. When a fishing bat detects a fish near the surface of the water, it swoops down, grabs the fish with its sharp claws, and flies to a tree to eat it before going back for more.

A few bats are **sanguinivorous** (sang gwin' ih vor us), which means they feed on blood. There are only three kinds of sanguinivorous bats in the whole world, and none of them live in the United States. They are sometimes called **vampire bats** and live in the tropical regions of South and Central

America. Two of the three types of vampire bats will *only* eat the blood of birds. These tiny bats make an itty bitty cut in the skin of chickens or other large birds that are sleeping, and they lap up the blood that flows from the wound. Because the bat is so miniscule, this doesn't even wake the bird, and it probably hurts less than a mosquito bite.

The one vampire bat that drinks the blood of mammals usually chooses cows and other large sleeping creatures. It will land on the ground nearby and hop over to the sleeping mammal. It will then make a tiny cut in the animal's skin and lap up the blood. Because the bat is tiny, the cut is tiny as well. It is likely never to be noticed by either the animal or anyone caring for the animal. Sometimes the vampire bats get so full of blood that they can't fly. They have to wait a few hours for the blood to digest before they can hop up and fly back to the roost.

Although this vampire bat feeds on blood, it is afraid of moving animals. As a result, it tends to feed on the blood of sleeping animals.

Vampire bats are feared by people, but this is only because people don't understand that they are not flying around looking for a person walking around on the street. They are afraid of moving animals and usually won't come anywhere near them.

What Big Ears You Have

You already know that microbats use echolocation to hunt for food, but you may not realize they also have another advantage when it comes to hearing. Their large ear size is designed by God to give them the ability to hear even the slightest sound. This helps them when they are trying to find prey. After all, if an insect is flying around, its wings will probably make a buzzing or rustling sound. You and I won't even hear such a soft sound, but a microbat might, and that helps it find food!

Microbats come in a wide variety of shapes and sizes and are usually pretty easy to tell apart. With their large, sometimes strangely shaped ears and their leafy, wrinkled noses, microbats aren't always considered cute. However, they are often so small that people mistake them for large moths circling the lights at night. Of course, they are not moths at all. Instead, they are *eating* the moths that are circling the lights.

Try This!

Take a sheet of notebook paper and roll it into a cone. Put the narrow end of the cone in your ear. Have someone talk to you from the other side of the room, and point the wide end of the cone towards him. Have him talk rather softly. While he is talking, remove the cone from your ear. Were you able to hear better with or without the cone? Most likely, you heard better with the cone. This is why sometimes people cup their ear when they are having difficulty hearing. This is also why God gave bats large ears!

Megabats

Since the bats that feed on animals are called microchiropterans, the bats that feed on plants are called **megachiropterans**, or **megabats**. They are pretty big compared to the tiny microbats. Megabats can have wingspans of up to six feet! That might be longer than your dad is tall!

Megabats have many features that are different from microbats. For example, megabats aren't as diverse as microbats when it comes to looks. They mostly have cute faces, resembling dogs or foxes. In fact, people call many megabats **flying foxes**. In addition, when a microbat roosts, it draws its wings in, closing them like a fan next to its body. A megabat folds its wings around its body when it roosts. The main difference between the two types of bats, however, is what they eat. While microbats eat animals, megabats are mostly vegetarians. They prefer ripe fruit, pollen, and nectar, but they will sometimes gobble up a wayward insect.

Notice how the microbat on the left folds its wings against its side, while the megabat on the right folds its wings around its body.

Another very important difference between these two types of bats is that most megabats don't have the ability to echolocate. They don't need it. Ripe fruit and blooming flowers don't run fast or fly away. In order to eat, a megabat simply needs the eyes with excellent vision that God provided, as well as its keen nose. Fruit-eaters are drawn by the sight and smell of ripe fruit.

Unlike the sharp teeth of the microbats, megabats have mostly flat teeth for chewing fruit. They also have an extra claw sticking out on the second finger. This helps them clutch the fruit that they like to eat. Most megabats eat only ripe fruit, so they are often called **fruit bats**. You have now heard four different names for these bats: megachiropterans, megabats, flying foxes, and fruit bats.

Do you remember that bats are a keystone species? This is especially true for megabats, as they help keep some of our favorite foods on the table. When they fly off with their fruit, they drop the seeds in a new spot where the seeds can grow roots and develop into new fruit trees. This is called **seed dispersal**, and it is an important step in plant reproduction. In fact, some seeds will actually not even sprout unless they have first passed through a bat's digestive system. Some bats can deposit up to 60,000 seeds in a single night of feeding! This shows you how important they are to the survival of certain plants!

Although most megabats eat fruit, some eat nectar and pollen. Nectar is the sweet juice that plants make in their flowers to attract bats, birds, and insects. Pollen is a powdery substance that flowers make for reproduction. In order to make a new plant, the pollen from one flower must travel to another flower. This process is called **pollination**. When a bat, bird, or insect comes to a flower to eat the nectar or pollen, some of the pollen gets on the animal, and when the animal goes to the next flower, some of that pollen may wipe off onto the next flower. In this way, bats, birds, and insects help the pollination of plants. Flowers that God created to rely on bat-assisted pollination often open at the setting of the sun and begin producing their scent around this time. This works out perfectly, since bats are nocturnal. Their scent and pretty colors attract bats, which help them in pollination.

Many plant species would not survive without bat pollinators. Megabats pollinate avocados, bananas, dates, figs, mangoes, and peaches. Did you know that the fruits you eat actually start out as flowers? It's true! If you ate a banana today, it was once a flower, and that flower was probably visited by a bat. Do you see how important bats are? Without bats, bananas wouldn't grow as easily, which would make them rare. If something is rare, it is much more expensive. Without bats, bananas would cost a lot more than they do today! In fact, banana plants might become extinct without bats.

There are more than 150 different kinds of megabats. None live in the United States, except in zoos. All of them live in tropical climates where there are a lot of fruits, nectar, and pollen for them to eat. You usually find these beautiful creatures in Africa, Asia, Australia, and Indonesia. Because megabats are typically found in what used to be called the "Old World" (Columbus discovered the "New World"), they are often called **Old World bats**, while microbats are called **New World bats**. That makes a total of five different names for megabats! Can you list them all?

Explain in your own words the differences between microbats and megabats.

Bat Habitats

Do you have bats in your town? Well, unless you live in Antarctica or the northernmost parts of the Arctic Circle, you probably do. There are over 900 species of bats, and they live pretty much everywhere.

Bats usually roost during the day, and they use that time to sleep, nurse their young, and groom themselves. They mostly groom themselves, spending a long time every day – sometimes several hours – cleaning themselves. Do you spend that much time cleaning yourself? Why not? When a bat cleans itself, it will hang by one foot and use the other to comb and clean its fur. It also uses its thumb to clean its ears and face and its tongue to clean its wings.

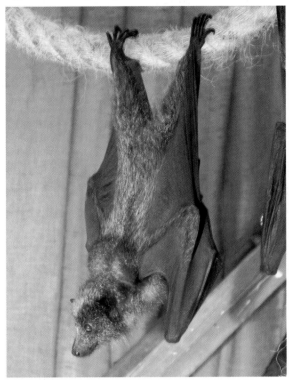

Bats hang upside down without effort or discomfort.

You know that a bat hangs by its toes, don't you? It is equipped with sharp, curved claws that can get a tight hold on even the smallest crack in a cave wall or a plank of wood. When a bat hangs, the weight of its body pulls on some tendons, which close the bat's claws automatically. There are no muscles involved. When you and I grip something, we must clench with our hand muscles. That takes effort. The bat doesn't need to do this, so it can hang without any effort.

God did not create us to hang upside down. When a person spends too much time upside down, his blood tends to rush to his head, but this doesn't happen to bats. God created the circulatory system (the blood vessels and heart) of a bat differently than He created the circulatory system of a person. As a result, a bat can hang upside down without having the blood rush to its head.

You might wonder *why* bats hang upside down. Well, that's because it's an ideal position from which to take off. Remember, bat wings are different from bird wings. Bird wings have more lift but do not allow for as much maneuvering as bat wings. Since bat wings don't have as much lift as bird wings, it is harder for bats to get started flying. Hanging in a high place upside down, however, gives them a perfect launch!

Where do you think bats live? You probably imagine them living in a cave, and in many cases, that's true. Many species of bats love to roost in dark, safe caves. But these **cave-dwelling bats** also like any dark crevice, such as the crevices under a bridge, in an attic, under the eaves of buildings, or inside hollow trees. Because of this, bats in the United States are often dependent on people for their homes.

Bats are very social animals. That means that they love to be around others of their same kind. As a result, you often find them in huge colonies. There are some magnificently large bat colonies in the Southwest United States. One of the biggest bat colonies in the world is in Bracken Cave, near San Antonio, Texas. Each year, 20 million Brazilian free-tailed bats go there to give birth to and raise their young. There is also a large colony of about a million bats that spend the summer under the Congress Avenue Bridge in Austin, Texas. These bats are called **city bats** because they live in the city, only a few blocks from the state capital. Tourists can watch one of the most spectacular sights in nature as these bats emerge from under the bridge to eat over 200 tons of flying insects each night. I'm sure there are very few mosquitoes in the area.

Unlike cave-dwelling bats, tree-roosting bats sleep out in the open, hanging from branches.

Many bats don't live in caves or cavities. They prefer to roost out in the open, usually in trees. In fact, most megabats are tree roosters. When bats roost on a tree branch, they often hang by one foot, looking like a small dead leaf. This makes it hard for predators to spot them. Most tree-roosting bats avoid grouping in large colonies. They tend to roost in small groups, alone, or with their young. When threatened, they will gather their young under their wings to protect them.

Try This!

So how do they know how many bats are in a colony? They do a bat count. It's not as hard as you might imagine counting twenty million bats. Try it yourself. I want you to estimate the number of bats in the drawing to the right. Use a 1-in x 1-in square from your math supplies or cut one out of paper. Count the number of bats that fit inside the square. It is easiest to count their heads. If any part of a head is in the square, it should count. Now count how many squares you can fit in the drawing. Multiply the number of bats in one square by the number of squares that fit in the drawing, and you have an estimate of the number of bats in the picture. If you want to make an even better estimate, count the number of bats that are in four different squares. Then multiply that number by the number of squares you can fit in the drawing, and then divide by four.

Guano

At the bottom of bat roosts, you will find bat waste. Bats usually turn themselves right side up to eliminate waste. Remember, they like to remain very clean. Bat waste is called **guano** (gwah' noh). For many years guano has been harvested for fertilizer because it is filled with many of the nutrients plants need. Scientists are also able to take certain chemicals out of guano and use it in laundry detergent and other products.

Explain all that you have learned in this lesson about the different habitats of bats.

Winter Homes

When is the best time of year to catch insects, and when can you pick fruit that is growing on trees? The spring and summer are the best seasons for these activities. If your main source of food were insects and fruit, you would have a hard time surviving cold winters. So, when the fall begins to turn to winter, bats decide its time to leave (migrate), or take a long winter's nap (**hibernate**).

These bats are hibernating in a cave.

Some bats find a cave, attic, tree hole, or human-made bat house and sleep all winter long. Some hibernate deep in cliff crevices, tree hollows, or even in woodpiles. The place an animal hibernates is called a **hibernaculum** (hi' bur nak' yoo lum), the plural of which is **hibernacula**. About 95% of all gray bats (*Myotis* [my oh' tis] *grisescens* [grih sess' sens]) hibernate each winter in one of only eight caves: three in Missouri, two in Tennessee, and one each in Kentucky, Alabama, and Arkansas.

If you live in the far north and find a bat hibernating in your home or yard, it is almost certainly a big brown bat (*Eptesicus* [ep tess' uh kus] *fuscus* [fuss' kus]). This bat is the only one known that can survive at temperatures below freezing. Merlin D. Tuttle, a scientist who studies bats, found one on a cave wall trapped completely in ice except for its nose. When he freed it from the ice, it aroused from its sleep and flew off, deeper into the cave to find another spot to sleep.

When a bat hibernates, its breathing slows down, and its body becomes almost the same temperature as the air around it. Its heartbeat drops from about 400 beats per minute to less than 25 beats per minute. This conserves a lot of energy, allowing the bat to stay alive until the spring brings back the food it needs to survive. Unlike bears, bats are true hibernators. You might have learned that bears hibernate in the winter, but they really don't. They just take long winter naps. You see, a hibernating animal's breathing and heart rate drop *a lot*, and its body temperature lowers to where it is almost as cold as the air around it. Bears reduce their breathing, heart rate, and body temperature a bit, but not nearly as much as a true hibernator.

It's important for a bat's hibernaculum to be moist. Otherwise, the little bat will dry up during its hibernation. In fact, a hibernating bat will wake up from time to time in order to drink, usually licking water off its fur or the cave wall. If the air warms above 55 degrees Fahrenheit or so, a bat may wake up to capture the few available insects and then go back to sleep. As the hibernation continues, the fat that the bat stored during the fall is slowly used up.

Bats are often threatened by cave explorers who sometime kill a whole colony of hibernating bats simply by disturbing them. This is because every time a hibernating bat is awakened, it loses many days worth of stored fat. If spring comes late, the bats may not have enough fat stored to stay alive throughout the hibernation period. This is why those who study bats try to learn where all the hibernacula are in the world so that they can place warning signs and put up fences that keep people out.

Although many bats hibernate for the winter, others migrate like birds. They fly long distances to a warmer climate for the winter so that they don't have to hibernate. Some will actually travel along the same routes as the birds. A bat will return in the spring to its cave, often to the very same spot in

Those who explore caves must be careful to avoid waking hibernating bats.

the cave that it roosted the year before and the year before that. In addition, some bats combine migration and hibernation. In the fall, they will fly to a warmer area and find a hibernaculum there. If a bat combines migration and hibernation, it doesn't travel as far as those that migrate but don't hibernate.

Breeding

At the end of the summer, the males begin seeking out females for mating. Some male bats will sing to attract a female. That should sound familiar. Some male birds sing to attract females. Once bats have mated (usually in the early fall) the males fly off alone to find their winter homes.

Most mother bats have only one bat pup each year, born in late spring or early summer. A few species, like the big brown bat, can have up to three at once, but that's rare. Tropical bats can have two pregnancies a year because the weather is warm all year long. Once the bat pups are born, they must have very warm temperatures to develop quickly.

One remarkable thing about bat pups is how big they are. They seem tiny to us, but they are as much as one third the size of the mother. If you were one third the size of your mother when you were born, how much would you have weighed?

Many bats, especially megabats, are born with a body covered with fur and wide open eyes. Other bats (like the little brown bat on the right) are born naked with closed eyes. Bats born completely naked are altricial, while bats born with fur are precocial. Do you remember what those words mean? You learned them in the previous lesson.

Whether naked or furry, mother bats adore their young pups and coo to them, much like your mom cooed to you! Like all mammals, the mother nurses her newborn with milk from her milk glands. Some microbats carry their newborns wherever they go, but most leave their pups in a nursery when they need to go out to look for food. Even the microbats that carry their pups will eventually have to

Even though this little brown bat pup seems tiny to you and me, it is about one third the size of its mother!

leave them in the nursery, once they get too heavy to carry around. Bat pups can nurse for as long as six months. That is a very long time for a mammal to keep feeding from its mother.

The Nursery

Infant bats stay in the bat nursery, where hundreds – sometimes millions – of baby bats snuggle together, keeping one another warm. Remember that most bats have only one pup. If there are several million young pups, that means there are several million bat mothers in the colony as well!

The pups are very tiny and fragile. God gave them the ability to clutch well to the mother or the wall from the day they are born. If a pup falls to the ground, it may die. After all, snakes, raccoons and other carnivores can get to the pup very easily if it is lying helpless on the ground. There might also be many feet of bat guano underneath where the bats roost, and the baby could sink into it and be completely covered up, unable to breathe. This is why it must stay very tightly hooked to the ceiling!

The mother bat comes to visit, nurse, clean, coo to, and nurture her young pup several times a day. For many years scientists thought that the mother probably just fed any little baby she could find, but experiments have shown that each mother can find her very own pup among the millions that might be in the nursery. She actually can tell his little squeal apart from all the other pups. She calls to her baby, and her baby answers. She can also recognize her pup by smell. Every bat mother has her own, unique scent that she rubs onto her baby. This allows her to recognize her baby even if the baby is not answering her calls.

As the weeks pass, the older pups begin to wave their wings back and forth, practicing for the day they will let go of the cave wall and fly for the first time. When they are about one or two months old, the pups must do a very frightening thing. They must let go, flying quickly into a cloud of fellow bats, and test out their echolocation system. The first flights are often just test flights for a young bat. It doesn't actually go out foraging for food for a few weeks more.

This bat pup is clinging to the wall because it is not ready to fly.

Explain what you remember from this lesson about bat babies and parents.

What Do You Remember?

Explain echolocation in your own words. What are the differences between microbats and megabats? What beneficial tasks do bats perform? Where are some of the different places that bats roost? What is interesting about bat hibernation and migration? How do mother bats care for their pups? Why would you want to attract bats to your neighborhood?

Notebook Activities

Record all the fascinating facts you learned about bats in this lesson. Be sure to explain what echolocation is, using a drawing like the one on page 106. Find pictures of bats to cut out (or print out) and put in your notebook. Also, write down the things you learned in this lesson about bat habitats, hibernation, migration, and how bats care for their young. Templates for these activities are provided in the *Zoology 1 Notebooking Journal.*

Older Students: Do a report on hibernation throughout the animal kingdom. What animals are true hibernators, and what animals take long winter naps but do not actually hibernate? If you have the *Zoology 1 Notebooking Journal,* a template for this activity is provided on page 94.

Make a Play of a Microbat Meeting a Megabat

Have you ever read a play? The written down version of a play is called a **script**. In a script, you indicate who is speaking by writing the person's name, followed by a colon. There is a page from a sample script on the right. This script is for a play that tells the story of Mark the microbat meeting Mary the megabat.

I want you to make a play about the same subject. In your play, a microbat and megabat will meet for the first time. Neither knows anything about the other kind of bat, so they will have to learn about their differences. That way, the people who watch your play will learn a lot about these two different kinds of bats. It might be fun for you to have them surprised by what the other bat eats. You may also have them discuss things like how and where they roost as well as whether they migrate or hibernate (or both). A page to complete this activity is provided in the *Zoology 1 Notebooking Journal*.

> **Microbat Mark**: My, aren't you a large bat!
>
> **Megabat Mary**: And you are so small that I thought you were a baby. But babies don't fly as well as you do.
>
> **Microbat Mark**: Well, I'm glad to meet you. Would you like to go hunting with me?
>
> **Megabat Mary**: Hunting? What is that? I'm really not interested in doing anything but getting a bite to eat.
>
> **Microbat Mark**: Yes. That's what I mean. Let's go hunt for some food.

Project
Find Your Pup

We are going to do an activity to see what it is like to find a baby pup in a crowded nursery.

You will need:

♦ A blindfold
♦ 20 cotton balls
♦ 20 different agents with characteristic smells such as vanilla, toothpaste, dish soap, hand lotion, coffee, juice, vinegar, oils, and perfumes.

1. Transfer the scent of each agent to one cotton ball. In the end, you will have 20 cotton balls, each with a different smell. Each cotton ball represents a pup in a nursery.
2. Choose one smell to be yours.
3. Mix all the cotton balls until you are sure you don't know which is yours.
4. Put on your blindfold and begin smelling until you think you have located your baby.

Were you able to locate the smell that you chose to be yours? Was it hard? Can you imagine if there were a million different smells? God gave bats an excellent sense of smell, don't you think?

Lesson 8
Flying Reptiles

Do you remember what we learned about **extinction** back in the first lesson? We learned that some animals have completely died out, and as far as we know, there are none of them alive anywhere on earth. When an animal becomes extinct, we can't study it up close anymore, but sometimes we can learn what the animal was like if people wrote down what they learned about the animal before it became extinct.

Today, there are people who study endangered animals and write down everything they know about them, just in case they become extinct. Another way we can learn about an extinct animal is to study a living animal that is similar to the extinct animal. If you studied a Mourning Dove, a bird much like the Passenger Pigeon, would you be able to learn something about the Passenger Pigeon? Perhaps. Since the two birds are similar, studying the one that is still alive might allow us to make educated guesses about the habits and behaviors of the one that is extinct.

Even if you are able to discover some things about extinct animals from written records or by studying similar animals, there are hundreds of other extinct animals that lived in places where there were no people to observe them. Others became extinct at a time when people didn't record information about them. And sometimes, whole groups of animals become extinct and there are no other animals still alive today that are similar to them. Can you think of any animals you have seen in books that became extinct long, long ago? Many different kinds of dinosaurs have been extinct for a long time and, as far as we know at this time, there are no other animals like them.

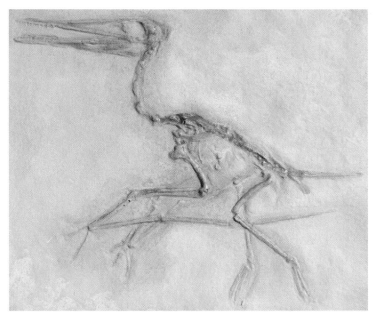

So how can we learn about animals like the dinosaurs? The only real way we can learn what they were like and how they lived is by studying their **fossils**. Do you remember what a fossil is? I told you about fossils in the first lesson. Fossils can tell us a lot about an animal, but there are many things that we can't learn from looking at fossils. Could you tell what color an animal was by looking at its fossilized bones? Would you know what

This is a fossil of *Pterodactylus kochi*, a pterosaur. Although scientists have learned a lot about pterosaurs from their fossils, there is much that they have not been able to learn.

kinds of sounds it made? Would you be able to tell whether it preferred to live alone (like the hawk) or in groups (like the penguin)? You probably could not, but you might be able to guess at some of these things. The study of fossils, called **paleontology** (pay' lee un tah' luh jee), is a difficult science. The scientists who study fossils have to make many guesses about the animals they are studying. Even though paleontologists have to make many guesses, they're still able to learn some things by studying just an animal's fossils. You will read about some of the things paleontologists have been able to learn in this lesson.

Try This!

Let's see how hard it is to be a paleontologist. This activity will help you understand how hard it is to guess with only a little information. Find an old photo of a family member that you don't know **and haven't heard much about**, but that your mom, dad, or grandma knows pretty well. Maybe it is someone who lives far away from you or someone who lived long ago and is now dead.

Study the photograph very carefully and look for clues that help you learn about this person. What kind of clothes is she wearing? What is she doing? Look at the background of the photo. Can you guess what this person was like? Take a piece of paper and make three columns on it. In one column write all the things you can know for sure from just looking at the picture. For example, you might know that the person is a girl with brown hair. Look very carefully at the photo and think very hard about all the things you know.

In the next column, write all the things that you can guess. For example, if she is cooking, you might guess that she enjoyed cooking. That may or may not be true. Can you guess whether she enjoyed being with people or preferred to be alone? What other kinds of guesses can you make about her habits and behavior?

After you have written down all of your guesses, ask a family member to tell you what he knows about the person in the photo. Write down this information in the third column. Were your guesses correct? Were you told things that you could never have guessed?

Do you now understand a little more about being a paleontologist? It is a difficult job to guess things based on only a small amount of information. Of course, unlike you had in this activity, paleontologists don't have the benefit of someone who can tell them whether or not their guesses are correct!

Pterosaurs

In this lesson we are going to learn about a group of flying animals called **pterosaurs** (tair' uh sorz). Look at how the word is spelled; the "p" is silent. The "ptero" at the beginning comes from the Greek word for "wing," and "saur" comes from the Greek word for lizard. Thus, a "pterosaur" is a "winged lizard."

The pterosaurs are all extinct, and unfortunately, there are no animals alive today that are similar to them. As a result, there are many things that we will never know for certain about them. Nevertheless, we'll study the facts we do know about pterosaurs and make good guesses about what pterosaurs were like. We will be like paleontologists, won't we?

On the fifth day of creation, God made all sorts of flying creatures. In the perfect world that He made, those flying creatures included the pterosaurs. These reptiles had wings and could fly. Even though the name means "winged lizard," they were not really lizards. In fact, scientists disagree about whether or not they were even reptiles. The bones in the skull of a pterosaur have the same arrangement and pattern as some reptiles, like crocodiles. On the other hand, the body of a reptile and the body of a pterosaur are very different. Not only do specific aspects of their skeletons differ, there have been some pterosaur fossils found that indicate at least some pterosaurs had hair (or at least a hair-like substance) on their bodies. Reptiles, of course, do not have hair. So even though we call pterosaurs flying reptiles, they may not have been reptiles at all!

On the fifth day of creation, pterosaurs like this one from genus *Rhamphorhynchus* graced the skies.

Like bird bones, pterosaur bones were mostly hollow. Why do you think God made them like that? Well, if their bones were not mostly hollow, pterosaurs would have been too heavy to fly. Unlike birds, pterosaurs didn't have feathers. Their wings were more like those of a bat, composed of a thin membrane that connected the arms and fingers to the sides of the body.

Many people think that pterosaurs were dinosaurs, but that's not correct either. Dinosaurs were upright land animals that moved about on either two or four legs. Dinosaur bones were built solid and heavy to support their weight as they walk around. They could never have gotten off the ground, even if they had wings. Pterosaurs were not designed that way, so a pterosaur wasn't a flying dinosaur. What were pterosaurs? Pterosaurs were flying, reptile-*like* animals. They make up their own group of creatures in God's creation, separate from the reptiles, birds, and dinosaurs.

Pterosaurs in History

The Bible mentions flying animals that sound very much like pterosaurs. The prophet Isaiah, who lived about three thousand years ago, mentions "flying serpents" twice (Isaiah 14:29, 30:6), and a flying serpent describes a pterosaur very well! Many translations of the Bible add the word "fiery" to the description, but the more literal translations tend to leave it out. We do not know for sure whether or not Isaiah was describing pterosaurs or what "fiery" might mean in connection to the flying serpents Isaiah was describing. We may never know while we live here on earth.

Some scientists think that the dragons in the Bible and in certain legends were actually pterosaurs that people saw with their own eyes.

The Bible also speaks of dragons. Have you ever seen a drawing of a dragon? Look at the one on the left. It has many similarities to the drawing of the pterosaur on the previous page, doesn't it? People from many different parts of the world have been describing dragons and flying serpents for thousands of years. They are mentioned in the writings of people who wrote history books, like Herodotus (huh rod' uh tus) and Josephus (joh see' fus). It is possible that these people were actually writing about pterosaurs.

Herodotus was a very well known and trustworthy Greek historian who lived about 450 years before Christ. He writes:

> There is a place in Arabia...to which I went, on hearing of some winged serpents; and when I arrived there, I saw bones and spines of serpents, in such quantities as it would be impossible to describe. The form of the serpent is like that of a water-snake; but he has wings without feathers, and as like as possible to the wings of a bat. (Herodotus, (1850 reprint), *Historiae*, trans. Henry Clay (London: Henry G. Bohn). 1850, pp. 75-76).

Josephus was also a very reliable writer of history, who lived about 500 years after Herodotus. He actually lived during the time of Jesus and wrote much about Him and His followers. A lot of what we know about what happened to Christians in Rome and the Jewish people during the first century after Christ's birth comes from the writings of Josephus.

Josephus often studied ancient texts and recorded information recounted in them. In those ancient texts, flying reptiles were mentioned as being very vicious. Were Isaiah, Herodotus, Josephus, and other ancient writers really describing the animals we call pterosaurs today? Could they have been talking about animals that other people called dragons? Now remember, the name "pterosaur" was invented fairly recently. If ancient people ever saw a pterosaur, they wouldn't have called it that. Perhaps the name "dragon" was not invented from people's imaginations after all. It might have been used to describe pterosaurs, which ancient people had seen with their own eyes.

So, did all the pterosaurs become extinct? Well, we think they did, but even today, people in far away, remote jungles in Africa and South America report seeing ferocious flying serpents with wingspans of several feet. Some people living in Africa today report seeing two pterosaur-like creatures. They do not call them pterosaurs, of course. They call them "Olitu" and "Kongamato," but their descriptions of the animals match that of what scientists think pterosaurs looked like. So far, there have been no pictures taken of these animals, though people have made drawings of them, supposedly from what they saw with their own eyes. Would you one day be willing to go on a hunt for these animals in the dense African jungle? You would need to be very brave and careful. There are a lot of dangers in the jungle.

Tell someone what you have learned so far about flying reptiles. Why are they not dinosaurs? Which people have written about them?

Types of Pterosaurs

God made two different types of pterosaurs: the **rhamphorhynchoids** (ram' foh ring' koydz) and the **pterodactyloids** (tehr uh dak' tuh loydz), which are sometimes mistakenly called "pterodactyls." Studying these animals can become confusing because some people make a mistake and call any pterosaur a pterodactyl. They make this mistake because the first pterosaur ever discovered was a pterodactyloid. In 1784, a man named Collini found a fossil skeleton in Germany. At first, he thought it was some sort of a lizard that swam in the water. When other scientists looked at the skeleton, they thought it was half bird and half bat. Can you see how easy it is to make mistakes about fossils?

For almost 20 years no one could agree on what this strange looking creature really was. In 1801, a man named Cuvier found similar fossils and believed the odd creature was a flying reptile. He named the animal "ptero-dactyle" which means "wing finger." That was a very good name for this animal because the membrane that forms its wing is stretched between its very long fourth finger and the rest of its body, as shown in the drawing to the right. Does this wing design look familiar? It should.

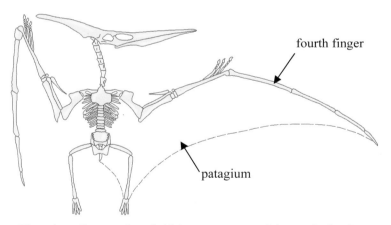

The wing of a pterodactyloid (or any pterosaur) is attached to its very long fourth finger.

It looks a lot like a bat's wing, doesn't it? The membrane that forms the wing is even called a patagium, just like the membrane that forms a bat's wing.

For many years, all pterosaurs were called pterodactyls, but now scientists recognize several different species. The species that have short tails belong to the pterodactyloid group, while species with long tails belong to the rhamphorhynchoid group.

Pterodactyloids generally had long necks and long beaks. Some had sharp pointy teeth, but some did not have any teeth at all. A few had big, fancy crests on top of their heads (like the one in the drawing below). No one knows if these crests served a purpose or if they were just decoration. Maybe the crests had something to do with attracting a mate. They might have been brightly colored like the beaks of puffins. On the other hand, the crests might have helped the animals to stay balanced and steer better while they were flying.

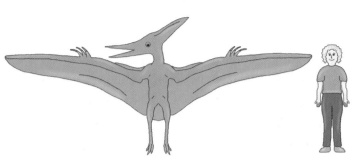

The smallest pterodactyloids had wingspans of about 16 inches, but some kinds of pterodactyloids, like the **pteranodon** (tuh ran' uh don), were very large. The pteranodon had a wingspan of up to 25 feet! If your foot is about six inches long (it might be an inch or two longer or shorter), you would have to take 50 steps with one foot in front of the other to measure out 25 feet. Do that to get an idea of just how big a pteranodon's wingspan was!

This drawing illustrates the size of a pteranodon compared to an adult.

Pteranodons weren't the largest of the pterodactyloids, however. That title belongs to **quetzalcoatlus** (ket' sahl koh aht' lus), a pterosaur that is named after one of the Aztecs' false gods.

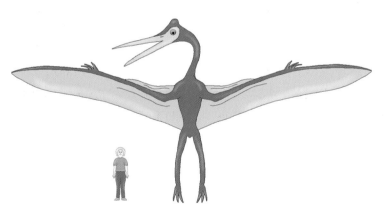

This drawing illustrates the size of Quetzalcoatlus compared to an adult.

You will need to use your imagination to understand just how big this pterodactyloid was. Do you know anyone who is over six feet tall? Well, just the head of a quetzalcoatlus is over six feet long! Can you imagine an animal whose head is bigger than a person's whole body? Now in your imagination add on to that big head a neck that is another 10 feet and a torso that is still another 10 feet. Then imagine a wingspan of 40 feet – that's as long as a school bus! You need a great imagination to picture an animal that big, don't you? If your imagination needs a little help, stop reading, go outside, and measure out the size of quetzalcoatlus for yourself. Lay out branches, rope, or string, until the line stretches for 40 feet. That's how wide the wings were when the animal stretched them out!

Can you imagine what it would have been like to discover such an amazing creature? The first quetzalcoatlus fossil was found in Big Bend National Park in Texas by a college student from the University of Texas in Austin. His name was Douglas Lawson. When he was in the park one day in 1971, he noticed a fossilized bone sticking out from a rock. The bone had a very thin wall and appeared to be hollow, like the bone of a bird, so he guessed that it was part of a flying creature. Since you have learned about bird bones would you have made the same guess?

With the help of his professor, he kept digging until many bones from an arm and wing were uncovered. Unfortunately, the rest of the animal's body was missing! Many other people have looked for the rest of that huge fossilized pterosaur, but it has never been found. If you go to Big Bend National Park in Texas, will you look for the missing quetzalcoatlus? Other quetzalcoatlus fossils have been found there, but they are much smaller than the one discovered by Lawson.

To make the study of pterodactyloids just a little more confusing, there is actually a *specific* pterodactyloid called a **pterodactyl**. Now remember, at one time all pterosaurs were called pterodactyls. Nowadays, we split the pterosaurs into two major groups: rhamphorhynchoids and pterodactyloids. There are many specific pterosaurs in each group. Pteranodons and quetzalcoatlus are two examples of *specific* pterodactyloids. Well, it turns out that the pterodactyl is another specific pterodactyloid. Pterodactyls belong in genus ***Pterodactylus***, and they were small compared to the pteranodon and quetzalcoatlus, with wingspans of about 2½ feet and no head crest. The fossil pictured on the first page of this lesson is an example of a species from this genus. The only time you really should use the term "pterodactyl" is when you are talking about members of this genus.

Now that I've told you a bit about the pterodactyloids, I want to move on to the rhamphorhynchoids. Their name comes from the Greek words *rhamphos*, which means "beak," and *rhygkhos*, which means "snout." These animals, then, are the "beak snouts." The beak is probably the first thing you would notice if you were able to see creatures in this group of pterosaurs, because they all had large, sometimes odd teeth. Have you ever heard the term "snaggletooth?" That's a good description of these creatures, because they looked like they needed to wear braces! They had a lot of teeth sticking out at all angles from their beaks. This might have looked strange, but those snaggleteeth would have been just perfect for snapping up insects while they were flying, or for catching slippery little fish.

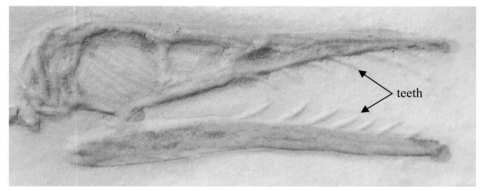

This fossil of a rhamphorhynchoid skull shows the large teeth that are in the beak

Rhamphorhynchoids were smaller the than pterodactyloids. They had long tails that often ended with diamond-shaped paddles at the end of them. No one really knows what the purpose of these paddles were, but they may have helped the creature to change direction while flying just like a rudder helps a boat to change direction in a stream. What is your guess about why God made the paddle on the end of its tail?

Just as there is a specific kind of pterodactyloid put in genus ***Pterodactylus***, there is also a specific kind of rhamphorhynchoid that is put into genus ***Rhamphorhynchus***. This particular rhamphorhynchoid was about the size of a Turkey Vulture and probably ate other animals for food.

Tell someone what you remember so far about each of the pterosaurs I discussed above.

Pterosaur Lifestyle

Since no one has ever been able to study a living pterosaur, it is very hard for us to know exactly what their lives were like. Pterosaurs probably ate other animals for food. Their mouths were well suited for snatching insects from the air. It is often believed that pterodactyls were fish eaters because their fossils are found near fossils of sea creatures. These animals, however, were likely buried during the worldwide flood of Noah's day. During that flood, sea life and other creatures were probably mixed together as the ocean tides swept over the land. Because of this, we really do not know what these flying reptiles ate, though it could have been fish.

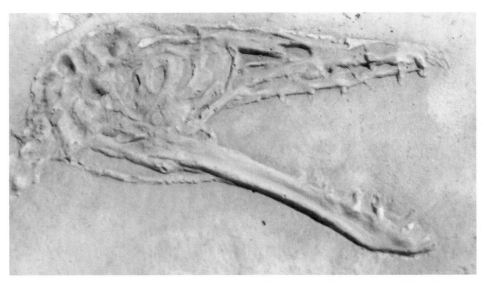

As this fossil shows, pterosaur mouths seem to have been able to open wide. Can you tell whether this is a pterodactyloid or a rhamphorhynchoid?

Pterosaur jaws look as if they could open very wide, and fossil evidence indicates that at least some of them might have had a throat pouch (like a pelican) for storing food. In addition, some pterosaurs did not have teeth. Those pterosaurs probably didn't chew their food. Of course, they would not necessarily have to. Some birds, like the cormorant, toss fish into their beaks and swallow them whole. Pterosaurs without teeth might have done the same thing. Fossils indicate that one pterosaur, the pterodaustro (tehr uh daw' stroh) found in Argentina, had comb-like strainers in its mouth. This pterosaur probably ate by filling its lower jaw with water and pushing the water out of its mouth through the strainers. The strainers probably caught any small fish or other creatures that were in the water, and once all of the water was gone, the pterodaustro ate what was left in the strainers.

Powered Flight

Do you remember the differences among flying, gliding, and soaring? You learned about them in Lesson 4. It was once thought that pterosaurs did not fly well, but instead relied on gliding and soaring to move through the air. Scientists don't believe that anymore. Pterosaurs may have jumped from high ocean cliffs and glided through the air, or they might have caught an updraft and soared on a warm day. In order to catch food, however, they surely had the ability to flap their wings and move around in the sky using controlled, powered flight. In other words, they couldn't have relied just on gliding or soaring.

As I already mentioned, the design of a pterosaur's wing is very similar to the design of a bat's wing, with a patagium stretched between the long, fourth finger and the body. This patagium was reinforced with stretchy fibers called **actinofibrillae** (act' in oh fib' ruh lay), which were spaced very close together. This helped to protect the wing and keep it from tearing or getting damaged. Reinforced wings like that would certainly be capable of powered flight. In addition, fossils indicate that several of their bones had

Most scientists now agree that pterosaurs like this pteranodon were excellent flyers.

places to which flight muscles attached. In the end, then, most scientists today think that many (if not all) of the pterosaurs were capable of true flight, like birds and bats.

Pterosaurs also had special bones. They were lightweight, even lighter than a bird's bones. The walls of a pterosaur's bones were very thin. Some of them were not much thicker than a piece of paper. In addition, the bones were almost hollow. Inside these hollow spaces were special supporting rods that crisscrossed like the steel beams on a bridge. These were the bone struts. Bone struts made the bones much stronger! With these special bones, even a large pterosaur like a pteranodon would have weighed less than 40 pounds. The largest of the pterosaurs, quetzalcoatlus, probably weighed less than 200 pounds!

Try This!

Find two different kinds of tape: masking tape and strapping tape. Strapping tape is the kind of tape that has small fibers embedded in it. Tear off a small piece of masking tape. Was it easy to tear? Now tear off a piece of strapping tape. Were you able to tear it? Which kind of tape is more like a pterosaur's wing? Do you understand why God designed pterosaurs with their very special wings?

Next, find a shipping box made of corrugated cardboard and tear it apart. Look in between the inside and outside layers of one of the pieces you tore. Do you see the ridge of cardboard that waves up and down between the layers? It acts like a bone strut, making the box strong. Since the area in between the layers is mostly empty, however, the box is still pretty light. The strength of the corrugated box is like the strength of pterosaur (and bird) bones that God made. God is a great designer. We should always remember to study His designs and learn from them. That is one reason He gave us so many animals to learn about. Inventors often mimic the designs God made in creation. Perhaps you will grow up to be an inventor, studying God's creation and allowing Him to inspire you to recreate His design for mankind to use.

Other Pterosaur Lifestyle Issues

Though pterosaurs had lightweight bones, their brains were very large. One region of their brain, called the **flocculus** (flok' yuh lus), was especially big. This area is believed to be the part of the brain that helps an animal balance and sends balance-related information to the eyes. The fact that pterosaurs had a large flocculus indicates that they were probably excellent flyers, capable of making acrobatic maneuvers in the sky. Compared to pterosaurs, people have a small flocculus, because people are not designed to fly.

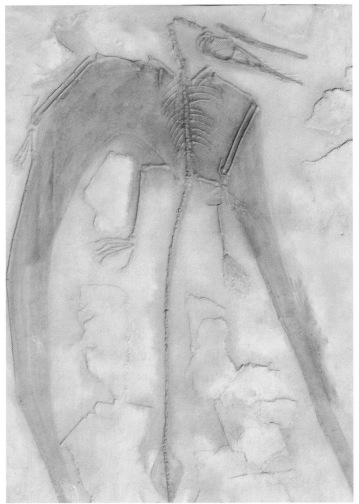

This rhamphorhynchoid fossil tells us much about its physical characteristics but little about how it lived and reproduced. Because of how the animal fossilized, its head is upside down.

When pterosaurs had to move along the ground, scientists aren't sure whether they pulled themselves along like a bat or walked upright like a bird. There are different opinions on this. There is evidence that when they were resting they may have hung upside down like a bat, with their wings folded alongside the body. Their long, skinny feet seem to be well suited for hanging this way. Can you imagine a whole bunch of pterosaurs hanging around upside down in a tree?

We do not know much about pterosaur family life. Pterosaur fossils are sometimes found in groups that may be family groups. We find fossils of smaller pterosaurs, which appear to be juveniles, mixed in with larger pterosaur bones that appear to be from adults, so we think that they may have lived together in colonies like penguins.

There has been a lot of disagreement over whether pterosaurs laid eggs, like birds and reptiles, or gave birth to live young, like bats. There was little evidence either way until recently. During the summer of 2004, two teams of scientists working in different parts of the world, one in China, one in Argentina, both claimed to have discovered pterosaur eggs. The eggshells were cracked but the hatchlings were still inside! Perhaps they were just hatching out. These discoveries are still being verified by **peer review**. Do you know what peer review is? A peer is someone that is your equal. To review is evaluate something. Peer review, then, is to have an equal look over and study your work. When one scientist learns something new, many other scientists who are skilled in the same area of science examine the discovery very carefully to make sure that the original discoverer did not make a mistake. Peer review is a very important part of the scientific process. If the peer review on these egg discoveries ends up confirming that they are pterosaur eggs, we will finally know that at least some pterosaurs laid eggs!

What Do You Remember?

Explain what it is a like to be a paleontologist. Which ancient people wrote about animals that may have been pterosaurs? Which modern day people talk about and draw pictures of animals that look like pterosaurs? What are the two basic groups of pterosaurs? Which group had the largest pterosaurs? Which group had the smallest? What were a pterosaur's bones like? What part of a pterosaur's brain is very large? What does this tell us about pterosaurs?

Notebook Activities

Record all the fascinating facts you learned about pterosaurs in your notebook. The *Zoology 1 Notebooking Journal* provides pages for you to record your learning.

Make a small book about pterosaurs. A template is provided for you to cut out and assemble a small book on page 105 of the *Zoology 1 Notebooking Journal*. On each page, illustrate pictures of each kind of pterosaur you learned about in this lesson or print images from the computer. Record facts about each pterosaur in your book.

Older Students: Do some research on the current status of the pterosaur eggs I discussed in this lesson. Have they been accepted as real eggs? If so, what were the eggs like? Were they hard, like bird eggs, or soft and leathery, like reptile eggs?

Activity
Make a Fossil Egg

You will need:

♦ A hardboiled egg

♦ A paper plate

♦ A piece of wax paper

♦ Clay or Play-doh®

♦ Plaster of Paris

♦ Water

♦ A paint brush

♦ A tea bag

♦ Hot water

♦ An old toothbrush (optional)

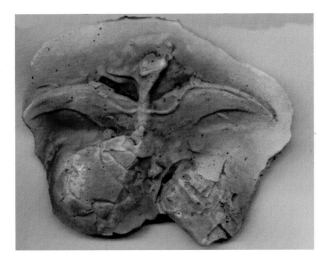

Let's assume that pterosaurs did lay eggs. I want you to make a fake fossil of a baby pterosaur just hatching from its egg.

1. Spread the clay or Play-doh out on the paper plate until you have an inch thick circle about the size of your hand.

2. Make some cracks in the hardboiled egg.

3. Firmly but gently press the egg into the center of the dough until you leave a nice imprint of the egg. (If you are using clay, you may want to coat the egg with a little oil first so the clay will not stick to it.) If you do not get a good impression the first time, try again.

4. You can be creative with your egg replica. You might want to make the impressions of a "nest" around the egg by pressing sticks or twigs into the clay. You could try pressing broken eggshell pieces into the clay to leave an impression of an egg that has just hatched.

5. Sculpt the clay so that you have an impression of what looks like a baby pterosaur just coming out of the egg. You can use the hard end of the paintbrush to help you make the impression.

6. After you have made a good impression, mix the plaster with water. Mix about ½ cup of plaster with ¼ cup of water. Stir it until it is smooth and creamy.

7. Pour the plaster over the impression and allow it to dry. This should take about an hour, but it might take longer.

8. While you are waiting for the plaster to dry, prepare a tea stain. You will use this stain to make the plaster fossil look more like a real fossil. Simply place the tea bag in a cup of hot water.

9. After the plaster is dry, peel the dough from the plaster and clean all the dough off the plaster. You might use an old toothbrush to do this.

10. Use a paint brush to paint the fossil with the tea you made. When you paint the tea on the plaster, it will stain the plaster, making it look old. Apply several coats of stain until the replica is just the color that you want. Allow time for the stain to soak into the plaster and dry before applying a new coat. Hopefully, your fossil will look something like the one in the picture above.

Lesson 9
A First Look at Insects

What do you think about insects? People usually either love them or hate them. I hope you don't hate them. If you do, maybe you won't by the time you're done with this part of zoology, called **entomology** (en' tuh mahl' uh jee), which is the study of insects.

This dragonfly is a part of class Insecta, which contains more species than any other class in creation.

You see, insects are a delightful group of animals. They are small, fascinating, and so numerous! In fact, class **Insecta**, which contains the insects, is larger than any other class in creation. That means there are more species of insects living on earth than that of any other type of animal. One thing insects do really well is produce a lot of young. In other words, they make big families. Each insect might lay hundreds of eggs at once, sometimes thousands in a day. It's no wonder there are so many of them. Of course, most live for only a short time, usually for less than a year, sometimes for less than a day!

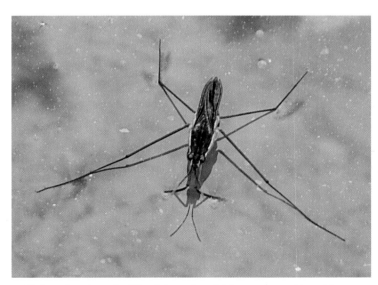

Only a few insects, like this water strider, are considered bugs.

Most people aren't very interested in studying insects. They prefer warm, furry animals over the creatures they see as bothersome bugs. But – here's a fact most people don't know – insects are not necessarily bugs. Bugs are a special group of insects that have interesting wings. Their front two wings are thick near where they attach to the body and thin towards the tip. We will learn all about bugs later on in the course. For right now, you only need to know that not every small creature that crawls or flies is a bug! As a matter of a fact, not every creature that crawls is an insect either! So what is an insect, anyway?

Identifying Insects

Insects are easy to recognize, because they have specific features. Counting the legs is always the first step to identifying insects, because all adult insects have six legs. In addition, adult insects have an exoskeleton (a hard covering on the outside), and body with three major sections to it. Most adult insects also have compound eyes (eyes made up of many, tiny lenses) and wings. There are some insects that never have wings, and there are some (like ants) in which certain adults have wings while the rest do not. Since we are studying the winged creatures of creation, I will concentrate on insect species in which at least some of the adults have wings.

From what I just told you, do you think that an ant is an insect? What about a spider, earthworm, centipede, or scorpion? I'll give you a clue; count the legs. Look at each creature below and decide whether or not it is an insect. You can check your answers by looking at the answers to the narrative questions in the back of the book.

All these creatures (A-F) are invertebrates, but as you found out when you looked at the answers in the back of the book, not all of them are insects. Remember the discussion about backbones way back at the beginning of this course? Well, we have spent all of our time so far studying vertebrates, which are creatures with backbones. From now on, we will be studying invertebrates, which don't have backbones. Of course, we will be studying only one type of invertebrates: insects. These creatures are classified in phylum **Arthropoda** and class **Insecta**.

Like all classes, Insecta has been divided into orders, but that's where we reach a problem. Have you ever had a disagreement with a friend that just could not be solved? Well, that's what happens with classifying insects. Entomologists cannot completely agree on how to classify insects. Because of this, there are disagreements from one book to another as to what kinds of insects go into what orders. For example, cockroaches are sometimes put in their own order called Blattaria (bluh tair' ee uh), and praying mantises are put in their own order, called Mantodae (man toh' day uh). But in other systems, the mantises are put in the same order with cockroaches, called Dictyoptera (dik' tee ahp' tur uh). This gets even more confusing when you find that other scientists put praying mantises with crickets and grasshoppers into an order called Orthoptera (or thahp' tur uh)!

Because there is so much disagreement among scientists when it comes to classifying insects, I won't discuss it in any detail. I'll just say that in general, scientists try to put insects in orders based on the type of wings they have, because wing types vary greatly from insect to insect. Usually, the name of the order is a Latin or Greek word that describes the wings. For example, flies have two wings that they use to fly. Because of this, flies are in the order Diptera (dip' tur uh), which means "two wings" in Greek.

What Good are They?

You may be wondering why God made insects. After all, many people will tell you that they could do without insects. But the truth is that we need insects, because God created them with very important and necessary jobs in our world. If all insects were to suddenly disappear, the world would simply become a disaster! In fact, humans may not even be able to survive on the planet without insects. It has been reported that Albert Einstein (a great scientist) once said, "If the bee disappeared off the surface of the globe then man would only have four years of life left." [Adrian Higgins, "Honeybees in a Mite More Than Trouble," *The Washington Post*, Tuesday, May 14, 2002, p. A01]

Bees are beneficial to people because they help plants reproduce, and people need plants in order to live. This bee is covered with a yellow powder called pollen, which it will transport to several other flowers, helping the plants reproduce. If you take a botany course, you will learn all about this amazing process.

In fact, there are really two kinds of insects: ones that are beneficial to people, and ones that are not beneficial to people, which we usually call **pests**. Sometimes, it really depends on what the insect is doing as to whether or not it is a pest. Termites, for example, are sometimes called pests because they can harm our homes. However, they also help break down the trees and branches that fall to the forest floor. Without the work done by termites, dead trees would cover the ground wherever you went. This would choke off the growth of plants, which we need in order to live. In other words, termites help to clean the earth for us. They do all the dirty work!

In some cases, if we did not have beneficial insects, the pest insects would eat all our food. Ladybugs, certain wasps, and praying mantises feed on the pests that destroy our crops and gardens. Without beneficial insects, we would also not have fruits and vegetables to eat, since almost all fruit and vegetable plants need insects to pollinate them, which is how plants reproduce. In fact, some farmers keep bees just so that there will be an ample supply of insects to pollinate their crops.

Insects are food for many birds, including this Summer Tanager.

Have you ever felt a cloth called silk? It's a strong, light fabric that is very soft. It used to be worn only by the wealthiest people on earth: kings and royalty. Without insects, there would be no silk, because silk is made by insects! You'll learn all about silk-making insects in the final lesson of this book.

Insects are even used to solve crimes. By studying the insects present on a dead body, entomologists can determine how long the body has been dead or whether the body has been moved. Insects are also used in medicine. Maggots, which are young flies, are used to help heal wounds that won't heal by themselves. Doctors call this "maggot debridement (dih breed' munt) therapy."

Another very important reason we need insects (both the beneficial ones and the pests) is that they are food for birds, fish, and many other animals that we enjoy. Without insects, woodpeckers, swallows, bluebirds, many owls, and hundreds of other birds would become extinct, never to be seen again. So let's here it for insects! (You should be clapping.)

Cold-Blooded

Do you remember that bats and birds are warm-blooded animals? What does being warm-blooded mean? It means that these animals are able to control their body temperatures and stay warm even when it's cold outside. Cold-blooded animals can't control the temperature of their bodies. If it is warm outside, their bodies are warm. If it is cold outside, their bodies are cold. They need warmth to be able to move around. If they are cold, they begin to slow down. Their bodies just can't move very fast in cold weather. You may have already guessed that insects are cold-blooded, like snakes and frogs.

Try This!

Catch an insect in a jar and put on the lid. Have an adult poke some holes in the lid so that air can get into the jar. Notice how much the insect moves around. Next, place the jar in the refrigerator. After a few hours, take it out and watch the insect again. Most likely, the insect is not moving very much anymore. That's because it is cold-blooded, and the cold temperature of the refrigerator cooled its body temperature so that it could not move around much. You could probably even take off the lid, and the insect wouldn't escape. If you do this, be careful! The insect can warm up pretty quickly and begin moving again.

Get an Insect

For the rest of this lesson, we will be looking closely at the different body segments of an insect. It would be helpful to have a real insect to study. A dead one would be much better than a living one, but don't kill one! If you can't find or prefer not to hold a dead insect, you can still enjoy this section, because there are pictures of what we are studying. A real insect will make the rest of the lesson better, however. If you have a real insect you can study, get it now.

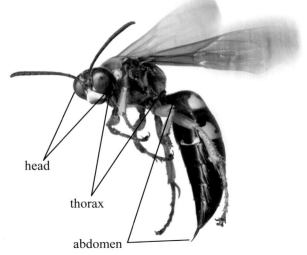

head

thorax

abdomen

Insects have three body segments: the **head**, **thorax** (thor' aks) and **abdomen** (ab' duh muhn). Try to find these body segments on the insect that you have. It is easier to see them if you turn the insect over, because the thorax and abdomen are often covered by the wings. All three parts are covered by a hard shell, called the **exoskeleton** (ek' so skel' ih tuhn).

Exoskeleton

The word exoskeleton means "outside skeleton." This is the perfect description for an insect, because its skeleton is the outside of its body. This is a great place for it, considering the behavior of some insects. Have you ever seen a June bug hit against your porch light again and again, never becoming injured? If you or I placed our finger on the light bulb, even for a split-second, it would burn us. What about the fly that became trapped in your home? Did you watch it hit against the window again and again, seeking to escape? If a bird were to do that, it would certainly become injured and possibly even die. That's not the case for God's little armor-coated insects, however. Much like a suit of armor, the insect's exoskeleton protects it from many things, including toxic chemicals, injury during a fall, or excessive heat, such as that from a light bulb.

Although all insects have an exoskeleton, some are harder than others. Beetles have a very tough exoskeleton, while butterflies have a softer exoskeleton. Praying mantis and grasshopper exoskeletons are somewhere in between. How hard is your insect's exoskeleton?

Have you ever heard that an ant can lift many times its own weight? It's true. If a person were as strong as an ant, he could lift two cars without any help! The muscles found underneath the ant's exoskeleton allow it to lift heavy items for its little size. Have you heard about a flea's ability to jump? It's the highest jumper in the animal kingdom – for its size that is. If we could jump as well as a flea, we could jump across three football fields in a single leap, or we could jump over a 30-story building without any problem. Yes, insects are given incredible strength for their small size, and their exoskeletons protect the muscles that give them such strength!

One thing an exoskeleton can't do, however, is grow. This presents a real problem for insects, and it's one reason why insects are small. Because of this, an insect must shed its exoskeleton from time to time. It does this by **molting**.

Molting

You should remember that birds molt; their feathers fall out and new ones grow back in. Well, an insect molts its entire exoskeleton all at once! Have you ever found a small shell attached to a tree or a rock that was in the shape of an insect? That was the insect's molted exoskeleton. It is called a **cast**. You can begin collecting casts and labeling them for an insect display, which we'll discuss in a later lesson.

The molting process of insects is very interesting. As an insect grows and its exoskeleton gets too tight, it starts to form a new exoskeleton *under* the old one. This new exoskeleton actually produces chemicals that eat away at the old one on the outside. As the old exoskeleton gets weak, the insect takes in air and flexes its strong muscles to crack it. The insect then crawls out of the old exoskeleton through the cracks. The new

This exoskeleton was left behind when a cicada molted.

exoskeleton is still soft and flexible, so the insect can make itself even bigger by taking in more air. This expands the exoskeleton so that it becomes bigger than the old one. The new exoskeleton then hardens, and the insect lets out the air it took in so it returns to its normal size. Now the insect's exoskeleton is bigger than the rest of its body, giving the insect room to grow before it has to molt again. This whole time is a dangerous one for the insect. After all, once it leaves its old exoskeleton and before its new exoskeleton has hardened, it does not have much protection, and any little animal could harm it.

Insect Heads

Every type of insect has its own specially shaped head. The exoskeleton plates on the head are sealed together to protect what is inside. What do you think is inside the head? Well, what's inside your head? Your brain, of course!

An insect's brain is not as complicated as your brain, but it is still pretty complex. The brain controls the insect by sending messages down a nerve cord. That nerve cord is attached to nerves that send those messages throughout the insect's body. Unlike your main nerve cord (the spinal cord), an insect's main nerve cord is not protected by a backbone, because insects are invertebrates. In addition to sending signals that control the body, the brain gets signals from the various nerves of the body, telling the brain about what's going on outside.

This is a grasshopper's head.

You may wonder whether or not insects feel pain. They have a brain that gets signals from nerves in the body, and some of those nerves are very similar to the nerves in our bodies that give us our sense of pain. However, researchers have done several experiments to indicate that insects probably do not feel pain, at least not as we know it. For example, even when an insect has a crushed foot, it does not stop walking. It doesn't even limp. If an insect were able to feel pain, you would think that it would at least limp on a crushed foot.

Insect Eyes

Take a close look at your insect's eyes. They are amazing! An insect looks at the world through eyes that are made up of hundreds – sometimes thousands – of separate lenses. These eyes are called **compound eyes**. "Compound" means "different parts coming together to form one thing." Look at the photo on the right. Can you see tiny, regularly repeating shapes in the eyes? Each one of those shapes is a little lens, and each little lens sees a separate image.

individual lenses

Each of these deerfly's eyes is made up of many lenses.

Have you ever been to a store that sells TVs? If so, were all the televisions showing the same channel? Scientists believe that an insect's vision might be a bit like trying to watch the same channel on a thousand different televisions sets at one time. Scientists can't know exactly what an insect sees, but they know that each lens within the compound eye sends its own signal to the brain. The brain then interprets all the signals coming from all the lenses to form some kind of picture. This makes the insect especially good at detecting movement, like our swatting hand. Wouldn't it be amazing to have a compound eye?

Simple Eyes

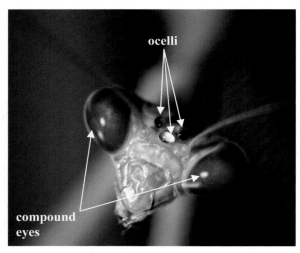

This picture of a praying mantis head shows the insect's three simple eyes and its two compound eyes.

Take a look at the close-up of the praying mantis head on the left. The three structures pointed out in the photo are **simple eyes**, which are also called **ocelli** (oh suhl' eye). Many insects have ocelli at some point in their lives, and some have them throughout their lives. Ocelli are relatively simple; they are not nearly as complex as compound eyes. In fact, they are so simple that they can only tell light from dark. Does your insect have ocelli?

Young insects, which are called **larvae** (lar' vee), do not have compound eyes. Many have simple eyes, and some have no eyes at all!

Antennae

Most adult insects also have a pair of **antennae** (an ten' ee), usually found between the compound eyes. Can you find the antennae on your insect? They function as the insect's nose! Believe it or not, insects use their antennae to "smell," and they can smell much better than we can! They use their antennae to smell a good place to lay eggs, smell out food, and pick up messages sent from their friends and family.

These messages are sent when insects give off a 'scent' in the form of chemicals, called **pheromones** (fair' uh mohnz), that travel through the air. An insect's antennae are able to "read" messages from these pheromones. For example, when a bee thinks it is in danger, it releases a danger pheromone. Other bees from many feet away smell that pheromone with their antennae and come to help the bee that is threatened. Usually, they sting whatever is making the bee feel threatened.

This butterfly uses its antennae to smell and touch.

Not only do insects use their antennae to smell, they can also use them to get a sense of touch. Some insects can actually "hear" with their antennae as well! As you can tell, antennae are very important to insects.

Mouths

Most people don't take the time to study insect mouths, but if you do, you will be amazed at how strange and interesting they are. There are three different kinds of insect mouths: **chewing mouths**, **sucking mouths**, and **sponging mouths**. After reading about each kind of mouth, use a magnifying glass to look at your insect's mouth and try to guess which kind of mouth it has.

Chewing Mouths

Most insects (like grasshoppers, beetles, crickets, dragonflies, and praying mantises) have chewing mouths, which are generally dominated by **mandibles** (man' duh buls) that the insect uses to chop the food into tiny pieces. Some insects also use their mandibles to cut wood or dig in the soil.

This tiger beetle has a chewing mouth.

On either side of the mouth are little feelers, called **palps**. They are used for touching and tasting food before it is eaten. Insects with chewing mouths typically have four palps. Insects that chew usually prefer solid food, some, like the mantis, even prefer other insects; they are predators.

Sucking Mouths

This female mosquito has sucked up so much blood that its abdomen has turned red!

Sucking insects live on liquids: sometimes plant juices, sometimes nectar, sometimes the blood of other insects, and sometimes the blood of warm-blooded animals. I'm sure you can guess which insect prefers your blood. Our old enemy, the mosquito, is a classic example of a sucking insect. Although you might not know this, only *female* mosquitoes suck our blood. They need it to develop their eggs. The male mosquitoes (and sometimes the females as well) feed on nectar and fruits.

The mosquito has a long, tubular mouthpart called a **proboscis** (proh bos' kis) with four cutting and piercing tools, which are often called **stylets** (sty lets'). When a female is feeding on blood, these tools stab into the skin, and then the proboscis is inserted into the wound and is used to suck blood from the victim. In the picture on the previous page, you can see the proboscis running down from the mosquito's head into the skin of the victim. The mosquito also injects her saliva into the wound to keep the blood from clotting. Most people have an allergic reaction to this saliva, and that's what makes a mosquito bite itch.

Other insects that have this piercing, sword-like mouth are bugs (remember, not all insects are bugs), leafhoppers, treehoppers, fleas, sucking lice, and some flies. Most use it to eat other insects or plant juices, but fleas, lice, and some biting flies enjoy a nice meal of blood.

Another type of sucking insect is quite a bit more pleasant in its approach to feeding. The butterfly does not pierce or cut; it simply unfurls its rolled up proboscis and draws up the sweet nectar of flowers. It's a good thing butterflies have such pleasant sucking mouth parts. If they were anything like the mosquito's mouth parts, we wouldn't plant any flowers that might attract them to our yard, and the sight of them would cultivate fear instead of delight!

A butterfly's proboscis stays rolled up until it is ready to suck nectar from a flower.

Sponging Mouths

This fly uses its proboscis to sponge up liquids.

Have you ever noticed the activities of a fly in your house or at your picnic? It lands on everything, sometimes staying for a while, sometimes flying away instantly. It tastes everything with its feet and mouth, hoping for something edible. When a fly finds something to eat, it extends its proboscis, which is like a sponge that absorbs any liquid it touches. Because of this, we say that flies have sponging mouths.

Because their mouths are designed to sponge up liquids, flies are incapable of chewing solid foods. Nevertheless, you can find them on solid food, seeming to eat. This is because they are able to liquefy the solids they want to eat. They do this by vomiting chemicals onto the solid material, whether it is trash, feces, or your hamburger. The chemicals in the vomit start to digest the solid food, making it watery. At that point, the fly sticks out its spongy proboscis and sops up the soupy material. Disgusting, huh? Well, it's even more disgusting when you realize that when the fly vomits, germs come out with the chemicals. When a fly eats something then, it contaminates it with lots of germs. You'll get to learn a little more about these despicable enemies of good health later on.

Thorax

Now that you have learned a bit about an insect's head, let's turn to the mid section of the insect's body, the thorax. Can you see your insect's thorax? It's in the middle – behind the head and in front of the abdomen. The thorax is known as the insect's center of movement because the parts that move the body (the legs and wings) are attached to the thorax.

Six Jointed Legs

As I mentioned, every insect has three pairs of legs, six legs in all. The legs are jointed, which splits them into five parts: the **coxa** (kok' suh), **trochanter** (troh kan' tur), **femur** (fee' mur), **tibia** (tib' ee uh) and the **foot**, called the **tarsus** (tar' sus).

The tarsus (foot) is often made up of many little joints and usually has small claws at the tip. A fly has little sticky suction cups on its tarsus, which allow it to walk on glass and ceilings, even upside down!

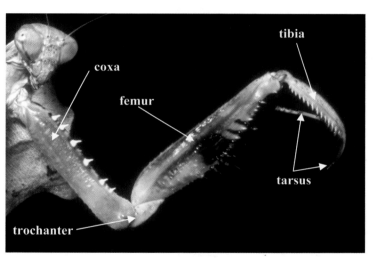

This photo shows you the five segments on the front leg of a praying mantis.

Insect legs are used for walking, jumping, grasping, climbing, and even for tasting. That's right: some insects can taste with their legs! There are hundreds of little projections, called **setae** (see' tee), that give some insect legs a hairy appearance. Although setae are not hairs, they do allow the insect legs to taste, smell, and even sense movement. Do you remember that insects also use their antennae to taste? Well, that's because their antennae are covered with setae as well. In other words, the same structures that allow the insect to taste things with its antennae also allow it to taste things with its legs.

Every insect has been given the legs it needs to do that which God created it to do. Crickets and grasshoppers have powerful spring-like designs that help them jump great distances. The mole cricket has front legs equipped with little fat shovels for digging, because it spends a lot of time digging. Bees have pouches on their legs into which they put pollen to carry home to the hive so that the hive will have plenty of food.

Wings

Many insects (except the flightless ones) have two sets of wings. Some insects have two sets of identical wings; others have one set that serves as a covering under which the other wings are housed. These insects lift up the hard wings, and unfold the second set of wings used for flying. If you have ever watched a ladybug crawl around and then fly away, you might have noticed that this is exactly what they do. Still others (like flies) have only one set of wings. They also have a set of small, wing-like structures called **halteres** (hal tir' eez) that they use for balance, but they are not true wings.

This ladybug (which is not really a bug) has two sets of wings. One set is hard and covers the second set, which is thin and membranous.

A dragonfly has two sets of membranous wings.

Do you know what a membrane (mem' brayn) is? It is a thin, moveable sheet. The wings underneath a ladybug's hard wings are called **membranous** (mem' bruh nus) **wings**. Look at the membranous wing in the pictures above and to the left. Do you see the lines running through the wings? They are called **veins**. They reinforce the thin wings and contain both nerves and blood. Most species have their own pattern of veins running through their membranous wings. This often helps **entomologists** (en' tuh mol' uh jists – scientists who study insects) tell one species from another.

Not all insects have membranous wings. Butterflies and moths, for example, have **scaled wings**. Have you ever touched a butterfly's wings and noticed that your fingers were covered in a powder? That powder is actually made up of the scales that cover the wings. These scales provide the beautiful colors and patterns on butterflies.

The striking colors on this Rajah Brooke's birdwing are due to the scales on the butterfly's wings.

The Abdomen

And finally, we reach the last segment of the insect: the abdomen! God placed your abdomen right in the center of your body, but on an insect, He placed this very important feature on the very back end. Can you find the abdomen on your insect?

This part of the body seems so uninteresting, but really, much activity goes on there. In addition to housing the male and female parts, this is the main place through which the insect breathes! You see, insects don't have lungs. They have little holes called **spiracles** (spear' uh kuhls) all over the abdomen (and some in the thorax) that let air into the body. Each spiracle is attached to a tube, called a **trachea** (tray' kee uh), which branches out into smaller and smaller tubes, reaching every part of the insect's body. As the air flows through these tubes, the oxygen that the insect needs is just pulled from the air. In addition, the waste gases that the insect needs to get rid of flow through the tubes and out the spiracles. This type of breathing, called **passive breathing**, is not very efficient, and it is one reason why insects are small. If an insect were large, it would have a hard time getting enough oxygen this way.

Try This!
Lazarus Experiment

Find a living insect. Any insect will do, even an ant. Put it in a bowl of water and hold it underwater with a spoon. It's tricky to get the insect to submit to this, but eventually it will. Keep the insect under the water for about three or more minutes, until you think it is dead.

Carefully spoon out the insect and lay it on a paper towel. Pour salt over the insect, covering it completely. After the insect is covered with salt, blow the salt off. Be careful if you have an ant or you may blow away the ant as well! Wait about five to ten minutes, watching the insect for signs of life. The insect should "come back to life" and crawl away!

Why didn't the insect drown in the water? Well, insects are able to close the spiracles in their abdomen when faced with heavy rains or other unfortunate meetings with water. When they come out of the water and dry off enough, they can reopen their spiracles and breathe again! The reason you used salt in the experiment is that it speeds up the absorption of water from the insect, causing it to start moving more quickly.

Ovipositors, Claspers, and Cerci

At the very tip of the abdomen in many insects are two little appendages called **cerci** (sur' sye). These give the insect a sense of touch at the back of the body. They are very different from insect to insect, and some insects don't have cerci at all.

One way you can tell female insects from male insects is to look for an **ovipositor** (oh' vuh poz' ih tur). The ovipositor is easy to spot, because it looks like a spike on the end of the abdomen. Sometimes it is long and pointy, sometimes it is short and stout. The insect's tiny little eggs come out of the ovipositor. Since the female lays eggs, if an insect has an ovipositor, it is a female. Look for an ovipositor sticking out of the abdomen of your insect. It might not be as long as the one in the cricket pictured to the right, but if you have a female, you should see something pointy sticking out of its abdomen. That's the ovipositor.

cerci

ovipositor

You can tell this cricket is a female because it has an ovipositor.

Often, people see the ovipositor and are afraid that it is a stinger. Only wasps and bees use the ovipositor to sting. The ovipositor on most bees is equipped with little barbs that get stuck in the victim. When the bee stings, these barbs keep the ovipositor lodged in the skin of the victim. When the bee tries to yank out its ovipositor, a little bit of its abdomen comes out as well, and it dies. Wasps don't have this problem. They can safely insert their ovipositor for a sting and remove it. We'll learn more about this in our social insect lesson.

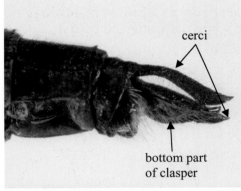

cerci

bottom part of clasper

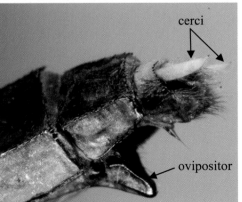

cerci

ovipositor

These are the rear ends of dragonfly abdomens from a male (top) and a female (bottom).

A male insect does not have an ovipositor, but it usually has a **clasper** instead. This clasper is often used to hold onto the female during mating. The clasper is usually made of the male's cerci and sometimes other parts of the abdomen. Notice the dragonfly abdomens shown on the left. The top one is from a male, while the bottom one is from a female. Notice the curved structure underneath the cerci in the male. This curved structure and the cerci make up the male dragonfly's clasper. You can see the difference between this and the female dragonfly's abdomen, which has cerci, but they are not part of a clasper. Also, you can see the ovipositor that tells you the abdomen on the bottom is from a female.

You have already learned so much about insects, and there is still more to come! You are certainly on your way to becoming an entomologist. It's time to add some information to your notebook and begin some projects and activities like a professional entomologist.

What Do You Remember?

How can you tell the difference between insects and other crawling creatures? What are the three segments of an insect's body? What is interesting about an insect's eyes? What are they called? What are simple eyes? What are the three kinds of insect mouths? To what part of an insect's body are the legs and wings attached? How does an insect breathe? What is an ovipositor? What are cerci?

Nature Points

When you are out in nature, keep a look out for every creepy crawly thing you see. Try to tell if it is an insect. You might have to use a magnifying glass on smaller creatures. If you have trouble, try to capture it or turn it over on its back so you can see if its body is segmented. Count its legs. Does it have wings? If you have a field guide, see if you can identify it.

Notebook Activities

Write down what you remember from the lesson in your notebook. If you have the *Zoology 1 Notebooking Journal*, use the Fascinating Facts pages for this activity. Then, draw an insect with every feature that makes an insect an insect (include wings even though there are a few without wings). Try to be as accurate as possible. Use some of the pictures in this lesson for guides if you need them. Label each part as you remember it. A template is provided in the *Zoology 1 Notebooking Journal* on page 117.

Project

Create an Insect Zoo

The best way to study insects is to see them up close, living out their lives before you. Of course, insects don't generally live out their lives in front of us, so entomologists have to work so that they can spend their days with living bugs. Often, they go out in the field to observe bugs, but they also keep bugs in indoor habitats, usually in their laboratories. An entomologist's laboratory is just as scientific as a chemist's lab. It is filled with transparent jars, containers, aquariums, magnifying glasses, microscopes, and other instruments, all for studying insects. A lot of what we know about insects comes from these laboratories.

I want you to start a laboratory study of insects by capturing at least one live insect and making a home for it. Most of you probably have experience catching insects, but if you need help, the course website I told you about in the introduction to the course has links to information on the many ways you can capture insects. You might want to look at some of these links, because if you use different methods, you can capture different kinds of insects. If it is not warm outside, it will be hard to find insects. If you really want to get started on your insect zoo, however, you can buy live insects. The course website has links to show you where you can buy them.

Once you have captured at least one insect, you need to make a home for it. Most of the time, when we catch an insect, we simply keep it in a jar. This is a fine *first* home for an insect, but in order to really study and understand your insect (and keep it alive for longer than a day) you will want to create a home that looks more like its natural habitat, the environment from which it came.

There are many containers you can use for an insect home. The easiest thing to do is purchase a glass or plastic aquarium from a large discount department store or pet store. Make sure it comes with a tight-fitting lid, because insects like to get out and other pets like to get in. You can also use a clear plastic storage container that has a snap-on lid. Just have an adult punch holes in the lid so that air can get inside.

Try to make your insect's home like its natural environment, with soil or sand, rocks, sticks, and living plants. If you found the insect on a particular plant, take a cutting from that plant and put it in a small pot of soil. Sometimes the cutting will grow roots and stay alive if you keep it moist. To provide water for the insect, place a wet sponge in the container.

You will need to keep your insect's home clean, because the insect could die from living in too much of its own waste. You will want to keep different kinds of insects separate from one another unless you are conducting an experiment with the two in one cage. If you want to keep your insect alive long enough to lay eggs, you must provide an environment that is close to its natural environment, with just the right spot for it to lay eggs. Of course, you will need to make sure you have both a male and female insect if you want the female to lay eggs.

The most important thing to know is what your insect eats. Some insects eat plants, while some eat other insects. Check field guides, books, and the internet to learn about your insect's diet.

Some of the following lessons will include fun experiments that you will do with insects. They are experiments that don't harm the insect, but rather seek to teach you about your insect. These experiments will help you understand how insects behave as well as the environments and foods they prefer.

Lesson 10
Life Cycles and Life Styles

Life Cycles

Every life has a cycle: a beginning, a middle, and an end. In this lesson, we will study the cycle of an insect's life, along with many of the interesting things it does in its life, such as mate and defend itself with poison or other interesting techniques. Every insect life begins with an egg, and every egg begins with a female and her mate. So, how does an insect go about finding a mate?

Finding a Mate

There are many ways of finding a mate in class Insecta. Moths and many other insects send out pheromones. Do you remember what pheromones are? They are chemicals that insects use to send messages. Other insects "read" those messages with their antennae. Well, one message an insect can send with pheromones is, "I want a mate!" Usually, the female releases these pheromones, and when a male smells the pheromones with its antennae, it begins looking for the female that emitted the smell.

Some insects don't rely just on pheromones. Male mosquitoes locate a female by listening for the hum of her wings as she flies by. Other insects, including flies and butterflies, are known to congregate at odd locations called **leks**. A lek is a place where the males gather and wait for the females to arrive. There is no food, water, or anything else of interest here except other insects of the same species looking for a mate. When the females arrive at the lek, the males flitter around, displaying their wings and trying to attract the females' attention.

Some male insects gather together at leks and wait for females to come and "check them out."

After mating has occurred, the female looks for a good place to lay her eggs. God gave her the instincts she needs so that she knows exactly where to lay her eggs. She usually looks for a place that has a lot of food available to the young once they hatch. A female housefly, for example, will look for garbage, dung, or decaying animals, because that's what her young will want to eat once they hatch. A

This Colorado potato beetle is laying eggs on the underside of a leaf.

female fruit fly will look for fruit, because that's what her young want to eat. In the same way, monarch butterflies look for milkweed plants, zebra heliconian (hel ih coh' nee uhn) butterflies look for passion vines, and painted lady butterflies look for thistle plants.

Once the female finds the perfect place, she uses her ovipositor to lay her eggs there. Some insects dig under the surface to lay their eggs. Certain fruit flies, for example, have sharp ovipositors that they use to drill into the fruit so that they can lay their eggs under the fruit's skin. Other fruit flies do not have these sharp ovipositors, because they lay their eggs on top of rotting fruit. Some insects lay their eggs right on the stems or leaves of the plants that their young will eat. Each egg is released with a little dab of glue that sticks it to the stem or leaf so it will stay there until it hatches.

Try This!
Be an Egg Detective

Insect eggs are everywhere in the spring and summer, and even in the winter you can find eggs hidden around your yard waiting for the spring weather to hatch. Most insect eggs don't look anything like the eggs you are used to. They come in all shapes and sizes. Some look like tiny golf balls, bullets, light bulbs, tear drops, bottles, barrels, etc.

Insect eggs come in all shapes and sizes. You can often find them on the underside of a leaf.

To be an egg detective, all you need is the outdoors and a magnifying glass. Go outside and begin searching high and low, in cracks and crevices, on tree trunks and fence posts. If there are leaves around, look on the underside of them.

If you look diligently, you will probably find at least one egg. Record your find in your notebook. If you desire, you can bring the egg indoors and place it in a jar that has holes punched in the lid. If it is winter, the warmth of your home will hasten its development. If it is able to hatch, you might be able to see how it develops into an adult! If you found the egg on an object (like a leaf), put at least some of the object in the jar with the egg. After all, insects usually lay their eggs on the things that their newly-hatched insects need to eat.

Although most insects lay eggs, there are some insects (certain flies, aphids, cockroaches, and beetles) in which the eggs are held inside the female's body. The eggs hatch inside her, and the young insects emerge from an opening in the female's abdomen. Even though this looks a little like the live births that occur in people (and mammals in general), it is not the same. The young develop in eggs and hatch from those eggs. The eggs just happen to stay inside the mother until they hatch.

Metamorphosis

After the eggs hatch, the little creature that comes out is usually called a **larva** (lar' vuh). Larvae (lar' vee – the plural of larva) don't look anything like their parents. That's because they must go through a great many changes in order to become adults. This series of changes is called **metamorphosis** (met' uh mor' fuh sis), which comes from a Greek word that means "to transform," and insects truly do transform as they grow up! There are two basic types of metamorphosis in class Insecta: **complete metamorphosis** and **incomplete metamorphosis**. Let's study each one.

Complete Metamorphosis

An insect that goes through complete metamorphosis has four distinct stages in its development: **egg**, **larva**, **pupa** (pyoo' puh), and **adult**. The best way to discuss this incredible process is to talk about how it happens in a specific insect, such as the monarch butterfly. The larva, pupa, and adult stages of this insect's life are shown below:

A monarch butterfly goes through complete metamorphosis. The egg hatches a larva (left), which forms a chrysalis to become a pupa (middle). When it comes out of the chrysalis, it is an adult (right).

After a monarch butterfly lays its eggs, the young are in their egg stage. This stage lasts until the eggs hatch. At that point, the young are larvae. As you can see from the picture on the left, a larva looks more like a worm than a butterfly. At this stage, it is often called a caterpillar. The caterpillar eats and grows, molting several times. During its last molt, the caterpillar will hang upside down and encase itself in a **chrysalis** (kris' uh lis). You might have heard this called a "cocoon," but a moth larva usually makes a cocoon. A butterfly larva usually makes a chrysalis. Once in the chrysalis, the butterfly is in its pupa stage. During the pupa stage, it goes through an amazing change. Once the change is complete, it comes out of its chrysalis as a beautiful adult butterfly!

Complete metamorphosis is absolutely astounding. Even though a caterpillar looks nothing like a butterfly, an individual butterfly is *both*! It starts out as a caterpillar and ends up as a butterfly. Isn't that amazing? Only through God's miraculous design could this occur!

Not only is metamorphosis amazing, it contains an incredible spiritual truth. God says in His Word that all created things point to Him and His truths. Romans 1:20 tells us, "For since the creation of the world His invisible attributes, His eternal power and divine nature, have been clearly seen, being understood through what has been made..."

Metamorphosis is nature's illustration of what happens to you in your spirit once you become a Christian. You begin your life as a humble little caterpillar with simple eyes that cannot see anything but shades of light and dark. Remember, if insect larvae have eyes, they are the simple ocelli that cannot see images but can only sense light and dark. Once you receive Christ, the Bible says you are "...a new creature; the old things passed away; behold, new things have come." (2 Corinthians 5:17) Wow! When we accept Christ, we become a totally new creature. Suddenly, we are like the amazingly beautiful butterfly that emerges from the chrysalis. We have new eyes, too, just like the butterfly. We can see clearly, not just shades of light and dark. We have suddenly developed compound eyes that see things in an eternal perspective! God's amazing process of the transformation of a caterpillar into a butterfly is a picture of the transformation a person experiences in Christ.

Although a butterfly gives us the most dramatic example of complete metamorphosis, most insects go through the same kind of life cycle. Moths, for example, have almost the same life cycle, but they typically encase the pupa stage in a cocoon rather than a chrysalis. What's the difference between a cocoon and a chrysalis? Well, a cocoon is something that the larva weaves out of silk, while the chrysalis is actually a part of the larva's exoskeleton. Not only do moths go through complete metamorphosis, but so do many other

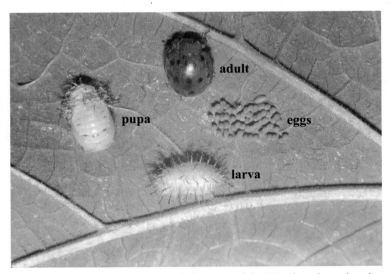

These are the four stages in the life cycle of the Mexican bean beetle.

insects, including the Mexican bean beetle. The Mexican bean beetle larva doesn't cover itself in anything when it reaches the pupa stage, however. It just attaches itself to the underside of the leaf and begins its transformation into an adult. Since most insects go through the four stages of complete metamorphosis (egg, larva, pupa, and adult), we should look at each stage individually.

If a female insect lays her eggs in the spring or summer, the egg stage usually lasts a week or two. Many insects, however, have eggs that **overwinter** and hatch in the spring. Can you guess what "overwinter" means? It means the egg is dormant (doesn't do anything) over the winter and begins developing once spring arrives.

When the egg hatches, out comes the larva. Usually larvae look like some kind of worm and therefore don't seem to have the features of an insect! Do you remember what the features of an insect are? Insects have six legs, a body in three segments, usually compound eyes, and usually wings. An insect larva usually has a long body, simple eyes (ocelli), and no wings. The body usually has many segments, but sometimes it's hard to see them. The larvae of flies (called maggots) don't even have eyes. The larva sometimes has three pairs of little stumpy legs or feet, but sometimes it has no feet at all. Occasionally a larva will have little bumps along the bottom of the body that look like feet, but they aren't true feet. Insect larva may or may not have antennae. Even though insect larvae look nothing like their parents, they contain all of the material they need to be able to transform into something that looks like their parents later on.

These creatures are commonly called mealworms, but they are not worms. They are the larvae of a beetle (*Tenebrio molitor*).

A newly hatched larva is sometimes the size of an eyelash or smaller, but within a few weeks it becomes hundreds of times bigger. It can grow like that because it spends most of its time eating. The larva stage of some insects (like many flies) lasts only a few days. Other insects (like some moths) have a larva stage of several weeks, while some (like the biting midge fly) have a larva stage of several months. Finally, there are even some insects (like chironomids – ky' ron uh midz) in which the larva stage lasts for up to two years. The larva stage usually ends with the little creature forming protective covering so that it can enter the pupa stage. There are many different kids of coverings. Some are little silk cocoons, some are chrysalises, others are little shell-like structures, and some larvae make no covering for themselves at all.

During the pupa stage, the creature does not eat. It simply begins to change. Every part of the creature changes, transforming the larva (which looks nothing like an insect) into the adult (which has all of the traits of an insect). In some insects, the pupa stage lasts a few days, and for others it can last up to several months. Some can even overwinter as a pupa, not completing their change until spring arrives.

After living as a pupa for as long as it takes to make the necessary changes, the totally transformed creature is ready to break free of its protective shell (if it had one). This process is called **eclosion** (ih kloh' shun).

As the newly formed adult begins to move about, the protective covering splits open, and the adult slowly struggles out. The wings are crumpled and soft because they have been encased for so long. The adult will sit still, breathing through the spiracles in its new abdomen and pumping body fluid up through the veins of its wings to straighten them out. It can't fly until the wings are completely straightened in this manner. Once that's done, it spreads its wings and flies away! Can you imagine the difference between its former life and its new life?

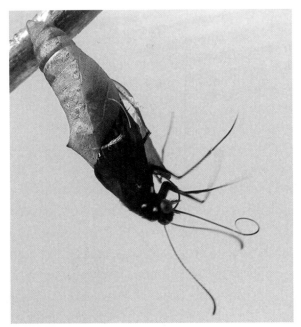

This is the moment of eclosion for a spicebush butterfly.

In some insects (like the mayfly), the adult stage might last only a few hours! Because the adult mayfly lives for such a short time, it is sometimes called the dayfly.   In other insects (such as termites), the adults can live for years. The average lifespan of an adult termite queen, for example, is 15 years.

Almost nine out of ten species of insect go through complete metamorphosis. That's almost all the insects. The rest of the insects go through incomplete metamorphosis.

Incomplete Metamorphosis

Incomplete metamorphosis has only three stages: **egg**, **nymph** (nimf), and **adult**. Now even though we call this "incomplete metamorphosis," there is *nothing* incomplete about it. It is a fully complete life cycle. The only reason we call it "incomplete" is that it has one less stage than complete metamorphosis.

Insects that experience incomplete metamorphosis usually lay lots of eggs enclosed inside an egg case, which holds all the eggs snuggled together. All the brother and sister

This praying mantis egg case has somewhere between 100 and 400 eggs in it.

insects will hatch together at the same time, emerging from inside the egg case. You might find a praying mantis egg case attached to a bush. Cockroach egg cases look like little black beans or pills.

When the egg hatches, a nymph emerges. The nymph looks similar to the adult, but it has no wings. Nymphs also behave much like adults. For example, they eat the same food that the adult eats. However, a nymph cannot produce young or fly.

Compare the praying mantis nymph (left) to the adult (right). They look similar, but the nymph has no wings.

As the nymphs eat, they begin to grow. Like all insects, they must molt once they reach a certain size so that they can grow more. With each molt, they look more and more like the adult. Their wings begin to develop in their own little cases made out of exoskeleton. With each molt, the wing cases get larger. On the nymph's last molt, the wings finally unfold, and the insect is officially an adult. The nymph stage usually lasts a few weeks, but it could last several years, which is the case for the seventeen year cicada (sih kay' duh). In addition to the insects I have already discussed, grasshoppers and stinkbugs also experience incomplete metamorphosis.

More Incomplete Metamorphosis

This adult dragonfly developed through a special kind of incomplete metamorphosis.

Believe it or not, there is yet another kind of metamorphosis and yet another name for the young insects. This kind of metamorphosis, experienced by dragonflies, mayflies, and stoneflies, is not complete metamorphosis, because the insect does not go through a pupa stage. At the same time, however, it's also not like the incomplete metamorphosis that I just told you about, because the young do not look anything like the adults.

Here's what happens: The adult flying insect lays its eggs in water. Each egg hatches into a young insect called a **naiad** (nay' uhd). It lives underwater throughout its entire youth. It even has gills with which to breathe, just like a fish! It molts while it lives underwater, growing into a larger and larger naiad. Then one day it crawls up a stick or branch sticking out of the water and sits still until its skin dries out. Then out crawls a winged flying creature that breathes air!

The naiad form of a dragonfly is shown on the left. It has already left the water and is starting to dry out. Once it is completely dried out, the adult emerges from the shell of the naiad, as shown on the right.

The adults are beautiful winged insects that spend much of their time in flight. Now that's a total metamorphosis, wouldn't you say? Strangely, it's still called incomplete metamorphosis because there is no pupa stage. Don't let that name fool you, however. The insect has done a lot of changing from the time it hatched to the time it became an adult. This entire life cycle can last from six months to seven years. Most dragonflies spend most of their lives in the naiad stage.

Explain the two (or three) kinds of metamorphosis that you have learned about. Give the name for the immature insect in each stage.

Insect Life Styles
Designed for Defense

God, in His great wisdom and knowledge about how the earth would be after the fall of Adam, designed all animals with defenses that help protect them from predators. Snakes bite, birds fly away, cats have claws and can climb into trees, porcupines have quills that hurt when they stick a predator, etc. These are ways animals protect themselves so that they can survive. Can you think of any other animal defenses? All these defenses were designed by God.

God's first defense for an insect is its hard outer skeleton. Do you remember what it is called? It's called an exoskeleton. The second defense is its ability to fly away from a predator. Even the flight pattern of some insects helps in their defense. A butterfly's erratic flight pattern, for example, keeps it from being easily snatched out of the air by a passing bird or bat.

God created other means of protection for insects as well. Some insects are protected by the special design that makes them blend in with their background. This is called **camouflage** (kam' uh flahj) or **crypsis** (krip' sis). Other insects simply taste bad or are poisonous to eat. Still others were created to look like other insects that are dangerous. Others are able to defend themselves by producing an offensive smell or noise. Have you ever been stung by a bee? If so, you know that other insects actually attack as a means of defense. As you can see, then, God created many kinds of defenses for insects. Let's look at some of them in detail.

Crypsis

Crypsis is a good way for an insect to protect itself, because it can go about its life without being noticed by animals that would harm it. When walking through tall grass, you don't even notice the grasshoppers until they hop out of the way. A great camouflage for katydids and grasshoppers is that they look a lot like grass and leaves. Many katydids look identical to a leaf, with wings that even have vein patterns on them! Can you think of any creatures that you have seen that use camouflage? Look at the insects below to see some specific examples of insect crypsis.

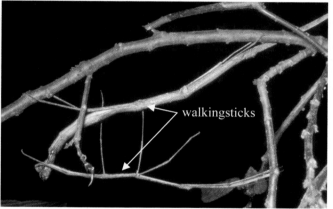

Can you see the grasshopper in this photo? It might be hard, because it is the same color as the grass.

There are two walkingstick insects pictured here. They look so much like sticks that it is hard to notice them.

Can you see why this insect is called a "leaf insect?"

This caterpillar not only looks like a twig, but it actually knows how to rest on the tree limb to make it look like a branch on the limb.

Advertisement

The exact opposite of crypsis is **advertisement**. This form of protection says, "Look at me!" Why would an insect want predators to look at it? Because the animal is either toxic (will make a predator sick) or foul tasting. So, the advertisement is actually a warning to predators. It says, "Don't mistake me for something good to eat!" When an insect has colors that advertise its presence, we say that it has **aposematic** (ap' uh suh mat' ik) **coloration**.

Usually insects that have aposematic coloration are orange and black, red and black, or yellow and black. Can you think of a yellow and black insect that might sting you? Bees, wasps, and hornets are colored that way. No one, not even an animal, likes to get stung by them. When animals see those colors, then, they usually avoid them.

The beautiful colors of a monarch butterfly tell predators that they will get sick if they eat it.

The orange and black monarch butterfly eats milkweed plants when it is a caterpillar. Milkweed contains a chemical that is poisonous to many animals, but not to the hungry monarch caterpillar. When the monarch becomes a butterfly, it no longer eats milkweed, but it still has those chemicals in its body. Birds that don't know better may try to eat a monarch, but when they become ill and vomit after eating it, they'll never eat another creature with those colors again!

It doesn't matter that you can see this ladybug so easily. Its colors tell predators that it tastes bad.

Two other insects, the milkweed bug and the milkweed beetle, are milkweed eaters. They are usually red and black or orange and black. Because they eat milkweed, they also make other animals sick, and their colors warn predators of this fact.

An insect doesn't have to have stingers or eat milkweed to use aposematic coloration. A ladybug has a bright red or orange body and black dots that make it very easy to see. However, this insect tastes bad to predators. Its colors warn ants and birds that they will not like a ladybug meal.

Mimicry

Another defense that animals use is called **mimicry** (mim' ih kree). This is when an insect that is not dangerous, toxic, or foul tasting looks like an insect that is. Certainly this is not the intention of the insect, for it has no choice about the features it was given by God. Nevertheless, these insects benefit from the experience that animals have with insects that look similar.

If a bird that has had the bad experience of eating a monarch butterfly sees a viceroy butterfly, it will keep its distance and leave the butterfly alone. Although a viceroy doesn't have the toxic milkweed poisons in its body, it does have the same coloring as the monarch. Look at the pictures of the two butterflies on the left. Which one is the monarch and which is the viceroy? It's hard to tell, isn't it?

The insect on the left is a viceroy butterfly, while the one on the right is a monarch butterfly. The best way to tell them apart is to look for a stripe running over the lower part of the wings. Only the viceroy has that stripe.

Another example of mimicry involves the robber fly, which looks just like a bee. Getting stung by a bee isn't a pleasant experience for anyone, even animals. So animals and people stay far away from the robber fly for fear of getting stung. There are more than 20 different kinds of robber flies. Some look like honeybees, some look like bumblebees, and some look like wasps. Robber flies often capture prey as large as or larger than themselves. They're especially fond of bees. These little mimics got their name because of their habit of hanging out on top of bee hives and catching bees as they leave the nest – robbing the nest of its inhabitants.

Trickery

Some insects avoid predators using other kinds of tricks. For example, some insects have **eye spots** on their bodies. Eye spots are colorations on the insect that look like eyes. Birds don't really like eyes that stare at them, especially if they look like the eyes of something that eats them, like an owl. Because of this, many moths and butterflies were given eye spots as protection.

Some moths have two big eye spots on their hind wings. When one of these moths is at rest, it covers the eye spots with its upper wings. When a predator comes close, it will suddenly flash its eye spots by lifting its upper wings, surprising the predator. The element of surprise startles the predator, giving the moth enough time to escape.

This io moth covers its eyespots when it is at rest so that it can use them to surprise predators.

This spicebush swallowtail butterfly has spots and spikes that make a predator think that its rear is its face.

Some butterflies have several small eye spots on the edges of their wings. This helps because most predators grab the face of their prey to make a quick kill. When the bird grabs the butterfly by its fake "eyes," it will only take off a bit of its wing, giving the butterfly a chance to escape with only a little bit of loss. Sometimes you will find butterflies with small pieces missing from the edges of their wing, because they were bitten off by a bird. Some butterflies (like the swallowtails) also trick predators another way. Besides having eye spots, these pretty little creatures have two spikes near the bottom of their wings. These little spikes look like antennae, increasing the illusion that the rear of the butterfly is its face. If you have some swallowtail butterflies in your yard, see if some are missing parts of their wings!

Caterpillars are often equipped with eye spots as well. These make them look frightening to many predators. Birds have an instinct to stay away from snakes, and these caterpillars look more like snakes because of their eyespots. Some even rear up their head, acting like a snake might when it is about to strike!

Chemical Defense

Some insects have a **chemical defense** that is very offensive. Do you know what "offensive" means? It is used to describe something that will attack or something that gives unpleasant sensations like pain or a terrible smell. God gave many insects the ability to protect themselves against predators by offending them with chemicals that it stores in its body. Instead of hiding, advertising, or mimicking, these insects protect themselves with chemicals that smell, surprise the predator, or hurt the predator.

If you are a nature person who loves insects, you may have smelled the odd smell that comes from some creatures when you handle them. It might be as faint as the strange smell coming from a walkingstick insect or as strong as that which comes from a stinkbug. Have you ever handled a stinkbug? When a stinkbug feels threatened, it releases a fluid that it stores in its body. The smell of the fluid is so offensive that it keeps most predators away. A frog will even struggle to get the creature off its sticky tongue to be rid of the smell.

When threatened, this stinkbug releases a foul smelling fluid.

Many insects use this kind of defense. One entomologist noticed a moth that was caught in a spider's web. The spider ran to the moth and cut it loose, not the least bit interested in eating it.

"What happened?" this scientist wondered. After many studies, he realized that when it got caught, the moth released such an unpleasant smell that the spider just wanted to get rid of it. Chemical defense is a great defense isn't it? Only a very wise God could have thought of such a great way for insects to protect themselves!

Some ants have their own chemical defense in which they spray formic acid on predators. This is a chemical that not only has a very obvious smell to other animals, but it can irritate many insects and other animals. As you learned in a previous lesson, some birds will crush ants and rub them on their feathers, using the formic acid to keep away lice and other pests.

The grasshopper has an interesting chemical defense. It actually *vomits* the contents of its stomach from its mouth. This brown juice, often called tobacco juice, smells bad and tastes awful, making the predator let go of the grasshopper, giving it just enough time for escape. If the predator can recover from the disgusting surprise in time and catch the grasshopper again, it can enjoy a nice meal, since the grasshopper must build up the contents of its stomach before it can vomit a second time. If you happen to catch a grasshopper, you may be able to cause it to spit out this fluid for you. If it does, smell it and record your experience in your notebook.

This blister beetle can release a blister-causing fluid when threatened.

Have you ever heard of a blister beetle? Stay far, far away from blister beetles! When spooked, these beetles will release a toxic, blister-causing fluid from their joints. This colorless, odorless fluid is so harmful that it will cause a long lasting and painful blister to form on any skin that it touches. You will learn how to spot a blister beetle in a later lesson.

Creation Confirmation

Have you been amazed by all of the different ways that insects can defend themselves? How could you not be? However, if you thought all of that was amazing, wait until I tell you about the **bombardier** (bom' bar deer) **beetle**. When this little insect feels threatened, it shoots boiling-hot, noxious gases in the direction of the danger! How does it make these boiling-hot gases? The answer is nothing short of amazing.

The bombardier beetle has two chambers in its body that contain at least five different chemicals. When the beetle feels threatened, it opens a valve between the chambers, allowing the chemicals to mix. The chemicals react together, producing oxygen and enough heat to boil the resulting liquid. This builds up pressure in the chamber, and at the last moment, the boiling-hot gases are released through openings in the abdomen, shooting whatever was threatening the bombardier beetle. You can bet that any animal that tried to cause this beetle harm will never do so again!

Think about the amazing design behind this weapon. The bombardier beetle makes all of the chemicals it needs to get the weapon to work, it stores them in separate chambers so that they don't make the boiling-hot gases until they are needed, and it has all of the "plumbing" it needs to connect the chambers and release the boiling-hot gases. When we see a weapon like a rifle or a flame-thrower, we know that it couldn't have happened by chance. It is simply too complicated. We know that someone had to have designed and built it. When we see the amazing weapon that the bombardier beetle has, we know that there is no way it could have happened by chance. It must have been designed by God!

Bites and Stings

As I mentioned, bees, wasps, and hornets can sting, which is a very good way for them to defend themselves. Although not a lot of other insects sting, you do have to beware of certain furry caterpillars. A few of the innocent looking "hairs" on these caterpillars are really tubes that, when touched, will stab into your skin and inject an irritating chemical. That's a pretty good defense, huh?

Although some caterpillars look cuddly, a few of them have "hairs" that will sting you and inject a chemical under your skin.

What Do You Remember?

Explain what a lek is. What is complete metamorphosis, and what are its stages? What is the difference between complete metamorphosis and incomplete metamorphosis? What are the stages of incomplete metamorphosis? What is an immature dragonfly called? List the six different kinds of insect defenses that I discussed in this lesson. Explain how the bombardier beetle defends itself.

Nature Points

When you are out in nature, begin to take note of the different ways God designed individual insects to defend themselves. Can it hop really far, really quickly? Does it blend in with its environment? Does it have eyespots or other trickery? Write these observations in your notebook. There is a template provided on page 129 of the *Zoology 1 Notebooking Journal* for you to use.

Notebook Activities

Record all that you remember from the lesson for your notebook. I also want you to draw three life cycle charts. What's a life cycle chart? Well, look at the drawing on the right. It shows the four stages in a fly's life, and it puts them in a circle, to show that the cycle repeats over and over again. I want you to draw a life cycle chart for a butterfly, a praying mantis, and a dragonfly. All three of your life charts should reflect the insect beginning with an egg and then going through the stages of metamorphosis to an adult. Be sure to draw pictures of each stage. The *Zoology 1 Notebooking Journal* provides templates for this activity on pages 130-131.

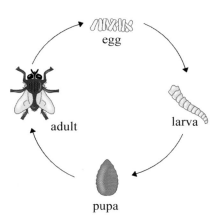

egg

larva

pupa

adult

Projects

Insect Display

Most insects don't have a very long life cycle and often perish as soon as the weather turns or after they have mated. In nature, it is common to find dead insects at forests, parks, or even the beach. I want you to make a display of dead insects so that they can be studied.

Take a cigar box or shoebox and have an adult cut out a rectangle of Styrofoam® so it fits snugly in the bottom of the box. When you find a dead insect, pin it to the Styrofoam. It is best to pin insects in the thorax, just to the right of center. If the insect is dried out and hard, you will need to put it in the relaxer discussed below before you pin it. If you want to get really fancy, you can buy a professional display box, like the one pictured on the right. The website I told you about in the introduction to this book has links to where you can buy this kind of box.

Relaxer

You will often find that dead insects are dry, hard, and difficult to pin or display. You can fix this with a relaxer, which puts moisture back into dry insects so they will be more flexible.

You will need:
♦ A wide-mouth jar
♦ Clean sand
♦ Liquid disinfectant (Lysol® or a similar product, but not bleach or household cleaner)
♦ Cardboard

- Water
- Measuring cup
- Scissors

1. Pour a few inches of sand in the bottom of the jar.
2. Make ½ cup of a 50/50 solution of water and disinfectant (to prevent mold).
3. Pour enough of the solution on the sand in the jar to wet it thoroughly.
4. Cut a piece of cardboard to fit tightly in the jar over the sand.
5. Place an insect in the jar, close lid, and let it stand for a few days. Check for mold and make sure the insect doesn't get too soggy.
6. When you remove the insect, it should be much more flexible, allowing you to stretch out its wings and pin it to your display.

Experiment
Can Trap Experiment

You will need:

- Two soup cans
- Something to punch holes into the soup cans
- Fruit, meat, or other possible insect baits
- Cheesecloth
- A small board or boards that will cover the openings of both soup cans with room to spare

This lesson's experiment will be done with can traps. To make a can trap, have an adult punch small holes into the bottom of a soup can. This will make sure the can won't fill up with water if it rains. Choose a spot in your yard that is rich in insect life, such as near or under a pile of leaves or grass clippings. Dig a can-sized hole in the ground and place the can in it so that its top is at ground level. Wrap some bait (like fruit or meat) in cheesecloth and put it on the bottom of the can. To protect the captured insects from the sun (and predators), put a small board over the top of the can, lifted a few inches above the ground with rocks or blocks.

You can choose one of two experiments to do with the cans. You can choose to answer the question, "Which bait will attract the most insects?" or "Which location will have the most insects?" You can do both experiments, but you will have to conduct them separately. You cannot do both different locations and different baits. Do you understand why?

The reason you can't do both experiments at the same time is because you will not get accurate results. If you have bananas in a can near a water hole and meat near a grass pile, no matter which one catches more insects, you won't know if it was because of the food or the location. You must keep every aspect of the experiment identical except the one variable you are testing. Count the number of insects in each can trap to determine which was the best bait or location. Use a Scientific Speculation Sheet to record your experiment procedures, your hypothesis, and your results.

Lesson 11
Social Insects

Many insects are loners. They don't spend time with other insects of the same species except to mate. They don't even take care of their young; they simply lay their eggs somewhere and leave forever. Some insects, like the praying mantis, will even eat its mate and its siblings if food is scarce! Other insects don't mind spending time with insects of the same species, but they don't help one another out or have special relationships with each other.

Interestingly, there are some insects that do form close relationships and depend on one another for survival. They all work together, having different jobs that keep the colony alive. These insects are called **social insects**. Only two orders of insects are considered social: Hymenoptera (hi men op' tur uh) and Isoptera (eye sop' tur uh). Order Hymenoptera contains bees, wasps, and ants, while order Isoptera contains termites.

Many bees are social insects. They live in large groups, and each bee has a specific job that helps the group survive.

Although there are several kinds of social insects, they tend to create colonies that operate in a similar manner. One insect is the **queen**, and she lays all the eggs. She is fed and taken care of by the other insects in the colony. With those in order Hymenoptera (bees, wasps, and ants), the males are called **drones** and only have one job: to mate with the queen. The rest of the colony is made up of females, called **workers**. These are the ants, bees, and wasps that you see. Termites have both a queen and a **king**, and they also have both male and female workers. They also have **soldiers** that protect the colony. Let's start our study of these interesting creatures by looking at bees, wasps, and ants.

Hymenoptera

The word "hymen" means "membrane," and the word "pteron" means "wing." The members of order Hymenoptera, then, have wings that are like thin membranes. Some ants don't have wings, but they do have little humps on their back where wings would have formed had they been fed the right food. Insects in this order usually have a "wasp waist," called a **petiole** (pet' ee ohl), which is a thin stalk on the front of the abdomen that connects to the thorax (see photo on the next page). They also have antennae that are used for smell and touch, and they all experience complete metamorphosis.

The ant's petiole is easy to see in this photo.

Ants are both beneficial insects and pests. They tunnel into the ground, which improves the soil, and many species also eat harmful insects. The ants that prefer to live in your home, however, are considered pests. The fire ant, with its terribly painful bite, is a serious pest to humans and animals in the southern United States as well as Central and South America.

Ants live in a colony that is "ruled" by a queen. Have you ever heard the saying, "You are what you eat"? Well, this is especially true with ants. Any female ant larva can become a queen if it is fed the proper diet. Most ant larvae are not fed that diet, however, so they do not become queens. If the larva is fed the proper diet, she will emerge from the pupa stage with wings. Larvae that are not fed the "royal diet" will come out of the pupa stage without wings, which means they cannot make eggs or produce young. Male ants, on the other hand, usually have wings when they emerge from their pupa stage and are ready to mate. They are called drones.

Usually, the queens and drones will emerge from their pupa stage at the same time. These male and female winged ants are called **alates** (ay' laytz). In order for the male and female alates to mate, they must **swarm**. How do they do that? Well, all the alates come out of their home (their anthill) at once, flying this way and that way. They pair off together and mate so that the new queen can lay eggs. After they mate, the male dies. His only job is done. He has no other reason to live.

Winged ants, whether they are male or female, are called alates.

After she mates, a queen usually looks for a nice place to begin a colony; she will become the mother of every ant in her colony. Some will simply drop to the ground wherever they finished mating and begin the colony there. Most ants prefer to nest in tunnels in the ground, building mounds that are called anthills. Other species nest in dead wood, in plants, in buildings and ships, or in papery nests attached to branches or rocks.

Once the queen has found her spot, she scrapes off her wings and starts to build her anthill. She tunnels into the earth (or whatever she prefers to tunnel into) and builds a little room where she lays her first eggs. These are the only young she will ever have to care for, because when they are adults, her children will do all the work. The queen feeds this little brood with her own saliva.

After a few days, the eggs hatch into little wormlike larvae, called **grubs**. They are white and can't move or feed themselves. They are completely and totally dependent on adult ants to care for them. They are constantly fed, and will molt and grow several times. Then, each larva will form a pupa, which often looks like an ant egg but is much bigger. If you happen to open an anthill and see the ants scurrying about carrying off what look like ant eggs, they are probably carrying the ant pupae (pyoo' pee – plural of pupa)! They are trying to save the pupae.

At eclosion (when the ant emerges from the pupa), it is often transparent, with a very soft body. It takes a few days for its exoskeleton to harden. The first group of eggs laid by the queen will all hatch **worker** ants. These are female ants that don't have wings and cannot mate. They will begin looking for food immediately. The queen will lay more eggs, and from that point on, that's all she will do. The eggs, larvae, pupae, and queen will all be cared for by the workers. The queen ant will live like that for several years, but worker ants typically live for somewhere between a few months and five years.

When the colony begins, the queen will produce only worker ants. Each worker begins its adult life with the safest job: caring for the eggs, grubs, pupae, or the queen. As they get older, they are given the harder job of making tunnels and keeping the nest clean by taking out the trash. Finally, when they are much older, they are sent out to look for food – the most dangerous job of all.

The big ant in the center is the queen, and the others are the workers that care for her and her young.

As the colony grows, the queen will lay eggs that produce male ants (drones), and the workers will create more queens by feeding the grubs with the diet necessary to produce queens. When these alates become adults, they will swarm and start the process all over again.

Worker Ant Jobs

Worker ants have several specific jobs. **Interior workers** tend to the queen and the brood (eggs, larvae, and pupae). These servants move the eggs, larvae, and pupae around all over the nest, finding just the right amount of warmth and moisture for them. The larva are licked, touched, and fed all day long. The interior workers chew insect parts or other food into a gooey mixture and feed it to the larvae. They also feed the larvae regurgitated food that they store in an organ called the crop. The workers also help open the pupae when they are ready to emerge as adults.

Nest maintenance workers help build the nest. The nest might be twenty feet deep and may cover thousands of square feet. These workers make the tunnels, called **galleries**, and rooms, called **chambers**, where everything is kept. The queen's chamber is usually a large room near the center of the colony. Other chambers are used for storing food, raising the larvae, or storing trash. As the colony grows, galleries and chambers are added. The nest maintenance ants may move many tons (a ton is two thousand pounds) of soil to build the anthill! All of this soil is moved one grain at a time, held in an ant's mandibles.

Scouts are single ants that go out and look for food. When food is found, they leave a scented trail from the food back to the anthill and tell the **foragers** to follow the trail. Once a scout tells the foragers about food, they march out and follow the scent the scout left behind all the way to the food source. The scout doesn't always leave a straight trail back to the food, which is why ants often zigzag as they are heading to get food.

Ants are extremely clean creatures and have designated trash men (actually, they are trash women because worker ants are all female). These **midden ants** take all waste (feces, left over food parts, and dead ants) out of the anthill and heap it into a pile called the **midden**. Not only do ants keep their anthill clean, they spend a lot of time cleaning themselves and each other.

All ants will fight to defend their colony, but some species of ant actually have designated warriors.

Although all ants defend the colony from attack or disaster, some species of ant have special fighting ants whose *only* job is to fight other ants. While other ants are busy keeping everything nice and clean and everyone well fed, these ants are busying watching out for the enemy. Who is the enemy? Usually, any ant from another colony is the enemy.

You see, ants like to find weaker ant colonies and destroy them. Because of this, ants are always on the lookout for attacks from other ants.

They are also looking for other ant colonies to attack. If a foreign ant comes too close to an ant colony, it will be attacked. When this happens, the ant will release an alarm pheromone, and all the ants will come to defend the colony.

Ants have several ways to defend themselves and fight other ants. They have sharp-toothed, biting mandibles. Some South American ant mouths are so strong they can even slice into the skin of animals. Ants also produce **formic acid** in special glands. The spray of formic acid can irritate or blind other insects. They spray the acid before and after they bite. This is part of what makes an ant bite so painful.

Ants can use their sharp mandibles in combat.

Ant Talk

Ants don't talk of course, but they do communicate very well. They communicate with one another by releasing pheromones, which you learned about in Lesson #9. Scientists have detected many different pheromones that ants produce, and each pheromone has its own meaning. One pheromone could mean, "There is food on the trail behind me," while another could mean, "Danger! Run away!" Another might say "Danger! Attack!" Other pheromones let the workers know what they need to do to take care of the colony.

When ants meet, they smell each other with their antennae.

Ants don't have good vision, so pheromones are very important to them. They also tend to recognize each other by scent. When two ants meet, they will often investigate each other with their antennae to smell whether or not they are members of the same colony. An ant can also sense vibrations with tiny hairlike projections on its body, head, and legs. Do you remember what these projections are called? They are called setae.

Ant Food

Most ants eat other insects. Some also like to eat seeds and fruits, but almost all ants like sweet stuff. Many drink flower nectar, for example. Interestingly enough, ants can only swallow liquids. They cannot eat solids. When they eat another insect, they swallow the liquids inside the insect; they don't eat the solid parts. If they find solid food, they cut it up into small pieces and take it back to the anthill, because the larvae can eat solid food at certain times.

Occasionally you will see a lone ant searching around your house or yard. That ant is a scout. It has been sent out to find food. It looks everywhere and loves it when you drop cereal or other food on the floor. When a scout finds a good food source, it heads back to the colony, squirting chemicals out as it goes to make a very smelly trail that the other ants can use to find the food source. When it runs into other ants, it speaks to them with its pheromones, telling them to head on down the trail. That ant tells other ants, and so on and so on until before you know it, there are hundreds of ants (forager ants) following the same path to the piece of cereal you dropped under the table.

Foragers have the hardest job of the colony. They have to face bad weather, other ants, and predators while gathering food for the colony. Because of their dangerous job, many do not live very long. However, the forager actually does a lot of good in its short life. It can carry much more than its own weight, hauling huge quantities of food back to the colony.

The Ant Shepherds and Farmers

Would you believe that some ants actually care for and use another insect species the way humans use sheep and cattle? In the same way a shepherd cares for his sheep and milks them to drink their milk, ants shepherd **aphids** (ay' fidz). Many species of ant take good care of their aphids, guarding them, moving them to better food sources, and taking them home for the night.

This ant is getting a drop of honeydew from an aphid. If you look closely, you can see the drop coming out of the aphid's abdomen.

Aphids are small insects that feed on the sap of newly sprouted stems, leaves, and flowers. Eating the sap inside these fresh plants causes a special substance called **honeydew** to form inside the aphid's body. Ants will "milk" an aphid by rubbing the aphid's back with its antennae. The honeydew squeezes out of the aphid's abdomen, and the ant enjoys a nice taste. You may think that this is a lousy thing to happen to an aphid, but it is not. You see, ladybugs love to eat aphids, but they don't eat aphids that are being guarded by ants. So aphids that become "sheep" are actually a lot safer than aphids that are on their own! Do you have aphids on the plants in your yard? Are they guarded by ants?

In God's incredible creation, not only have some ants been designed to be shepherds, others have been designed to be farmers! Leaf-cutter ants cut up leaves and bring them back to the colony. The leaves are then cleaned (remember, ants are very clean) and chewed up into little bits. Those little bits of leaves are piled together and mixed with ant droppings (feces). This mixture is perfect for a particular kind of fungus, which grows on the mixture. The ants tend their "fungus farm," keeping it free of anything else except the fungus, and they eat the fungus for food. Isn't that amazing?

Explain what you have learned about social insects, especially ants. What are the different ant jobs? Which one would you like to do if you were an ant? Why? Which one would you not like to do? Why?

The Honeybee

Let's explore another group of insects in order Hymenoptera that are almost as commonly seen on a warm summer day as the ant. Let's learn about bees! Do you realize that there are more than 20,000 different species of bee? Most of them are solitary bees that live alone, but a few are social bees that live with thousands of others, sometimes up to 80,000 in one colony!

Bees, including this honeybee, help flowering plants to reproduce.

Even though there are many different kinds of bees, I want to cover one type of bee in detail: the honeybee. It isn't native to America, but was brought here from Europe where it provided people with honey for thousands of years. The bumblebee is native to America, and I'll give this little forager an honorable mention at the end of the lesson.

Wherever you see flowers, you will usually see honeybees and bumblebees. Do you think bees are beneficial insects or pests? Sometimes they sting, so you might think they are pests. Most bees, however, are beneficial insects that keep us not only fed, but supplied with beautiful flowers. Bees are **pollinators** for flowers. Without bees, the world would look quite different, and we wouldn't have nearly as much food! You see, the fruits and vegetables we love to eat come from plants that produce flowers, and those flowers need pollination. If a flower does not get pollinated, it will not be able to make seeds.

If you have not yet taken a course on botany (the study of plants), let me take a moment to explain how pollination works: Many plants make seeds that start out as flowers. The flowers have male and female parts. The male part produces pollen, while the female part produces eggs. In order for a seed to form, the pollen must get from the male part of one flower to the female part of another

flower. So how does the pollen get from one flower to another? There are many ways, but the most common is the result of visiting insects, like bees and butterflies. A bee has little hairlike bristles on its body, and those bristles get all covered with pollen while the bee is collecting both pollen and nectar for the hive. When the bee goes to another flower of the same kind, some of the pollen falls off and finds its way to the female part of the flower. Once that happens, seeds are formed, and a big fruit (like an apple, peach, pear, cherry, or tomato) grows around the seeds to protect them. Then we eat the

The yellow powder that covers this bee is pollen. As the bee goes from flower to flower, the pollen will get transferred, allowing seeds to form.

fruit and plant the seeds! It is a wonderful thing that God created bees so that we could continue to have beautiful flowers to enjoy, fruits to eat, and seeds to plant.

Bees are feared by most people because their ovipositors are stingers that are outfitted with an internal venom chamber for injecting venom into their victims. This is how bees protect the hive and themselves. This sting is a painful reminder to keep your distance.

Honeybees have it a little more difficult than other stinging insects, because their stingers have barbs on them. When a worker honeybee stings a creature, the barb causes the stinger to get caught. As the bee yanks to get its ovipositor out of the creature, the entire ovipositor and part of the abdomen come off! Sadly, this causes the little bee to die. Wasps, other kinds of bees, and queen honeybees don't have these barbs. They can sting again and again because they simply pull out the stinger and it doesn't get stuck.

Why does a honeybee have a barbed stinger, if it kills the bee? Well, a honeybee sting hurts worse than a sting from most other insects, which is a powerful reminder to animals and people that they should avoid honeybees. The sting of a honeybee hurts so much because the stinger is left in the skin with the venom chamber attached. If you push on it, more venom goes into your skin. In the same way, if you try to get the stinger out with tweezers, you will inject more venom into you. To safely remove a honeybee's stinger from your skin, you need to scrape the stinger from the side with a blunt object. This will pull the stinger out without squeezing the venom chamber.

Royal Food

Bees build hives out of a waxy substance that they make themselves. Not surprisingly, this substance is called **beeswax**. A beehive is an elaborate, beautiful structure that contains hundreds of six-sided cells. Bees store food in most of the cells, but the queen also lays eggs in some of them.

Just like a queen ant, a queen bee lays eggs that mostly produce female bees. When they hatch, the larvae are fed by nurse bees. If the bee is to be a worker, the nurse bees feed it a substance called **royal jelly** for three days only. Royal jelly is a special white substance made by worker bees. It has nutritional properties that make the bee develop and grow a lot in just three days. After three days, however, the nurse bees will change the larvae's diet to pollen and honey to make sure it is a worker. The hive needs *lots* of workers. If a larva is fed royal jelly beyond three days, it will develop into a queen. Since a queen bee is bigger than a worker bee, the walls of the developing larva's cells must be broken down to give the developing queen more room.

A beehive is made up of many six-sided cells.

The Queen Bee

The large bee near the center of this photo is the queen.

Even after the queen bee is an adult, she is given a diet of royal jelly her entire life, which is usually about five years. The queen bee is easy to spot, because she is larger than the worker bees.

Even though a hive can have only one queen, nurse bees still feed some larvae royal jelly. Those larvae do not survive, however, because the queen kills them before they mature. When the queen dies, however, there is nothing to kill the developing queen larvae, so they will continue to develop. When the first queen matures, she will kill the remaining queen larvae. This interesting process makes sure that the hive will never be without a queen for long and that there will never be more than one queen at a time.

After a new queen has killed all of the other potential queens, she goes on a vacation to mate, much like an ant queen. Unlike an ant queen, however, this queen returns to her hive to lay the eggs.

Now remember, both the workers and the queens are females. What about the males? Well, male bees are called **drones**, and their sole purpose in life is to mate with the queen so that she can lay eggs. Since they can't do anything else, they don't live for very long, and before winter, they are all kicked out of the hive and are not allowed back in. Since they don't know how to find food, they die of starvation outside of the hive. That's kind of sad, huh?

Worker Bees

When a worker metamorphoses into an adult, she gets to work immediately. If she is born early in the year, she will live for only about five or six weeks. If she is born in the fall, she will live through winter but die soon after spring arrives. Worker bees have a short, but very busy, important life. Each worker bee begins with one job, and graduates to the next job, much like a worker ant. Every job is just as important as the next, but they do get progressively harder as the bee moves up the job ladder.

This worker bee will have a short but busy life.

Most female worker bees begin their lives as the **nurse bees,** feeding the young larvae and making royal jelly for new larvae and the queen. A few are assigned the all important job of queen's attendant, and they feed and clean the queen every day.

The next job is to be the **storekeeper**. The storekeeper does three things. First, she makes sure the hive doesn't get too hot. As the hive temperature increases, she flaps her wings, which makes her like a little fan that cools the hive. Second, she packs the pollen brought in by the gatherer bees into the cells of the hive so that it can be stored for future use. Third, she makes honey.

After spending time as a storekeeper, the bee graduates to become a **waxmaker**. This is a very hard job, much harder than feeding bees, cooling the hive, or even making honey. The waxmaker is the architect and builder of the hive, producing beeswax and forming the six-sided cells of which the hive is made.

When the waxmakers are ready to add more structures to the hive, they gather into a group and hang, waiting for the wax to ooze out of them from glands in their abdomens. Then, with their back legs, they pull it out and shove it into their mouths, chewing it for a while. This makes the waxy paste that becomes the hive. With the paste in its mouth, each bee is ready to spit it out, little by little, to create perfect six-sided (called **hexagonal** – hek sag' uh nuhl) cells.

After the bee has been a waxmaker for a while, it will then be put to work at the entrance to the hive as a guard, called a **sentry bee**. As a sentry, it protects the hive from intruders, including the drones that were kicked out of the hive. If anything that shouldn't be in the hive tries to get in, the sentry uses its venomous stinger on the intruder. This kills the sentry, but it also keeps the intruder away.

If a beehive has a rough time, like really bad weather, a severe lack of flowers, or a catastrophe such as a visiting bear, the queen bee will send out **robber bees**. Robber bees find and take honey from weaker hives so that their hive can continue to survive.

The last job that a worker bee has is usually that of a **scout** or a **gatherer bee**. Scouts go out each day searching for just the right flower. You see, most honeybees don't just visit the closest flowers. Instead, bees in a particular hive usually look for a specific kind of flower from which to gather nectar or pollen. The scout's job is to find that specific kind of flower. The gatherer bees are the ones that you usually see. They go to the flowers that the scouts have found, and they gather pollen and nectar to bring back to the hive.

Dancing Bees

When the right flowers are discovered by a scout, she rushes back to the hive to spread the news. Moments later, gatherer bees charge out of the hive and fly directly to the flowers. The astonishing thing about this is that the gatherer bees don't follow the scouts back to the flowers; they simply fly directly to them. How do they know where the flowers are?

Scientists have discovered that scouts tell the gatherers where the flowers are by *dancing*! The dance is done in the hive so that all the gatherers can see it. If the flowers are within 50 yards or so of the hive, the scouts dance the **circular dance**. If the flowers are farther away, the scouts dance the **waggle dance**, which is more

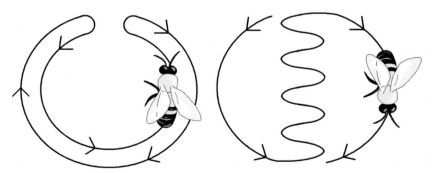

The circular dance (left) is used to tell the gatherers about flowers that are near the hive. The waggle dance (right) is used for flowers that are farther away.

like a figure-eight dance. First, the bee starts as if it is dancing in a circle, but then it waggles up the center and then completes the circle. The "waggle" part of the dance tells the gatherers what direction to fly, and the speed at which it travels in the circles tells the gatherers how far away the flowers are.

Flower Power

So why do gatherer bees visit flowers? Well, flowers provide the food that the members of the hive eat. The gatherer bees collect both pollen and nectar from flowers. Their back legs are covered with hairlike bristles and shaped like little spoons with little bags attached. The bee loads these bags up with pollen. Back at the hive, the bees use the collected pollen to make **bee bread**, which is a mixture of honey and pollen. This is the main food for the members of the hive. In addition to drinking some nectar for energy to make it through the day, the gatherer bee stores nectar in special sacs that are inside the bee's body. Nectar is used to make honey, which I will discuss in a moment.

Have you ever heard of a bee collecting **propolis** (prop' uh lis)? Most people don't know that gatherer bees collect this substance as well. It is a thick, sticky fluid that bees gather from the buds of trees. Back at the hive, it is used like glue to fill in the cracks in the hive. This makes the hive stronger, and it also keeps out the wind, making the hive warmer for the winter.

Making Honey

When the gatherers return to the hive, they vomit up the nectar into the mouths of other bees, and those bees mix the nectar with their saliva. This saliva contains chemicals that begin to convert the nectar into honey. Then, the nectar/saliva mixture is placed in a cell to dry. Bees stand over the cells and fan their wings to evaporate water from the nectar. As the nectar looses water, it becomes thicker and more solid until it is honey. Finally, the cells are capped and sealed with beeswax until the honey is needed. Because honey is stored in the cells that make up a hive, a collection of hive cells is often called a **honeycomb**.

This beekeeper is showing you her box of bees. Notice that she is not wearing gloves. This is because the bees have been calmed by smoke.

The bees use the honey to mix with pollen and make bee bread, which feeds the hive. Of course, we like to use the honey for ourselves. Do you enjoy eating honey? All our honey comes from bees. For thousands of years people have enjoyed eating this wonderful product made by busy bees. Today, beekeepers can be found in every state. One may even live near you. Beekeepers have boxes where they keep their colonies of bees.

Have you ever wondered how beekeepers are able to collect the honey without getting stung by the bees? Well, a long time ago, it was discovered that bees become very calm and unlikely to give off the alarm pheromone if they are first exposed to smoke from a fire. This is because they think they may have to leave the hive, so they start eating all they can in preparation for leaving. Because of this, beekeepers spray smoke on the hive before they open up the box to collect the honey. Usually a beekeeper will wear protective clothing anyway, just in case.

Honey isn't the only product we take from bees. We also take the hive and use the wax from which it is made. Some important uses for beeswax are cosmetics (make-up for women), candles, lotions, ointments, coatings for pills, floor and furniture polishes, crayons, and ski wax. Some people even eat the honeycomb, but now that you know how it is made, you may have a hard time doing that!

Bumblebees

Bumblebees are quite different from honeybees. They not only look different, but they also act differently. The main difference you notice with bumblebees is that they are much larger than honeybees. They are chubby, furry little creatures. They also don't seem to sting as much as a honeybee stings. When they do sting, however, they don't kill themselves stinging you, as honeybees do. This is because they don't have barbed stingers, so they can remove their stinger after they have stung and fly away.

Bumblebees are quite different from honeybees.

When a new queen bumblebee is born and becomes an adult, she looks for a drone (a male bumblebee) for a mate. After mating, the male dies. She then finds a place to hibernate (usually the soil) and sleeps through the winter. Once spring comes, she stops her hibernation and looks for an empty hole in the ground. This is where she will start her colony. In there, she will build a wax pot, and she will forage for nectar to make honey, which she will put in the pot. She also collects pollen and makes it into a ball, and she lays her eggs on that pollen ball. She keeps the eggs warm and does not leave them, using the honey in the honey pot for food.

The first set of eggs produce worker bees, which build cells for the nest, take care of the nest, and forage for nectar to make more honey. At this point, the queen does nothing but eat and lay eggs. Bumblebees are not as loyal to the queen as honeybees are, and they don't have nearly as organized a life. They don't have scouts that go out and search for flowers and then return to tell the others how to get to the flowers. The workers just all go out looking for them. Nevertheless, in the process of collecting nectar, they do pollinate flowers, just as honeybees do.

When the nest has made enough honey, the queen starts laying eggs that will make drones. Interestingly enough, some of the workers are also able to lay eggs that become drones. Once the drones have developed into adults, they may stay in the nest a few days, but they generally leave pretty quickly and do not come back. Unlike honeybee drones, bumblebee drones know how to find flowers and eat nectar from them.

In late summer, some eggs hatch into new queen bees, and once they have become adults, they leave the nest to mate. Then, like the previous queen, they will hibernate over the winter to start a nest next spring. The workers and the drones die off, leaving only the queen to survive the winter.

Badly Behaved Bees

Have you ever thought about being a scientist? Have you ever imagined doing experiments and discovering new things? That's the fun of being a scientist; you get to experiment. Well, sometimes experiments turn out bad. That is what happened about fifty years ago to a group of scientists that studied bees.

These scientists brought African bees and European bees to Brazil, in South America, to see if they could mate them. They wanted to do this so they could develop a bee that would produce more honey in a warmer climate. Scientists called these new bees **Africanized honeybees**. This new breed of bees, however, wouldn't stay in a beekeeper's box. Unlike regular honeybees, they would suddenly leave the colony and build a hive somewhere else. Scientists later discovered that the queen would decide to leave after a few months, often taking half the colony with her.

Africanized honeybees are much more protective of their beehive and more likely to sting. When one releases an alarm pheromone, they all attack together and sting the same animal or person with hundreds of stings. They tend to chase their target much farther than regular honeybees,

This is a photo of a colony of Africanized honeybees that is looking for a new place to build a hive. The inset shows an individual, which looks much like a normal honeybee.

and they stay angry and ready to attack much longer than a honeybee. As a result, some people call them **killer bees**. This was definitely an experiment that went badly, don't you think? I hope none of your experiments ever turn out like this one.

Because of the queen's strange behavior of leaving the hive and starting new colonies, Africanized honeybees have been spreading out from Brazil. They have moved northward so that they have spread through most of South America, Mexico, and the southern parts of Texas, New Mexico, Arizona, and California. Scientists are not sure how far north these bees will spread. Some suggest they cannot survive well in cold temperatures, but others disagree.

Even though some people call them killer bees, Africanized honeybees are not incredibly dangerous. The sting from one Africanized honeybee is no different from the sting of a regular honeybee. The only thing that makes them dangerous is that they tend to sting in much greater numbers. However, if you leave them alone, they will generally leave you alone.

Wasps

Now we are going to talk about another member of order Hymenoptera: the wasp. It's pretty easy to tell the difference between bees and wasps, because bees look hairy and wasps generally don't. Wasps also have a longer petiole, or wasp waist. Often, the petiole that separates the thorax from the abdomen is very long and thin. Some wasps also have such an extensively long ovipositor that it looks like a long needle!

Notice the long petiole and ovipositor on this wasp.

Many wasps are social insects, like bees and ants, but there are a few solitary, unsocial wasps. Social wasps include paper wasps, yellow jackets, and hornets. All three make **paper nests**. Wasps have known how to turn trees into paper for thousands of years, much longer than we have known how to do it! They create cells similar to the combs that bees make with wax, but they make them with paper! They chew up bits of wood and convert it into a paste which they use to construct their paper nests. Then the queen lays an egg in each cell. When it hatches the grub is fed regurgitated insects by the worker wasps. Many adult wasps will eat pollen and nectar, but they also eat other insects.

The cells that a wasp makes out of paper are similar to the cells a bee makes out of beeswax.

Unlike honeybees, but just like bumblebees, the only one in a social wasp colony that will survive the winter is the queen. She will find a place to hibernate – in the hollows of trees, under bark, or in the walls of buildings. In the spring, she crawls out and starts all over again, building a few cells, laying a few eggs, and nurturing them until they can become workers who will do all the work while she lays more eggs.

Solitary wasps do not live in colonies; they live alone. The mud dauber is probably the most common solitary wasp. It is easy to recognize because it has a really long petiole. The female gathers mud in her mouth and uses it to build a nest for her young. She uses her long ovipositor to sting and paralyze tiny spiders, caterpillars, crickets, and other creatures, which are then stuffed inside the mud nest. After each cell in the nest is well stocked with spiders and insects, the mud dauber lays

This mud dauber is a solitary wasp. Note the long petiole.

an egg in each cell, seals it up, and leaves. Then, when the eggs hatch, the larvae have a perfectly nice feast upon which they will dine until they become adults.

The balls on these leaves are galls, which contain wasp eggs.

Some solitary wasps make galls, which are abnormal growths on plants. They look like tumors or strange looking balls. They form when a wasp lays its eggs in the plant, and the plant develops a growth around the egg, encasing it. This actually protects the egg as it develops. Galls can be found everywhere in the late summer, especially on the branches of oak trees.

Other solitary wasps are even parasitic, laying their eggs inside the eggs or larvae of caterpillars. When the eggs hatch, the wasp larvae begin eating the flesh of the larvae in which they hatched. They eat their way into the inside of the larvae and feast until they pupate. The pupa is formed right inside the dying larvae, and the wasps turn into adults inside this creature. Farmers buy these parasitic wasps for insect control in their fields.

Some wasps deposit their eggs in wood so that the young wasp larvae will feed on the tree itself, making circular tunnels through the wood as it feeds, until it pupates and crawls out of the tree as an adult wasp.

Lesson 12
Beetles, Flies, and True Bugs

Throughout the summer, beetles are so plentiful that we usually don't stop to appreciate what amazing and beautiful creations they are. There's a good reason there are so many beetles around us all summer long: there are more species of beetle on earth than any other type of insect. Scientists have identified more than *three hundred thousand* species of beetle, and there are many others that have not been identified! Depending on where you live, you might have June beetles continually hitting against your porch light, Japanese beetles feeding on the plants in your garden, or bark beetles destroying the trees in your yard.

As with most insects, beetles have two pairs of wings. However, you might not consider the front pair wings, since they are not used in flight. These front wings, called **elytra** (el' ih truh)**,** usually cover the entire body of the beetle. This hard covering protects the beetle very well, making it like a little nut, hard to crack or hurt. In fact, beetles are put in order **Coleoptera** (koh' lee op' tur uh), which means "sheath wings," referring to the elytra. Under these protective "sheath wings," you find the membranous wings (the back wings) that the beetle uses in flight.

This dogwood calligrapha beetle is about to take flight, showing you its elytra and its membranous wings underneath.

If you know what you are looking for, it is usually easy to tell whether or not an insect is a beetle. Beetles have hard exoskeletons, and the front wings meet to form a single line down the center of the back. From that description, look at the insects below and see if you can tell which ones are beetles. You can check whether or not you are right by looking at the answers to the narrative questions in the back of the book.

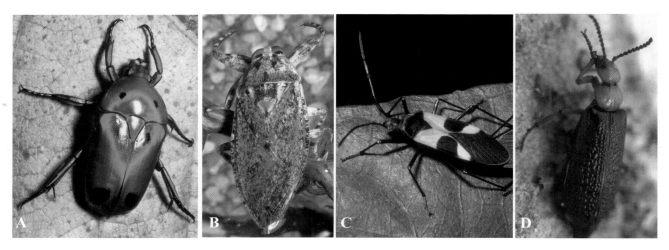

Beetle Behavior

Because there are so many beetles, there are many that have never been seen or studied. Some sources say that if you walk through a rainforest for an entire day, sweeping the ground with a net as you walk, you will pick up at least one beetle that has never been seen or studied before. Maybe you will get an opportunity to do that, but be sure to bring lots of mosquito repellant!

Beetles are fabulous little creatures, and because they are so numerous on the earth, you shouldn't have a difficult time finding one to study, especially in the spring, summer, or early fall. Many beetles are **nocturnal** (nok tur' nuhl), which means they are mostly active at night. They tend to spend the day sleeping, typically underneath rocks or logs or even in the dirt. At the end of this lesson, you will do an experiment in the hopes of finding beetles (and other insects) in dirt from your yard.

Beetles have biting-chewing mouths, and some can look quite fearsome. However, very few beetles actually bite people, and the ones that do typically only bite if they are handled. Although the majority of beetles won't hurt you, some have been given amazing weapons for defense. You already learned about how the bombardier beetle can squirt boiling-hot gases and how the blister beetle can release oil that causes blisters. Some can even suction themselves to a plant so birds can't pick them up to eat them. Despite examples like these, most beetles are safe to handle and study.

These ground beetles look fearsome with their large, curved mandibles. However, they will only bite you if they are handled.

All beetles go through complete metamorphosis. Once a beetle egg hatches, the young beetle may stay a larva only a few weeks, or it may stay a larva up to twelve years, depending on the kind of beetle it is. Some beetle larvae are legless, while others are worm-like creatures with six legs known as grubs. Yet, unlike bee and ant grubs, they are equipped with little beetle faces containing chewing mouthparts with which to eat plants or animals. After the pupa stage, they become adult beetles that can fly. Adults usually live until they have mated or laid eggs, which could be a few weeks or many years.

Both Beneficial and Pesky

A few beetles are truly beneficial and include some of our favorite flying creatures, like ladybugs and fireflies! Yes, it's true. A ladybug is not a bug, and a firefly is not a fly; they are both

These ladybugs are eating black aphids, which can destroy crops as well as garden plants.

beetles! Ladybeetles, as they should be called, are so helpful to farmers that they can be ordered and sent to farmers all over North America. These little creatures eat terrible pests that destroy both important food crops and decorative garden flowers.

At the same time, many beetles are major pests and are responsible for destroying crops that we need for food. Both the larvae and adults take part in this destruction. Colorado potato beetles, for example, can decimate a potato crop. Both the larvae and adults feed on the leaves of potato plants, and without enough leaves, the plants cannot survive.

A few species of beetle have come to America as a result of trade between countries and have spread rapidly. Japanese beetles, for example, accidentally came to the United States from Japan, probably as eggs in a plant. They eat up crops and garden plants all over the eastern United States.

Even though some beetles destroy crops and forests, they can be very beautiful and interesting to study. So I want to look at just a few of the many families of beetles. Of course, what I will talk about here only scratches the surface of the world of beetles. An entomologist can spend his whole life studying one single family, or even one single beetle in a family, and still not learn all there is to know about it!

Scarab Beetles

Scarab beetles belong to family Scarabaeidae (skair uh bee' ih dee), and they are easy to identify if you can look at their antennae. Scarab beetle antennae end in little clubs that can open and close. When open, they look like tiny fans, and when closed, they look like knobs at the end of the antennae. Aside from this common feature, scarab beetles can look very different from one another, especially in their faces and heads. Some scarab beetles have long, pinching mandibles, and some even have a big horn. June bugs, tumblebugs, Japanese beetles, rhinoceros beetles, stag beetles, Hercules beetles, dung beetles, elephant beetles, and Goliath beetles are all in this family.

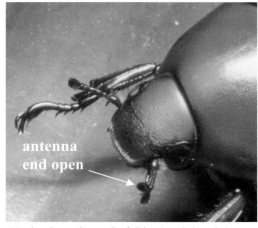

antenna end open

Notice how the end of this scarab beetle's antenna looks like a tiny fan. It can close to look like a tiny knob.

The beetles in this family are usually medium to large and sometimes very brightly colored. One of the largest beetles on earth is in this family. Look at the list of beetles on the previous page and guess what this very large beetle is called. Did you guess Goliath? That's right! The Goliath beetle is named after the giant in the Bible (1 Samuel 17:4), because it is so large. It can grow longer than six inches, which is *really* big for a beetle. Not surprisingly, elephant beetles are very large as well.

Although they look disgusting, the feeding habits of dung beetles are vitally important to creation.

So what's for dinner if you are a scarab beetle? Probably some flowers, fruits, or leaves, but if you are a dung beetle, you prefer animal droppings, also called dung. Sounds pretty disgusting, doesn't it? Well, even though it is disgusting, it is actually very helpful to people and animals because it cleans up the environment.

Both dung beetle larvae and adults love to feast on dung, and the way a dung beetle makes sure its larvae are fed is nothing short of remarkable. God designed this little creature to use its legs and mouth to shape some dung into round (sometimes pear-shaped) balls. After the dung is shaped, the beetle rolls and rolls and rolls the dung on the ground, this way and that way, until it reaches home. The ball of dung can be up to *50 times heavier* than the beetle rolling it!

Once the beetle gets the ball home (a hole in the ground), the female will lay an egg into it. When there are several balls of dung, each with an egg in it, the female will cover the hole up with soil and more dung. When the eggs hatch, the larvae can eat to their heart's desire. As time goes on, they eventually reach the pupa stage and then transform into adults. Most dung beetles live for 3-5 years.

Scientists believe that without the dung beetle, we would have piles of dung everywhere! There are thousands of species of dung beetle, and they are found wherever dung can be found – which is just about everywhere. Dung beetles are considered very beneficial and are even shipped places where too much dung begins to be a problem. I'm sure glad God made the dung beetle, aren't you?

Fireflies/Lightning Bugs

For who knows how long, children have loved to chase and collect **fireflies**, which are also called lightning bugs. They have collected fireflies in jars, and companies have even sold necklaces that consist of a string attached to a little plastic container into which you are supposed to put a firefly.

All these activities amount to loads of fun. Of course, it is probably not fun for the firefly, but it is definitely fun for kids. If you grow up to be an entomologist, you will still get to play with fireflies. Not only that, you will be paid to do it!

Were you surprised to learn that fireflies are not flies? Even though some people call them lightning bugs, they aren't bugs either. They are beetles; very special beetles. They create their own light! That's pretty special. They aren't pests either. They usually eat other insects, nectar, or pollen. One kind actually eats other fireflies. The larvae, which walk around on the ground and look nothing like the adults, eat mostly worms, snails, and slugs. So fireflies are quite beneficial to us, since snails and slugs eat crops and garden plants.

Firefly larvae, sometimes called "glow worms," walk along the ground eating worms, snails, and slugs.

The larvae actually eat their prey in an interesting way: they bite their prey and inject digestive juices into them. The digestive juices turn the prey into liquid, which the larvae then drink. The larva stage lasts quite a while, as the fireflies won't actually become adults until the following spring. The larvae continue to gobble up food until the fall, when they burrow under the ground and hibernate through the winter. In the spring, they emerge from the ground, eat a little bit more, and then enter the pupa stage, which usually lasts for two weeks. At the end of the pupa stage, the firefly is an adult, which is what gets caught and put into jars. Some species will actually hibernate for several years. If those are the kind of fireflies that live in your area, you will probably see more adults in some years than you do other years. Even though most adult fireflies eat small insects, pollen, or nectar, some actually eat nothing at all. They mate, lay eggs, and die all within a few days.

Fireflies are bioluminescent, and they can make light using much less energy than a light bulb.

Fireflies are **bioluminescent** (by' oh loo' muh nes' uhnt). That means they make their own light. They do this by producing certain chemicals and mixing them together. The reaction between those chemicals produces light but virtually no heat. As a result, it is often called "cold light." This is amazing, because that's not the way it is for the light bulbs that we use to make light. About 90% of the energy used by a non-fluorescent light bulb is converted into heat, while only about 10%

of the energy makes light. Even in fluorescent lights, which are more efficient, only about 15-20% of the energy is used to make light. Either way, that's a lot of wasted energy, which means it's a lot of wasted money. After all, we pay for all of the energy that comes into our homes.

The firefly doesn't waste energy like we do. Since it makes cold light, more than 90% of the energy it uses in bioluminescence ends up making light. Only about 4% is lost as heat. If we could light our homes as efficiently as fireflies light their abdomens, we would save a *lot* of money! Of course, it should be no surprise that the firefly is more efficient at making light than we are. After all, the firefly was designed by God. He makes wonderfully efficient, beautiful things.

I expect you have watched fireflies at night. If you have, you know that they don't leave their lights on all of the time. Instead, they flash them on and off. There are three reasons a firefly flashes its light. The main reason it flashes is to attract a mate. The male will flash first. If a female fancies what she sees, she will wait for a specific amount of time and flash her light in response. Every species of firefly has a different pattern and time frame for this flashing. The fireflies of each species know exactly what their pattern and time

Fireflies flash their lights for mating.

frame should be. So, after the female flashes, if it's the right pattern and time, the male will fly over to her and mate with her. However, there is one kind of female that doesn't play fair; she pretends to be another species in order to lure the male of that species over. When he arrives, she eats him. That's not nice!

Another reason the firefly flashes is to warn other fireflies of danger. If a firefly gets caught in a spider web, for example, it will flash a warning to others to steer clear of the area. Finally, a firefly might flash its light to warn predators that it is not a tasty meal. Many predators do not like the taste of fireflies, so they learn to avoid insects that emit flashes of light. Not all predators find fireflies distasteful, however, so flashing doesn't always help the firefly warn off predators.

Ladybugs

I've already mentioned the benefits of **ladybugs**, but I want to discuss them a little more in depth here. Ladybugs are also called ladybirds, but they are not bugs or birds, and they are not all ladies! After all, in order to produce eggs that will hatch into larvae, they must mate. That requires a male and a female. The very fact that there are ladybugs around, then, tells us that there are males as well as females. As I mentioned before, ladybugs are more properly called ladybeetles.

Both larva and adult ladybeetles eat aphids and similar insects. Aphids are a huge problem for farmers and gardeners. Do you remember which insect keeps aphids as pets? Ants herd them like sheep, and ants will also attack a ladybeetle that tries to eat one of their aphids.

Ladybeetle larvae look like strange adult insects.

Ladybeetle larvae are different from many other beetle larvae. Many beetles have legless grubs that spend the larva stage under the ground. Ladybeetle larvae look more like strange adult insects, crawling on plants and consuming aphids all the live long day. You might be frightened of this tiny insect if you were to see one in real life, not knowing it is a sweet baby ladybeetle.

Like all beetles, the ladybeetle goes through complete metamorphosis, which means it has a pupa stage as well. Ladybeetle pupae are little reddish and black bumps found on plants.

Ladybeetles can be red, orange, or yellow with black spots. They can also be black with red spots. Some are missing the spots altogether. There are even a few kinds of ladybeetles with metallic blue iridescence, and some have checkerboard markings or stripes. Which kind do you have in your yard?

Most people think the entire black bulge at the tip of the ladybeetle is its head. If you look closely, however, the head is the very tiny segment at the tip of the ladybeetle. Most of the black part of the ladybeetle is the thorax. It sometimes has spots on it, and sometimes it is all black. Can you tell the difference between the head and thorax in the photo on the right?

It only takes about four weeks for the ladybeetle to go from egg to adult. Compare that to the firefly I told you about earlier, which takes nearly a year, sometimes longer. Some females can lay up to 1,000 eggs in one summer. Of course, the ladybeetle will try to lay her eggs near an aphid colony so that the larvae will have a ready supply of food when they hatch.

Some ladybeetles can live as many as three years, hibernating during the winter. In the autumn, they will find a nice crack or crevice, usually in a sunny spot, and snuggle down for a long winter's nap. Some states, like Kentucky, have had problems with ladybeetles choosing living rooms as their preferred place of hibernation. Suddenly, the wonderful ladybeetle is transformed into a pest as people try to remove thousands from their curtains.

Ladybeetles have had the special honor of being astronauts for NASA, America's space program. Yes, four little ladybeetles were sent into space along with a host of aphids. Because aphids usually escape ladybeetles by falling from the plant onto the ground, scientists were very curious how the aphids would escape without the help of gravity (which pulls the aphids to the ground when they let go of the plant). It turns out that the aphids could not escape without the help of gravity. So the NASA ladybugs were quite well fed!

Flies

The haltere (singular of halteres) shown in this photo is used for balance when this fly is in the air.

It's time to discuss some of our least favorite animals: flies, gnats, and mosquitoes. Scientists usually lump all of these creatures into one order: **Diptera** (dip' tur uh), which means "two wings." Most insects have four wings, but members of this order have only two true wings. In addition to these wings, however, they do have two little paddles, called **halteres** (hal' tears), that look like tiny wings. Rather than working like wings, however halteres work to keep the insect's body balanced while it is flying. Let's start our discussion of this order by looking at flies.

Though many flies are considered pests, not all of them are. In fact, most flies are an important part of our world, benefiting us in many ways. Why, without them, our lives wouldn't be nearly as pleasant. One kind of fly, a midge in South America, is the size of the head of a pin, but there's a good chance that it makes your life more enjoyable. "How can that be?" you ask. Well, this tiny midge is the main pollinator of the cocoa plant. Do you know what that means? Without this fly, you would not have any chocolate to eat! So, I guess you like flies a little bit after all.

Some flies are beneficial because they feed on other pests. Marsh fly larvae, for example, feed on snails and slugs. Do you remember the beetle larvae that do this as well? Firefly larvae. Flies and

What Do You Remember?

How can you tell a beetle from other insects? Which beetles are beneficial? Describe the tip of a scarab beetle's antennae.   What is the term that describes the way a firefly makes light? What is special about a firefly's light? How many wings do flies have? Where are their halteres and what do they do? Why do mosquitoes feed on human blood? What attracts them? How can you keep their population down? How can you tell a robber fly from a wasp or bee? What makes a bug a true bug? What makes water striders able to walk on water? Why are giant water bugs sometimes called "toe biters?"

Nature Points

When you are out in nature, look for insects. Try to tell which order they belong to by examining their wings. Do they cross over the back like a true bug? Do they have a nice straight line down the middle like a beetle? Are there only two wings like a fly?

Notebook Activities

Write all the fascinating facts you remember about beetles, flies, and bugs in your notebook. Also, based on what you have learned about the habits of mosquitoes, write or dictate a letter informing citizens how they might best avoid mosquito bites. Templates for these assignments are provided in the *Zoology 1 Notebooking Journal.*

Experiment
Where do most insect prefer to live?

The soil in your yard is filled with life. Yes, it is! Under rocks, leaf piles, grass clipping, and virtually everywhere else you can find living creatures. Most of them are tiny. Many are small ground beetles that emerge at night to feed. Some are the larvae of insects, feeding on the rotting stuff in your soil. Even though these creatures like to remain hidden, there is a way to force these creatures to show their faces. It's a lot of fun!

You are going to conduct an experiment to determine which kind of earth environment insects prefer. Look for different areas in your yard that either receive different amounts of sun or have different materials, such as pine straw, dead leaves, bark, grass clippings, or just plain dirt. Choose at least two of these areas as test areas to see which one will have more creatures living in the soil. After you have chosen the areas you will test, decide which one you think ground-dwelling creatures will prefer. Use a Scientific Speculation Sheet to record your hypothesis, experiment, and results.

You will need:

♦   A large funnel with a pretty large drain hole (It is best to cut off the top of a plastic, 2-liter soda pop bottle to make one of these.)
♦   A lamp with the shade removed (A bendable-necked desk lamp works best.)
♦   A clear glass jar in which the funnel rests comfortably
♦   A trowel or very large serving spoon
♦   A couple of containers in which to collect your soil
♦   A set of measuring cups

1.   Dig up the soil by inserting the trowel fairly deep into the soil and lifting up as much soil as possible in one scoop.
2.   Put the soil into one container.
3.   Do steps 1 and 2 for both test areas, using different containers in which to collect your soil.
4.   Place the funnel so that it rests on the jar.
5.   Estimate how much soil your funnel can hold, measure out that amount of soil from one of your containers, and pour it into the funnel. Don't worry if some if it falls into the jar. Remember how much soil you measured, because you will need to add the same amount of soil when you repeat the experiment for the other test area.

6.   Shine the light directly onto the soil. As the light bulb heats up, the top surface of the soil will heat as well, and the insects will burrow further down to escape the heat. As they continue to burrow, they will find themselves falling through the hole in the funnel.
7.   You should see little creepy crawlies fall into the jar: spiders, larvae, beetles, and many other creatures. When you are done, make a count of these creatures and examine the ones that appear interesting to you.
8.   Repeat the experiment with the other soil sample. Now remember, a good scientific experiment keeps everything the same except what is being tested, so make sure that you use the same amount of soil this time as you did for the first test area.

Which soil did the creatures prefer? Did the two test areas have basically the same kinds of creatures in them, or did they have different kinds of creatures in them? These are the things that scientists find out through experimentation.

Lesson 13
Interesting Insects

Although all insects are interesting, the ones we will study in this lesson (praying mantises, dragonflies, grasshoppers, crickets, katydids, aphids, and cicadas) are especially fun to find in nature. Most of these creatures can be seen all summer long if you know where to look.

Praying Mantises

Scientists don't agree on the classification of **praying mantises**, which are also called **praying mantids** or sometimes just **mantids**. Some put them in the same order as cockroaches and call it Dictyoptera (dik' tee ahp' tur uh). Others put them with crickets and grasshoppers into an order called Orthoptera (or thahp' tur uh). Other scientists think they need to belong to their own order, and they typically call this order **Mantodae** (man toh' day uh). Many scientists compromise by putting praying mantises in either Dictyoptera or Orthoptera and then saying that they belong to their own special subgroup within that order called Mantodae.

With hands folded up in prayer-like fashion, a praying mantis is really a *preying* mantis. Any moving creature smaller than itself is fair game for a quick meal, and since praying mantises can grow quite lengthy when they are full grown, most insects are in danger. In some cases, praying mantises even eat things like salamanders, toads, frogs, small lizards, and

This praying mantis is feasting on a butterfly.

hummingbirds. They learn to sit still on a plant and wait, and wait, and wait, without moving an inch. The first insect that gets within grabbing distance experiences the unfortunate result of being snatched up by the long arms of this still, silent predator.

Their prey don't have a chance, for the mantises' front legs are spiked and endowed with claws that hook onto the creature. In addition to the advantage of claws and spikes, a praying mantis can turn its head from one side to the other, just like you can turn your head to look both ways before you cross the street. This makes it very easy for the praying mantis to look for an insect upon which to pounce. No other insect can do this with its head, which is one more reason that the praying mantis is one of the best hunters in class Insecta.

Since mantids prey on insects that are harmful to crops, they are considered beneficial. You can even order live praying mantises for insect control. Interestingly enough, praying mantises are such ferocious predators that they sometimes eat other praying mantises, even those of the same species. This is called **cannibalism**, and praying mantises are often referred to as **cannibalistic insects**. I told you in a previous lesson that when praying mantis nymphs hatch, they sometimes eat other nymphs that come from the same egg case. Also, in some cases, a female will eat the male after they mate. That is definitely not a nice thing to do! It doesn't happen all of the time or with all praying mantises, but it does happen, especially when the female is hungry.

Dragonflies and Damselflies

As you may have guessed, dragonflies and damselflies are not flies. They are in their own special order, called **Odonata** (oh doh nay' tuh). Odonata comes from the Greek word *odontos*, which means "tooth." Of course, insects don't really have teeth, but the mandibles that make up the chewing mouths of dragonflies are sharp and jagged, which makes it look like they have teeth. You can usually find the adults flying around in search of prey near bodies of water like ponds, lakes, and streams.

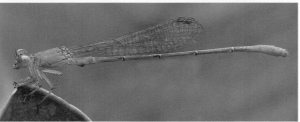

Based on what I just told you, can you tell the dragonfly from the damselfly? Check the answers to the narrative questions to see if you got it right.

Dragonflies and damselflies have many similarities: Neither dragonflies nor damselflies can lay their wings flat against their back as most other insects do. They both have large and beautiful transparent wings with intricate veins throughout. In addition, each of them has an abdomen that is a lot longer than the rest of its body.

Even though they have a lot in common, damselflies and dragonflies are put in different families within order Odonata. This is because there are differences between them as well. Adult damselflies, for example, have thinner, more delicate bodies than those of dragonflies. Also, while resting, adult damselflies fold their wings together over their backs, while dragonflies hold their wings spread out.

Winging It

God gave the beautiful dragonflies and damselflies an amazing gift: the ability to fly backward! They can also hover in midair for as long as they like, and then they can take off at speeds of up to 35 miles per hour! How can they do such amazing feats? Well, unlike most insects, the insects in this order can move each of their four wings independently. This gives these little creatures amazing flying abilities. Researchers have learned that these insects bend and twist their wings in just the right way to cause little whirlwinds that move the air even faster over the upper part of the airfoil, reducing air pressure even more than most flying animals can. This, of course, gives them a mighty lift, even in the face of powerful winds. Did you know that the United States Navy and Air Force pay researchers to study dragonflies in the hopes of learning how to create similar flying machines?

Seeing More than Double

Along with these amazing flight capabilities, members of order Odonata have tremendous eyesight. These two things combined make it a very hard to catch one! Birds, kids, and entomologists alike have trouble netting the dragonfly. Their compound eyes are very large and have up to 50,000 individual lenses. In dragonflies, the eyes are so large that they wrap all the way around the top of the head. As a result, they can see almost everywhere at once. A dragonfly can still be looking at you even after it flies by. Even though damselflies have large eyes, they are not quite as large as those of a dragonfly, so they do not wrap all the way around the head.

Notice how this dragonfly's eyes wrap all the way over the top of its head.

Most insects can be caught by swinging a net at them from the front, before they fly away. If you try to catch a dragonfly from its front, it can easily avoid your net. The best way to catch a dragonfly is to let it fly by and then swing your net like a baseball bat after it.

Feeding on the Fly

Dragonflies and damselflies can catch other insects while flying. They grab their prey with their legs, which have thorny bristles to help ensnare the unfortunate insect. If the insect is small, they can it eat as they fly. If the insect is large, they can lock their legs together to form a "basket" to carry the prey to a place where they can perch and eat it in smaller chunks.

Dragonflies and damselflies will even steal food from a spider's web! Consider this story, which comes from an article in *Creation* magazine:

For several minutes I stalked this little creature [a damselfly] as it fluttered from plant to plant. My plan was to get close enough for a good picture. Eventually, after the damsel had threaded its way through tangled stems, leaves, and flowers, it passed within a meter (3 feet) of a small spider's web that had a tiny object near its center. Then something very unusual happened. The damselfly hovered about 30 centimeters (one foot) in front of the web, seeming to study the spider's lair. Then, after a few seconds, it ever so deliberately moved forward until ... wham! It was caught, head first, right where the object was in the web! 'What a picture this will make', I exclaimed to myself as I thought about how clumsy this little fellow was to do such a thing. To my surprise, however, even though it looked like its head was hopelessly stuck to the sticky silk, it kept flying. The damsel hovered in place while tugging and tugging on the web until ... 'pop', it broke free—taking with it the object that was in the web. Soon I discovered that this little acrobatic thief had stolen the spider's meal out of the spider's web, without getting snagged itself! [Tom Wagner, "The acrobatic damselfly...A wonderful creation of God," *Creation*, Volume 18 (1): p. 15, December 1995]

As you can tell, these amazing creatures are excellent hunters, whether they are grabbing insects right out of the air or stealing the prey of other animals!

Water Babies

The white dots in the picture above are dragonfly eggs. Notice that they are in water. A naiad is shown in the lower photo.

As you have already learned, dragonflies and damselflies experience incomplete metamorphosis with a twist: the nymphs (called **naiads**) swim and live underwater, like fish! The female dragonfly lays her fertilized eggs near or right in the water. The naiads – which don't look much like dragonflies at all – hatch and immediately take to the water.

While living in the water, the naiads gorge themselves on aquatic insects as well other small living creatures like tadpoles and minnows. Hidden in the muck and mire, a naiad will lie in wait for little creatures to swim by. It can then squeeze water out the rear of its abdomen like a jet stream. This propels the naiad forward very quickly, allowing it to snatch its prey with its powerful jaws. Some naiads even have a long lower jaw that can shoot out and grab prey.

These carnivorous nymphs live in the water for weeks (or even years in some species) and undergo a series of molts to grow. When a naiad is ready for its final molt, it finds a stick or other object projecting out of the water, crawls out of the water, and waits for its exoskeleton to dry. As the exoskeleton cracks open at the seam, the beautiful adult dragonfly or damselfly crawls out.

Crickets, Grasshoppers, and Katydids

Like praying mantises, animals in order **Orthoptera** (or thahp' tur uh) begin life inside an egg case. After three weeks – or when spring arrives – the tiny nymphs emerge from the egg case and begin life with a greedy appetite. At the time of emergence, you may find a field littered with teeny nymphs numbering in the thousands. After four or five molts, they have wings that allow them to take flight. This signals that they are adults and are ready to reproduce.

Since this grasshopper has no wings, it is a nymph.

"Ortho" means "straight," so "Orthoptera" means "straight wings." This refers to the front wings, called **tegmina** (teg' men uh), that are stiff and straight and not used for flying. The back wings are membranous and are folded like a fan under the front wings when the creature is not flying. Many use their wings to make sounds, which we generally call "chirping" noises. They make these sounds by rubbing one body part against another, which is called **stridulation** (strij uh lay' shun). Grasshoppers typically stridulate by scraping a comb-like structure on their back legs against their wing or abdomen. It's a little bit like quickly running a stick along a fence. Crickets and katydids often stridulate by rubbing a comb-like scraper on a front wing against a file on the other front wing.

tegmina

The front wings of an adult member of order Orthoptera are tough and straight, while the back ones are membranous and used for flight.

Grasshoppers and katydids tend to buzz more than chirp. Grasshoppers tend to buzz during the day, and katydids usually get started in the late afternoon and continue until late into the night. Crickets, of course, charm us with their sweet chirps in the evening hours and through the night.

Every species makes its own unique sound, and in most cases only the male sings. He does so to attract females or to warn other males to stay away. Crickets have shorter wings than grasshoppers and katydids, so their chirping is higher and more pleasant to our ears. In China, singing crickets are so loved that they are sold as pets in tiny baskets from street vendors. People keep them just to listen to their nice sound.

Would you believe that a cricket can serve as a thermometer? It's true! Scientists have learned that a cricket (specifically the snowy tree cricket) chirps more when it is warmer and less when it is cooler. In fact, if you count the number of chirps in a 15 second period and then add 40 to that number, you get a number that is pretty close to the temperature (in degrees Fahrenheit). Isn't that amazing?

Try This!

To understand how a shorter wing can make a higher sound than a longer wing, get a drinking glass that is reasonably tall. Fill it about one-third full of water. Using a small spoon, gently tap the edge of the glass's lip to hear a ringing sound. Now add water so it is nearly half full. Make a guess as to whether the pitch of the sound will be higher or lower when you tap the glass. Now tap it the same way you did before. Which sound was higher in pitch? Add more water until the glass is about three-fourths full. Once again, tap the glass.

What happened? The more water you added to the glass, the lower pitch of the sound was. Why? Well, the glass makes sound because the glass and the water inside it vibrate. The more water you had in the glass, the *longer* the column of water was that vibrated in the glass. You found out that the longer the column of water, the lower the pitch of the sound. This means that the *shorter* the column of water, the *higher* the pitch of the sound. It is essentially the same with crickets and grasshoppers. The shorter the wings, the shorter the length of the thing that is vibrating, so the higher the pitch of the sound.

Hearing Legs and Abdomens

With all the chirping these animals do, they need to be able to hear. Do they have ears? Yes, in a way. Unlike you and me, however, their "ears," called **tympana** (tim' puh nuh), are not on their heads. Crickets, katydids, and some grasshoppers have tympana on their front legs. Many grasshoppers have their tympana on the front segment of their abdomen instead. The tympanum (singular of tympana) is a little hole with a thin membrane covering it. This is its "eardrum," which vibrates when sounds hit it. Of course, it can't really be called an eardrum if it's not in an ear, can it? Should it be called a legdrum or abdomendrum?

The tympanum allows this grasshopper to hear.

Chomp and Chew

This grasshopper is feasting on leaves.

Members of order Orthoptera chew their food. If you watch one closely, you can see that its jaws (mandibles) move sideways as it chews, not up and down like human jaws do. Crickets are **omnivores** (om' nuh vorz), which means they eat both plants and animals. In fact, they will eat almost anything: vegetables, cereal, and even their mate if they are hungry enough. Katydids are mostly **herbivores** (hur' buh vorz), which means they eat plants. However, they will eat aphids and other small, slow-moving insects, as well as insect eggs from time to time. If very hungry, they might also eat their mate. Grasshoppers, on the other hand, are pretty strict herbivores. If you have one as a pet, feed it fresh grass, wheat bran, and lettuce.

The fact that grasshoppers are herbivores is not necessarily good. They can be terrible crop pests, especially if they swarm. Most grasshoppers don't swarm, and therefore they don't do too much damage. But the swarmers, called **locusts**, can destroy thousands of crops in very little time. You've probably heard of locusts from the Bible (see Exodus 10).

Swarming

Even though locusts are identified as swarming grasshoppers, swarming is not their typical behavior. Generally they lead happy, solitary lives, visiting with other locusts only when they are ready to mate. However, if food becomes scarce, they tend to gather together around whatever food sources are left. As the number of locusts in a region begins to increase, a change in their behavior occurs, and they swarm. Now please realize that swarming in locusts is not the same as swarming in ants. When ants swarm, it is to mate. When locusts swarm, they are moving from one place to another in a *huge* group.

People that have lived through a locust swarm report that they saw what appeared to be a huge, dark cloud up in the sky slowly coming down to the earth. As they watched in perplexed amazement, they began to hear a faint noise that grew louder and louder as the "cloud" grew closer and closer. Swiftly, they would see that the "cloud" was really a huge group of locusts that would land, covering hundreds of square miles of vegetation. Amazingly, scientists have estimated that there can be more than *100 million locusts in each square mile*! That many locusts can completely destroy vast areas of crops and other plants in only a few hours.

Leg Power

Have you ever tried to catch a cricket, grasshopper, or katydid? It's hard, isn't it? As you slowly approach one, it's suddenly gone! You look around and see it a few feet away. The only way to catch it is to pounce on it quickly. These insects are hard to catch because God designed them with amazing legs so that they can really jump! In fact, a grasshopper can jump 20 times farther than the length of its body. If you could jump like a grasshopper, how far would you go? Have an adult measure how

This katydid's long hind legs give it an amazing jumping ability.

tall you are and multiply by 20. Don't you wish you could jump that far? If you study the insects in this order, you will notice how very large and long their back legs are. Those long, strong legs give these insects their amazing ability to jump.

Differences among Crickets, Grasshoppers, and Katydids

Crickets, katydids, and grasshoppers belong to the same order because they have many things in common. However, they are all different creatures, so it is important to be able to tell them apart. There are several different things you can look for in order to help you decide whether a member of this order is a grasshopper, cricket, or katydid.

First, you can look at the coloration. Since grasshoppers are active during the day, they tend to be colored so as to blend in with the grass or with brightly colored flowers. As a result, they tend to be either green, light brown, or multicolored. Crickets, however, are active at night. As a result, they tend to be dark so as to blend in with the shadows. Since katydids spend a lot of time on leaves, they often are leaf-colored, and their wings often look like leaves.

Second, you can look at the antennae. Katydids and crickets tend to have long antennae, while grasshoppers tend to have short ones. In general, katydids have the thinnest antennae, crickets have slightly thicker antennae, and grasshoppers have the thickest antennae.

Third, you can look at behavior. In general, grasshoppers are active all day, while katydids tend to be active in the late afternoon and evening. Crickets tend to be active at night. Now it is important to realize that there are exceptions to these general rules. For example, even though grasshoppers *usually* have short, thick antennae, the long-horned grasshopper has long, thin antennae, much like those of a cricket. As a result, it is sometimes hard to tell the members of this order apart.

Nevertheless, try it yourself. For each picture below, indicate whether you are looking at a grasshopper, katydid, or cricket. The answers can be found at the back of the book with the answers to the narrative questions.

Dangers and Defense

Birds, wasps, mammals, amphibians, reptiles, spiders, and other insects love to dine on members of order Orthoptera. Another very disgusting danger for these insects comes from certain species of flesh flies and tachinid flies. These flies lay their eggs on the back of a cricket or grasshopper. When the eggs hatch, the larvae eat their way into the body of the creature and live off its innards.

How do members of this order protect themselves from these dangers? Well, their primary means of defense is to simply jump and/or fly away. If that doesn't work, grasshoppers are actually equipped with one other important defense. Do you remember that they vomit a stinking juice, called **tobacco juice**, when they are threatened? If you catch a grasshopper, don't be surprised if it vomits tobacco juice on you. You may even be able to make it vomit the juice if you prod it enough.

Of course, camouflage is also a defense. God made katydids look so much like leaves that they are rarely seen by the casual observer. Their wings have the same vein patterns as leaves, and they often have imperfections and blemishes like the ones you might find on a leaf. They are very convincing imitators and well protected with this defense.

Looking for Members of Order Orthoptera

Hunting for these insects is a lot of fun. During summer months, grasshoppers are easy to find. Look for them in tall grass, weedy fields, gardens, or crops. A grasshopper might even startle you when it hops away from you as you walk by. You can even try to catch one. Although you can try to catch members of this order with your hands, you will probably have more success if you use a net. One of the best nets to use is a **sweep net**, which is designed to be swept through plants so that it can pick up the insects living there. The course website I mentioned in the introduction to this book has links to places where you can buy a sweep net.

You will need crickets to complete the experiment at the end of this lesson. Crickets can be found hiding during the day. Look under piles of damp leaves or grass clippings or under any soft mat found at ground level. If you can't find any, that's okay. You can buy them at virtually any bait shop.

Aphids

Now we reach another example of insects that cause scientists to disagree. **Aphids** and **cicadas** are often put in their own order, called **Homoptera** (hoh mop' tur uh). However, other scientists think they are similar enough to the true bugs that they should be in their order, Hemiptera. Now remember, order Hemiptera gets its name from the fact that true bugs have front wings that start off thick and tough but end up thin and membranous. Aphids and cicadas have front wings that are the same throughout, however. In fact, that's what "Homoptera" means. As a result, even scientists that put aphids and cicadas in order Hemiptera still put them in a subgroup of order Hemiptera, and they even call this subgroup Homoptera. The big disagreement, then, is whether aphids and cicadas deserve their own order or should be considered a subgroup of the true bugs. I think they deserve their own order, since their wings don't look like those of a true bug.

Aphids are tiny pests to gardeners and farmers alike. They come in many different colors, mostly green or red. Like all members of order Homoptera, they have piercing and sucking mouthparts so that they can cut into a plant and suck sap out of it. This, of course, can kill the plant. Some species also produce destructive galls on trees. Because they plague plants, they are also called **plant lice**.

These insects have a very complex life cycle. Some will overwinter in the egg and hatch in the spring. Typically, these eggs produce wingless females whose eggs develop and hatch inside their bodies. When a colony of aphids gets too crowded, winged aphids are produced, and they leave to start a new colony somewhere else. This kind of

This group of aphids has mostly wingless individuals, but there is one winged aphid in the picture.

reproduction can produce *huge* populations. At any given time, a farmer may have more than *four tons* of aphids in one field. Late in the summer, males and females mate, and the female lays eggs that will overwinter to start the process all over again.

Remember that aphids are often kept by ants. They produce honeydew for the ants, and the ants protect them. Ladybugs are the aphid's greatest predator, though other insects will feed on them as well. Some wasps lay their eggs inside an aphid's body. When the eggs hatch, the larvae feed on the aphid's internal organs, slowing killing the aphid.

Cicadas

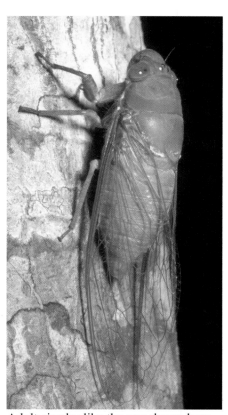

Adult cicadas like the one shown here are often called locusts, but they are not locusts. As you have already learned, locusts are swarming grasshoppers.

Have you ever heard an extremely loud buzzing coming from high in the trees on a warm summer day? It may have been the result of cicadas. They are the loudest of all insects and can be heard from more than four hundred yards away.

The buzz you hear is the male calling to the female using the vibrating panels, called **tymbals** (tim' buhls), on his sides. When the female, who isn't able to buzz, hears the buzz of a male, she searches for him. After they mate, the female will use her ovipositor to cut a slit in the branch of a tree and lay her eggs there. Adult cicadas often don't eat anything, and they don't bite. So they don't cause much damage except for that egg-laying business, and they are safe to collect and study. They live for only a few weeks, however, so they can be hard to find.

After the eggs in the tree hatch, the newborn nymphs instinctively drop to the ground and burrow down into the soil where they feed on the sap in plant roots.   They live like that for a long, long time. Some live underground for two to seven years and are called **dog-day cicadas** or **annual cicadas**. They are typically green or black.

Once the cicada nymphs crawl out of the ground, they crawl up a plant and molt for the last time, emerging as winged adults. Even though they stay in the ground for more than a year, they are not synchronized, so you can usually find adults every year. Of course, since they do not live for very long as adults, you often don't see them. However, you can usually find the empty exoskeletons (called **casts**) from the final molt. Have you ever found one? Next time you do, put it in your insect display box.

Adult cicadas don't have any defenses except the ability to fly. When facing a predator that also flies, the adult cicada usually becomes a meal. So as cicadas emerge, many are eaten by birds, bats, and other insects. In fact, some people eat cicadas! A certain kind of wasp, called the cicada killer, will place cicadas inside its nest for the hatching larvae to feed on.

Periodical cicadas are a bit different from annual cicadas, because the nymphs stay underground for *17 years* (13 for some species). In addition, the broods are mostly synchronized, so most of them tend to emerge at once every 13 or 17 years. This results in enormous droves of periodical cicadas. When the males all start singing, it produces quite a racket. The buzzing is incredibly loud, because the cicadas are simply everywhere. Thankfully, this happens only once every 13 or 17 years. The periodical cicadas can be identified by their black bodies with red eyes and orange legs.

An adult periodical cicada like this one appears once every 13 or 17 years.

Periodical cicadas are generally found in the eastern parts of North America. The 17-year cicadas tend to live in the northeast, while the 13-year cicadas live in the southeast and midwest. Like other cicadas, the adults live for only a few weeks. A period of 13 or 17 years as a youngster (nymph) and only a few weeks as an adult is quite unlike our lives! Nevertheless, it is "normal" for these interesting creatures.

Creation Confirmation

Periodical cicadas give us excellent evidence that they were designed by Almighty God. Think about it. The nymphs stay underground for 17 (or 13) years and then, all of the sudden, they *all* emerge from the ground. This happens for miles around, even though the nymphs have no means of communicating with one another (as far as we know). Of course it seems impossible for us to imagine what causes millions of creatures to "know" to emerge within days of one another all over an entire region of the country. Nevertheless, it happens!

As far as we can tell, cicadas have a built-in "clock" and preset "programming" so that they know when to emerge. How did they get these clocks and this programming? We know from experience that it takes intelligence to make clocks and program computers. These things don't happen by chance. The "clocks" and "programming" in periodical cicadas tell us that they were made by an intelligent, amazing Creator!

What Do You Remember?

What is another name for a praying mantis? Explain the metamorphosis of a dragonfly. What is the difference between a locust and a grasshopper? Where are a grasshopper's "ears"? How can you tell grasshoppers, crickets, and katydids apart? Which cicadas live for two years underground? Which cicadas live for 17 years under the ground?

Nature Points

As you observe members of order Orthoptera, try to determine whether you are looking at a cricket, grasshopper, or katydid. If you aren't sure, try to find a field guide that will help you identify the insect you are observing.

Notebook Activity

Write down all the interesting and new information you learned in this lesson. Include illustrations of the interesting insects you have studied. Of all the insects you have learned about so far, which do you like the least and which do you like the most? Give reasons for your answers in the Fascinating Facts section of the *Zoology 1 Notebooking Journal*, if you have one.

Older Students: Go back through the previous insect lessons and make a set of flash cards that have the name of each insect order on one side and the common names of the insects found in that order on the other side. Flashcard images are provided for you in the *Zoology 1 Notebooking Journal*, on pages A53-A57. Have someone quiz you to see if you can memorize them.

Experiment
Which environment does a cricket prefer?

Crickets make their homes in many different types of areas, but they may favor one kind of environment. By observing crickets in living spaces that provide options for hiding, we can learn more about what types of environments they prefer.

You will need:

♦ At least one cricket (You can either catch them yourself or buy them from a live bait or pet store.)
♦ Spray bottle of water
♦ Four different types of materials that you will test. Here are some suggestions: grass clippings, dried leaves, moss, bark mulch, pine shavings, a piece of a black plastic bag.
♦ A knife

♦   A shoebox or plastic box with a lid
♦   Sand
♦   A fresh potato

1. Cover the bottom of the box with sand.
2. Cut up the potato and put a few pieces in the center of the box. The potato pieces will provide the water and food the crickets need.
3. In each of the four corners of your container, place a different material for testing.
4. Spray all of the materials with water until they are just a bit moist. You need to do this because crickets like moist environments. Try to make sure one material is not wetter than another.
5. Make a hypothesis about which environment you think your cricket or crickets will prefer. Record it on a Scientific Speculation Sheet.

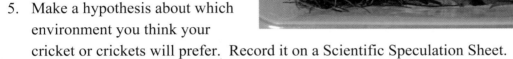

6. Add the cricket or crickets to the box, and cover the box with the lid.
7. Have an adult use the knife to cut several small holes in the lid so that air can get in the box.
8. Check on your crickets every few hours to see where they have chosen to dwell. Take the lid off slowly and watch for any crickets that try to jump out! Most likely, the crickets will have burrowed under the materials, so you might have to spend some time looking for them.
9. Mark your results in a table like the one shown below.
10. Was your hypothesis correct? Record the results on your Scientific Speculation Sheet.

	Grass Clippings	**Leaves**	**Pine Shavings**	**Spanish Moss**
First Check				
Second Check				
Third Check				
Fourth Check				
Fifth Check				

When you are done with this experiment, you can do more experiments if you like. For example, you can determine the crickets' food preferences or see if you can determine the temperature from their chirping.

Lesson 14
Order Lepidoptera

The sight of butterflies often elicits wonder and excitement. How many times have you seen a butterfly and felt the need to simply gaze at it? That's the response many people have when they encounter a butterfly. In fact, some people call butterflies "flying flowers" because of their beauty. Learning about these flying flowers is our last quest in Zoology I, and I think you will find them as fascinating as many of the other animals you have learned about in this book, if not more so.

Why are these wonderful insects called butterflies? There are many possibilities, but no one knows for sure. Some say that people started using the phrase "flutter by" to describe how they fly, and that phrase was eventually corrupted into "butterfly." In England, many of these insects are yellow, like butter. Some people say that they were called "butter-colored flies," and that eventually got shortened to butterflies. However the name came to be, we will call them **leps** in this book, because that's the nickname given to butterflies, moths, and skippers by those who study them. Because these insects belong in order **Lepidoptera** (lep' ud dop' tur uh), those who study them are often called **lepidopterists** (lep' uh dopt' tur ists).

Lepidoptera means "scale wings," and that's a good description of these insects because of the overlapping scales that cover their wings. These scales are so tiny and fragile that they look like little hairs, but when you touch a lep's wing, the scales can actually be rubbed off. When they come off, they look like a fine powder. These scales are what give leps their beautiful colors. Some people say that if you rub the scales off a lep's wings it can't fly. This is just a myth, however. A butterfly can fly with just half a wing, so a few missing scales certainly doesn't hurt it.

This closeup of a butterfly's wing shows the overlapping scales that give the butterfly its beautiful colors.

Order Lepidoptera has more species than any other order except Coleoptera, which contains the beetles. Just like beetles, there are probably thousands of undiscovered leps in the world, especially in tropical rainforests. Every year, new species of moths and butterflies are discovered. There are many leps, but there are not enough researchers to discover them all! Perhaps someday you will be a lepidopterist that discovers new species of butterflies, moths, or skippers.

The fat body and hooked antennae tell you this is a skipper.

Have you ever heard of **skippers**? They are overlooked by most people, but you have probably seen them more often than you realize. Skippers are smaller than most butterflies, but their bodies are generally fatter in comparison to their wings than are the bodies of most butterflies. Because of their fat bodies and often drab colors, skippers are sometimes mistaken for moths. However, they are not moths or butterflies. They are skippers.

You can usually tell a skipper by its antennae, which are often curled into a little upside down "J" at the end. They also skip when they fly, which is how they got the name "skipper." Their flight patterns look like a stone skimming the surface of the water. Look for them this summer, flitting from one dandelion to another.

Leps are very important pollinators. Many flowers are *only* pollinated by leps. This is because the petal isn't a large enough landing pad for a bee, and the flower's tube is so long that only a lep's long proboscis can reach down to extract the nectar within it. There are many flower-producing plants that would not exist today without certain leps that pollinate them. Remember that without pollination, a plant cannot produce seeds, which means that it would go extinct!

In fact, there are some plants that depend on a *specific* lep for pollination.   One such plant is the yucca plant. It depends on a specific moth, and guess what this moth is called: The **yucca moth**! You see, a female yucca moth will arrive at a yucca flower, collect some of its pollen, and shape the pollen into a little pellet. She will then travel to another flower on another yucca plant and rub the pollen against the part of the flower that needs it, which completes the pollination process. After that is done, she will place one or two eggs in the flower. When the egg or eggs hatch, the larvae (little caterpillars) will feed on the seeds, but they will not eat *all* of them. Instead, they leave some alone so that the seeds can become new yucca plants.

When the larvae are ready to enter their pupa stage, they drop from the flower and burrow into the ground. They surround themselves with silken cocoons that are usually covered with sand or dirt. Usually, they overwinter in the cocoons and emerge as adults in the spring, just when the flowers on the yucca plant are in bloom. This is important, because the adults live for only a few days, so if they emerged from their cocoons too soon, there would be no flowers to pollinate and lay eggs in. Although this is the typical life cycle of the yucca moth, the caterpillars have the incredible ability to delay their development into adults by as many as *30 years* if conditions require it.

Creation Confirmation

Think about how well the yucca plant and yucca moth work together so that both of them can reproduce. The yucca moth somehow "knows" that in order for its larvae to have something to eat, the yucca flower in which it lays its eggs must be pollinated. Because of this, it carries pollen from the flower of one plant to the flower of another to ensure that pollination occurs. It also places eggs only in empty flowers. If the yucca moth sees eggs already inside a flower, it will not leave eggs there. Otherwise there would be too many caterpillars when the eggs hatched, and they would consume all the seeds of the yucca plant. That, of course, would keep the yucca plant from reproducing. Once the eggs hatch, the caterpillars somehow "know" to eat only a few of the seeds, leaving the rest to become new plants.

This yucca plant is perfectly designed to work with the yucca moth so that both can reproduce.

That's not the end of the story, however. Once the caterpillars leave the yucca plant and form their cocoons, they somehow "know" exactly how long to stay in the pupa stage. They don't emerge until the yucca plant has made flowers. If they emerged too soon, they would die before they pollinated the plants. If they emerged too late, the flowers would be gone, and once again, they would not be able to pollinate the plants. Neither one of these things happens. Instead, the yucca plant life cycle and yucca moth life cycle are perfectly coordinated with one another.

Clearly this relationship could not have come about by chance. Just like a television and a remote control, the yucca moth and yucca plant have been designed to work together. Since it is obvious that the television and remote control are made by an intelligent designer, it should be clear that the yucca moth and yucca plant have been made by the most Intelligent Designer of them all!

Lep Anatomy

All leps have the same basic body features: a head, thorax, abdomen, and scaly wings. Leps have antennae, which are used for smell, touch, and navigation. The head is equipped with two compound eyes. Most leps cannot see the color red, but they are capable of seeing other colors like orange, yellow, blue, and violet. They can also see a certain type of light that we cannot see, called ultraviolet light.

Have you ever wondered why a moth will fly in circles around a light at night? Well, scientists have wondered that, too, and they are not sure. One possible explanation is that a moth tends to use the light of the moon to navigate at night. Since the moon's light comes from a fixed point far away, it can judge where it is going by keeping the moon on the same side of its body during its flight.

However, when there is another light that looks brighter than the moon (like your porch light), a moth will try to use it as a guide. If the moth gets too close, it looks like the light is coming from all directions. This confuses the moth, forcing it to fly in circles. We don't know that this is the correct explanation, but it is a possible one. If you become a lepidopterist, maybe you will find out whether or not this is true.

Antennae

How do you tell when a lep is a skipper, moth, or butterfly? Well, one way is to look at its antennae. The antennae of a butterfly are two long stalks with swollen ends. Often, those ends are so swollen that they look like little knobs. The antennae of skippers, on the other hand, are usually curved into the shape of a "J" at the end. The antennae of a moth often look feathery and typically don't have a knob on the end. Even if the antennae do not look feathery, the lep is still most likely a moth if they do not have swollen ends.

These are antennae from a butterfly (left), skipper (middle), and moth (right).

Like most insects, leps use their antennae for smell and touch. They also have a special organ at the base of each antenna called the **Johnston's organ**. This organ helps them maintain balance and orientation, especially while in flight. Most insects have this organ at the base of each antenna.

Drinking Straws

Adult leps eat nectar. Contrary to popular belief, adult moths don't eat clothing. Some species of moth, however, do have larvae that eat clothing. Not surprisingly, the leps that have such larvae are called **clothes moths**. Unlike chewing insects, most leps don't have a mouth that opens and closes. Instead, a lep usually has a long proboscis that uncurls when it lands on a flower or other food source.

A mosquito has a long proboscis, but it also has mouthparts that pierce into the food source so that the proboscis can be dipped into the fluid that the mosquito wants to eat. Because of this, we sometimes say that the mosquito has piercing/sucking mouthparts. A lep does not have piercing mouthparts; it has only sucking mouthparts. When it feeds, it gently unfurls its proboscis and drinks its food (usually nectar) the way we drink from a straw.

A lep's proboscis is usually curled up (see picture on page 140). When it feeds, however, it unfurls its proboscis, as seen here.

Though adult butterflies and skippers are hungry when they emerge from the pupa stage, they won't eat unless it is warm enough. They can't even fly around looking for flowers unless their bodies are warm enough. This is why you typically see them flying around flowers later in the day when it is warm. If it is not quite warm enough for them to fly, however, they can warm themselves up by sitting out in the sun and shivering their wings (moving them up and down quickly). If you happen to raise butterflies indoors, you will probably see them shivering, because most of us don't keep our homes warm enough for them to fly and eat.

This moth is hovering around the flowers as it uses its long proboscis to feed.

Butterflies tend to land on a flower to drink its nectar (as shown in the picture above), while moths often hover around the flower, like a hummingbird (as shown in the picture to the left). In fact, one kind of moth is so often mistaken for a hummingbird that it is called the **hummingbird moth**. In Europe, people sometimes report seeing hummingbirds, even though there are no wild hummingbirds in that part of the world. Most likely, they either saw a hummingbird that escaped captivity or a hummingbird moth!

Thorax

Behind a lep's head is its thorax, of course. Like all insects, a lep's wings and legs attach to it. Each leg is segmented, with a **tarsus** at the end. Do you remember what a tarsus is? It is an insect foot. The tarsi (plural of tarsus) of a butterfly are very helpful since they have little sensors on the bottom that can taste. Imagine if you could taste with your feet! I bet you would never walk outside without your shoes on, unless you were in a patch of flowers!

A lep's tarsi also have claws that help it grasp the surfaces on which it lands. Butterflies use them when they land on flowers to feed, for example. Moths use them to cling to almost anything while they rest during the day.

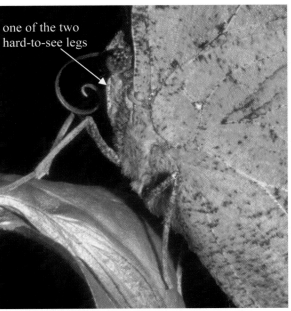

one of the two hard-to-see legs

This butterfly looks like it has only four legs because the fifth and sixth are being held next to the body.

Some butterflies (like the painted lady and monarch) have front legs that are so tiny it looks like they have only four legs. These butterflies are typically called **brushfooted butterflies**. Of course, if they really had only four legs, they would not be insects. All insects have how many legs? Six. However, if you examine them carefully, you will see the first set of legs tucked next to the body. They use them as brushes for cleaning their antennae and eyes. That's why they are called brushfooted butterflies.

forewings

hindwings

Leps have four wings: two front wings, called **forewings**, and two back wings, called **hindwings**. As I mentioned, lep wings are covered with scales that overlap one another. The scales are what form the patterns we see on a lep's wings. Some butterflies actually have patterns on their wings that look like letters in the alphabet or numbers. Can you guess what pattern the question mark butterfly has on its wings? Next time you see a butterfly, look to see if there is a pattern on its wings that resembles characters you have seen before.

Migration

Most butterflies spend their entire lives in the area where they hatched, but there are some exceptions. One of the most interesting exceptions is the monarch butterfly. This incredible butterfly migrates up to 2,500 miles from the farthest reaches of North America all the way down to Central Mexico. This was discovered by Dr. Fred Urquhart of the University of Toronto. He knew the monarchs migrated because he would stop seeing them after a certain time of the year. He didn't know where they went, however, so he clipped a little tag on every monarch he could. On this tag was his name address and a request to send him the butterfly if it was found.

Within a few months, butterflies were returned to him from all over North America and even Mexico. Aha! He had a clue. Mexico was the southernmost area from which he had gotten a butterfly returned, so he started traveling there to look for the monarchs. For many years, he traveled to Mexico, where he climbed through the jungles, tromped through forests, and talked to the people he found. He eventually heard there was a place west of Mexico City where people had seen large numbers of monarchs all together. He searched and searched for this place, and he eventually found it! There they were, millions of monarch butterflies covering every square inch of the area. There were so many monarchs that the trees looked orange and black from top to bottom!

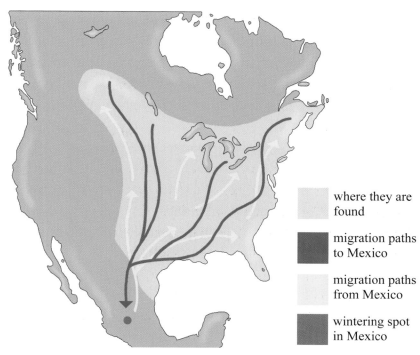

where they are found

migration paths to Mexico

migration paths from Mexico

wintering spot in Mexico

This map shows the migration paths of monarchs that winter in Mexico.

While in Mexico, the monarchs cling to everything they can find: trees, bushes, and even each other. This results in layer upon layer of resting monarchs in a state of hibernation. They stay like that from November through mid March, at which time they head back home, laying eggs along the way. Most never make it all the way home, but when the eggs hatch, pupate, and become butterflies, they will continue the journey north to the place where their parents spent the summer. Isn't that amazing?

Scientists have since found out that some monarch butterflies (especially those that live west of the Rocky Mountains) don't travel all the way to Mexico for the winter. Instead, they spend the winter in Southern California. There are other butterflies that migrate, including the painted lady, red admiral and common buckeye, but their flights are not as long and don't end with millions all in one spot.

Tell what you remember so far about butterflies. Can you name the parts of its body?
Tell the story of Dr. Urquhart.

More Metamorphosis

As you have already learned, leps go through complete metamorphosis. They begin as a tiny egg, sometimes smaller than the period at the end of this sentence. They hatch as caterpillar, molt in order to grow, form a chrysalis or cocoon, and transform into an amazing winged creature.

Have you been searching for eggs since you began your study of insects? If not, begin searching the underside of leaves whenever you go out. Insect eggs, including lep eggs, may be found in clusters or individually on one leaf. They can be as small as a speck of dust or as large as a pea. Some caterpillar eggs are so tiny you will need a magnifying glass to see them clearly. If you find an egg, you can try to raise it using a habitat you will make at the end of this lesson.

This caterpillar is munching on a leaf.

Within a few weeks, the caterpillar hatches from the egg. It's a very tiny creature that has only simple eyes to discern light from dark. Do you remember what those simple eyes are called? They are called **ocelli**. Most caterpillars have a total of six ocelli. They also have two antennae. Sometimes the antennae are not very noticeable and can shrink back into the body when the caterpillar is touched. Below the antennae are the chewing mouthparts. If you listen closely, you can sometimes hear caterpillars munching on leaves in the stillness of the night. Below their mouths are tiny silk-producing organs called **spinnerets** (spin uh rets'). The moth and skipper caterpillars use these to form a cocoon to enter their pupa stage.

Since a caterpillar has only ocelli (no compound eyes), it can't see anything but light and dark. If that's the case, how does it find food? Well, thankfully, the lep that laid the egg is programmed by God to know where to lay the eggs, and she lays them right on the food that the caterpillars will need to eat. That way, the caterpillar hatches right where it needs to be. Its first meal is often its own egg case, but then it goes about eating the plant on which it hatched. It usually crawls up to the top of the plant first. God designed caterpillars to crawl up because that is where the freshest, newest, most tender leaves are found on the plant.

Now you might be wondering about how the caterpillar knows which way is up. After all, it can't really see. It can only sense light and dark. How does it know which way to crawl to get to the top of a plant? Well, God might have programmed it to crawl opposite of **gravity**. Do you know what gravity is? It is the force that pulls you towards the earth so that you don't go flying off into space. When you drop a ball, it falls to the ground because gravity pulls it that way. Since gravity pulls things towards the ground, if a caterpillar crawls opposite of gravity, it will be crawling up. That's not the only possible explanation, however. Perhaps God programmed caterpillars to crawl towards light. Since the sun is up in the sky, does a caterpillar crawl up a plant because it is headed towards the sun? This is a great question, and you will find the answer to it in your very last experiment. Start thinking now about how you will conduct that experiment. If you haven't found any caterpillars in your yard, you can order them from the supply companies listed on the course website that I mentioned in the introduction to this book.

Caterpillars, with their simple eyes and tiny legs, aren't fast enough to escape predators. Most have some sort of defense. Do you remember some of the interesting defenses that caterpillars have? Some look and behave like snakes, and some have huge eye spots. Others are protected by their ability to blend in with their food source. In other words, they are camouflaged. Some look like bird droppings, while others look like twigs. The wavy-lined emerald moth caterpillar can be found biting off pieces of the flower it is eating and sticking them to its back. This makes it blend in with the flower! Some caterpillars also taste bad to most predators or are toxic. Many caterpillars even have poisonous spikes on their bodies. These spikes look like hair but are actually hollow tubes with needle-like tips that poke into predators. These tubes are filled with irritating or poisonous fluid.

If you brush up against this saddleback caterpillar, its spines will inject you with a poison that causes pain and irritation comparable to that of a bee sting.

Whether or not a caterpillar has poisonous spikes, it does have hair-like projections that cover its body. It uses these "hairs" to sense things about its surroundings. Do you remember what the sensory hairs on an insect are called? They are called **setae**. Some caterpillars appear smooth and shiny, but if you look closely with a magnifying glass, you will see setae.

Like all insects, a caterpillar has a head, thorax, and abdomen. You might have a hard time finding them, but they are there! The head is usually the easiest to spot. The thorax is usually made up of three segments right behind the head. This is where you find the caterpillar's six legs – its six **true** legs that is. These true legs are called **thoracic** (thuh ras' ik) **legs**, since they are attached to the thorax.

Many caterpillars appear to have more than six legs, because they have extra little appendages, called **prolegs**, which are not true legs. These prolegs have tiny hooks, called **crochets** (kroh shayz'), that can be used to grasp onto things. Caterpillars therefore use their prolegs to grip the surfaces on which they crawl. Most caterpillars have five pairs of prolegs.

Have you ever seen an **inchworm**? Believe it or not, inchworms are not worms. They are caterpillars! These specific caterpillars have only two or three pairs of prolegs, so they must crawl along a bit differently from other caterpillars. An inchworm holds on with its true legs and then draws its abdomen towards its head. This causes its body to curl into an upside-down "U." It then grips with its prolegs and lets go with its true legs, pushing the front of the body forward until its body is flat again. It then grips with its true legs, lets go with its prolegs, and draws its abdomen forward, starting the process all over again.

Notice that this inchworm has only two pairs of prolegs but three pairs of true legs.

With powerful mandibles, eating and eating and more eating is about all a caterpillar wants to do. It eats, gets bigger, then molts; eats, gets bigger, then molts, and so on until it is a large caterpillar ready to enter its pupa stage. Most butterfly caterpillars will molt four or five times, leaving behind a crumpled exoskeleton each time. The stages in between these molts are called **instars**. Notice the two caterpillars on this child's arm. They are in two different instars. You can tell because they look noticeably different from one another. The larger one looks like it might be in its last instar, almost ready to enter its pupa stage.

These two caterpillars are in two different instars.

Cocoon

Once a caterpillar has reached its last instar and is ready to enter its pupa stage, there is a big difference between a moth caterpillar and a butterfly caterpillar. Do you remember what that difference is? Moths usually spin a cocoon to enter the pupa stage, while butterflies usually form a chrysalis. Let's start by discussing moths. When a moth enters the pupa stage, it releases silk from spinnerets under its mouth, spinning the silk into a cocoon that surrounds it. Some even fasten leaves to their cocoons so that they are camouflaged while in their pupa stage.

Although most moths make cocoons out of silk, the **silk moth** (also called the **silkworm moth**) produces an especially strong kind of silk from its spinnerets. This silk has been woven into fabric for thousands of years to make silk garments. The Chinese were the first to discover how to make silk garments, several thousand years ago. They kept the secret to this amazingly soft, tough fabric for thousands of years. Only the emperors, their family, and certain servants knew how it was produced. Anyone suspected of telling the secret was immediately beheaded. This went on for thousands of years. Talk about a family tradition!

Silk is a wonderful fabric because it is soft and allows air to flow through it. This makes it feel light and comfortable. Because it is so wonderful and few people knew how to make it, silk used to be available only to the wealthy and powerful. About 1,500 years ago, however, Christian monks snuck silk moths out of the country in their hollow walking sticks, and the secret of silk making was revealed to the rest of the world. Now silk can be purchased by normal people, but it is still expensive. That's because it takes a lot of silk moth cocoons to make silk fabric. For example, it takes over 100 cocoons to make one tie. Does your father have any silk ties? Estimate how many silk moth cocoons it took to make the ties in his closet. That's a lot of caterpillars and a lot of cocoons!

It takes a lot of these silk moth cocoons to make silk fabric.

The silk moth caterpillar is often called the silkworm, but it's not a worm at all. How do we make silk from its cocoon? Well, once the silk moth caterpillar spins its cocoon, the silk maker dunks it in hot water and unravels the silk thread from the cocoon. This means that the caterpillar is sacrificed for the cocoon. Of course, if a silk maker did that with *all* of his cocoons, he wouldn't have any silk moth caterpillars left to make more silk, so some cocoons are left alone so that the caterpillars can become adults and mate. That way, there will always be more silkworms.

The silk moth caterpillar is often called a silkworm, even though it is not a worm.

Interestingly enough, because silk moths have been used for producing silk for so many years, the entire species has lost the ability to fly. You see, the adults are fed the mulberry leaves they need by the silk makers, so they don't need to use their wings to forage for food. As a result, whether or not a silk moth could fly did not affect whether or not it would live. If a flightless silk moth had been born in the wild, it would have died without producing offspring because of its inability to care for itself, but not so in the silk maker's care. In captivity, flightless silk moths are preferred, because they don't try to escape. Eventually, after thousands of years, all silk moths became flightless, even though they still have wings.

Chrysalis

A butterfly caterpillar is able to produce silk, but it doesn't use the silk to make a cocoon. Instead, it finds a nice place from which to hang. In some species, it just clasps on with its last pair of prolegs. In other species, it spins some silk into a pad that is attached to where it will hang. It then attaches a little hook on the tip of its abdomen, called a cremaster (kree' mas tur), to the pad. No matter how it attaches itself, the caterpillar will hang upside down and begin its final molt.

In this molt, the caterpillar sheds its exoskeleton, and the new exoskeleton underneath looks quite different from its previous exoskeletons. When exposed to the air, this new exoskeleton hardens, and that's the chrysalis. So rather than

These painted lady chrysalises are specialized exoskeletons that appear only in the pupa stage.

being something that the caterpillar covers itself in (like a cocoon), a chrysalis is a special exoskeleton. It is the exoskeleton that appears only for the pupa stage.

The chrysalis hangs there, so quiet and still, yet this is very deceptive. Inside the chrysalis, drastic things are happening. Every aspect of the caterpillar's body is changing into an adult butterfly! When conditions outside the chrysalis are favorable and all of the necessary changes have taken place, the chrysalis will break open. If the chrysalis formed in the fall, it might overwinter until spring before this happens.

When the chrysalis splits, the new adult butterfly struggles out. It sits quietly for hours, pumping fluid into its wings to expand them. When its wings are fully expanded, it is ready for flight. The first order of business is to look for food. Then it will be ready to mate.

How Long Do Leps Live?

It is most common for an adult lep to live only one or two weeks, because it lived most of its life as a caterpillar or a pupa. However, there are some leps that have a much longer adult life. Adult zebra heliconian butterflies living in warm climates, for example, can live for several months. Adult monarch butterflies live for up to nine months. Of course, monarchs must live longer than most adult butterflies in order to make the incredible migration you learned about earlier.

Though most adults live for only a few weeks, the pupa and egg stages may last for more than a year. For some species, the entire life cycle can be as short as one month. Though this is a short life, the good news is that short-lived leps can reproduce rapidly, and there can be several generations of young in one summer.

What's the Difference?

Now that you have learned about leps and their life cycles, let's concentrate on the differences among leps. Remember, order Lepidoptera has butterflies, skippers, and moths. Can you name a few of the differences among these three types of leps?

Let's start with the antennae. You already learned that a butterfly's antennae are long with thickened or knobbed ends, a skipper's antennae are usually curved into a "J" at the end, and a moth's antennae are often feathery and usually don't have knobs on the end.

There are other general differences as well. Butterflies and skippers usually hold their wings up while they rest, while moths usually hold their wings flat while resting. This generally means that the moth's body is covered by its wings when it is at rest. In addition, the bodies of butterflies are thinner than those of moths and skippers. Finally, moths are generally drab, while butterflies are usually quite colorful.

This is a moth, even though it is not drab.

You can sometimes distinguish leps by watching how they behave. Moths usually hover next to the flower to drink from the nectar, while butterflies and skippers often land on the flower. In addition, most moths are nocturnal (active at night), while most butterflies are **diurnal** (dye ur' nuhl – active during the day). Finally, butterflies generally form a chrysalis in their pupa stage, while moths and skippers usually spin cocoons around themselves.

Now it is important to understand that while these general rules I have just discussed are helpful in determining whether a lep is a moth, butterfly, or skipper, they are not foolproof. There are exceptions to nearly every one of these rules. Consider, for example, the luna moth pictured above. It is a moth, but it is not drab at all. In fact, it is quite beautiful. It does have the feathery antennae of a moth, however, and it does hold its wings flat when at rest.

Try This!

Identify each lep in the pictures below as a butterfly, moth, or skipper. The correct answers are with the answers to the narrative questions in the back of the book.

Try This!

A **Venn diagram** compares and contrasts different things. Make your own Venn diagram to compare and contrast butterflies and moths. Write the things that butterflies and moths have in common in the overlapping part of the diagram, and record those things that are different in the ovals outside the overlapping part. Place your Venn diagram in your notebook. If you have the *Zoology 1 Notebooking Journal*, a template is provided on page 177 for you to complete this activity.

In this space, write things that are true for butterflies but not for moths.

In this space, write things that are true for both butterflies and moths.

In this space, write things that are true for moths but not for butterflies.

Home Sweet Home

You can make your yard attractive to butterflies if you grow the plants that meet the needs of the butterfly in each stage of its life: the egg, caterpillar, chrysalis (cocoon), and adult. Butterflies will lay their eggs only on plants that their caterpillars will eat. Each species of caterpillar eats different plants. While in the chrysalis, the butterfly does not eat; however, it needs a sheltered environment. It usually hangs from a twig and is hidden from view by its coloring.

Each kind of caterpillar must have a particular kind of food. So, you must learn which butterflies are common to your area. If you have trouble learning the species common to your area and you live in the United States or Canada, you can build a garden for these very common species: painted ladies, swallowtails, whites and sulphurs, gossamer-wing butterflies, brush-footed butterflies, and skippers. Remember, if it gets too cool, butterflies cannot fly. Because of this, it is best to plant these flowers in a sunny place.

Once you learn which types of butterflies are common to your region, you need to grow two types of plants. First, you need to grow the kinds of plants that produce nectar that butterflies enjoy eating. Second, you will need to grow the kinds of plants on which the butterflies will lay eggs. These would be plants that the caterpillars enjoy eating. Since each species of butterfly tends to lay its eggs on specific plants, you need to make sure that you get the right kinds of plants. Your local nursery will be happy to help you, as many people ask them the same questions you will need answered. I have included some information on the next page to help you.

You also need to make water available for butterflies. You can use a bird bath (preferably one that sits on the ground rather than on a pedestal) with rocks covering the bottom and protruding above the water. The rocks will give the butterflies a place to land when they drink. You can often find butterflies hovering above muddy areas, landing down to enjoy a puddle. This is called **puddling**, and many butterflies enjoy it. Butterflies also love the salt and minerals found in beach sand. If you can find some beach sand and add it to your birdbath, it will be even more attractive to butterflies.

If you live in the city or an apartment, you can create a butterfly container garden right on your porch. Butterflies aren't particular about location; they just want the plants and water.

Plants that make flowers which produce nectar that most butterflies enjoy eating: butterfly bush, lantana, zinnia, bee balm, purple coneflower, penta, sage, milkweed or butterfly weed, lilac, sunflower, marjoram

Plants and Trees with Leaves That Are Eaten
by the Caterpillars of Different Species of Butterfly

Butterfly	Plant	Butterfly	Plant	Butterfly	Plant
painted lady	thistle	Diana fritillary or regal fritillary	violet	California sister	live oak
tiger swallowtail	tulip, cottonwood, aspen	orange-barred sulphur	pea plant, alfalfa	American copper	sheep sorrel
spicebush swallowtail	sassafras, spicebush	cloudless sulphur	wild senna and other Cassia species	eastern tailed-blue, Mellissa blue	legumes
anise swallowtail	parsnip, fennel, carrot, parsley	question mark	elm	spring azure	dogwood flower
pipevine swallowtail	pipevine	green comma	birch	marine blue	wisteria, alfalfa, legumes
black swallowtail	fennel, dill, carrot, parsley, parsnip	southern dogface	wild indigo, clover	southern cloudywing, northern cloudywing	clover
common buckeye	snapdragon	great southern white	mustard	Pacific orangetip	wild mustard
monarch	milkweed, butterfly weed	Julia, gulf fritillary, zebra (heliconian)	passion flower leaf	silver-spotted skipper	wisteria, black locust, honey locust
field crescent	aster	mourning cloak	elm, willow, poplar	west coast lady	mallow

Butterfly Pets

In the winter months or even just for fun in the spring or summer, you can raise a few butterflies in your home as pets.

You will need:
- Caterpillars (You can either find them outside or order them from a supplier. Several suppliers are listed on the course website I discussed in the introduction to this book.)
- A potted plant that the caterpillar likes to eat
- Two coat hangers
- Tulle or netting (found at any fabric or craft store)
- Rubber band
- Sugar

♦ Water
♦ Clean lid from a jar
♦ Cotton balls

1. Put the caterpillars on the host plant.
2. Bend two coat hangers into "bridges" (see the picture on the right) and insert the ends in the soil.
3. Cover the "bridges" with tulle or netting
4. Place a rubber band around the bottom to hold the netting.
5. Keep the plant watered and in the sun.
6. When your caterpillars form pupae, remove the tulle. If the chrysalises or cocoons fall or are not attached to anything, use white school glue to glue them onto a twig.
7. Keep watch for when the adults emerge from the chrysalises or cocoons.
8. When the adults emerge, provide sugar-rich foods for them to eat by following the instructions in steps 9-12.
9. Mix one cup of warm water with 1 teaspoon of table sugar.
10. Place cotton balls on an upside down lid from a jar.
11. Pour the sugar water on top of the cotton balls. The butterfly will enjoy this treat.
12. You can also cut an orange, watermelon, or other juicy fruit and make little slits in it where the juice will pool. A butterfly will sit on the fruit, uncoil its proboscis, and sip the tasty juice.
13. If your house is clear of cats, birds, and dogs, you can allow the butterflies to roam free in your home.
14. It is fine to pick up your butterfly, but do so by holding its "shoulders" with its wings closed over its back, as close to the head as possible. This is shown in the picture on the right.
15. You can even hand feed your butterfly by dipping a Q-tip® into sugar water and holding it up to the butterfly. When its feet touch the Q-top and taste the delicious treat, it will unfurl its proboscis and drink from the Q-tip.

Notebook Activities

You have learned so much about butterflies, moths, and skippers. Record and illustrate all that you learned. If you have the *Zoology 1 Notebooking Journal*, use the Fascinating Facts templates.

Make a poster of the butterflies in your area. Cut out pictures from magazines or print them from the Internet. Get poster board and glue the pictures to the board. Write the name of the butterfly under each picture. Include the scientific name if possible. You can use a butterfly field guide to help you identify the butterflies, or you can go to the course website where there are links to places that will help you identify the butterflies in your area. Take a picture of your poster and put it in your notebook.

Experiment
Do Caterpillars Use Gravity or Light to Determine Which Way Is Up?

You may remember that I said you were going to design your own experiment with caterpillars. We discussed the fact that caterpillars tend to climb upward, towards the top of the plant in order to reach the most nutritious and juiciest leaves. The purpose of this experiment is to try to determine what causes caterpillars to do this. Remember, they can't really see. Their eyes can only tell light from dark, so how do they know which way is up? Is it the light of the sun or moon that attracts them upward, or, like plants, do they actually sense gravity?

What is your hypothesis? Which one do you think it is? Write it down on a Scientific Speculation Sheet. Now you need to determine how you will test this hypothesis. Think about it for a while. Talk it over with your mom or dad, but try to come up with the idea yourself. Be sure that you keep everything the same except the one variable that you are testing. If you have trouble determining how to do this experiment, visit the course website that I discussed in the introduction to this book.

Design and plan your experiment; then perform it. Do it several times to make sure that the results are reliable. Fill out the rest of the Scientific Speculation Sheet once your experiment is done.

Answers to the Narrative Questions

Your child should not be expected to know the answer to every question. These questions are designed to jog the child's memory and help him put the concepts into his own words. *The questions are highlighted in bold and italic type*. The answers are in plain type.

Lesson 1

What is instinct? It is built in need to do something for survival. *Can you think of any animal instincts?* Answers will vary, but any behavior that is done for survival is an instinct. *What is one reason the dinosaurs may have become extinct?* They probably died out because of changes to the earth that were caused by the worldwide Flood.

Lesson 2

Hummingbird identification: Left: Calliope Hummingbird, Middle: Ruby-throated Hummingbird, Right: Rufous Hummingbird. *What are the benefits of birds?* They eat insects. This reduces the number of annoying insects and reduces insect-caused problems such as famines. They also help pollinate certain plants (this isn't discussed in the lesson). *Why is it important to know what habitat a bird prefers?* It helps you identify the bird, and you can attract the birds you desire by giving them the right habitat. *What are some reasons a bird sings?* A bird sings to attract a mate and mark territory. *What are some reasons a bird might call?* A bird calls to alert others to danger, to help in feeding, and to help in migration. *What is the history of bird banding?* It began with King Henry of England in the late 1500s. It used to be to mark the birds a person owns. In the early 1800s, John James Audubon started using it to track migrating birds. It is still used for that purpose today. *What are passerines?* They are birds in order Passeriformes. They have feet with three toes pointing forward and one toe pointing backwards, are singing birds, and are born without feathers, blind, and completely dependent on their parents for food and protection.

Lesson 3

What does it mean for a bird to molt? It means the bird sheds its feathers. *What is the hard, stick-like structure that runs the length of some types of feather?* It is called the shaft. *What part of the feather attaches to the bird's body?* The quill attaches to the bird's body. *What is the soft part of a feather called?* It is called the vane. *What does it mean to have hooked barbules?* It means that the barbules can hook to other barbules, making a smooth vane. It also means the feather is a contour feather. *What is preening?* It is when a bird oils and cleans its feathers, rehooking any barbules that have become unhooked. *Where are flight feathers located?* They are located on the wings and the tail. *What are the five basic types of feathers?* They are contour feathers, down feathers, semiplumes, filoplumes, and bristles. *What do some birds bathe in other than water?* Some bathe in the dust and others sunbathe. *Why do scientists think they do this?* Some think that dust bathing gets rid of extra preen oil or lice. The sunbathing is most likely to get warm or to dry wet feathers.

Lesson 4

How are bird bones different from the bones of other animals? They are light and hollow. *Where are a bird's flight muscles located?* They are on the breast of the bird. *Tell about the different kinds of flying birds do.* Birds flap to overcome drag, glide to save energy, and soar by catching a thermal that rises from the ground. Some can soar on gusts of wind as well. *What does a bird use its tail for when flying?* A bird uses its tail to steer. *What causes a bird to migrate?* The best answer is that their instincts tell them to go where there will be plenty of food. *How does a bird find its way while migrating?* They use landmarks, the sun and the stars, and the earth's magnetic field. *Why do some birds flock together while migrating?* They do so for protection. *Why do others migrate alone?* They don't need the protection. *What is the benefit of flying in formation?* It saves energy. *Which birds abandon their young when they migrate?* The Bristle-thighed Curlew (*Numenius tahitiensis*) does this.

Lesson 5

Name a few birds that don't build nests. Emperor Penguins, Short-eared Owls, White Terns, potoos, Common Murres, European Cuckoos, and cowbirds don't build nests. *What is a mound nest?* It is a mound that sits on the ground. *What is the difference between an earth-hole nest and a cavity nest?* An earth-hole nest is built in a tunnel underground or on the side of a cliff. A cavity nest is a nest inside holes in things like trees, fence posts, or birdhouses. *How long is the tunnel in which a puffin builds its nest?* It is usually 2 to 3 feet long. *Where does a Red-headed Woodpecker like to nest?* It likes to nest in a cavity about 65 feet above ground. *Where does a cardinal like to nest?* It prefers to nest in bushes near the ground. *Which birds build platform nests?* Raptors (birds of prey like hawks and eagles) and other large birds build platform nests. Some water birds, like grebes and loons, do as well. *Which is the most common type of nest?* The cup nest is probably the most common of all bird nests.

Lesson 6

Which is usually more colorful, a male or female bird? The male bird is usually more colorful. *What do you call a group of eggs in a nest?* You call it a clutch. *What is it called when a mother bird sits on her eggs?* It is called incubation. *What are the patches of featherless skin called that a bird develops when incubating its eggs, and what is their purpose?* They are called "brood patches," and birds use them to warm their eggs. *Can you name the parts of an egg?* See the illustration on page 94. *What is the name of the bump on the bird's beak that helps it break out of the shell?* It is called an "egg tooth." *If a bird is completely dependent on its parents, what is it called?* It is called altricial. *If a bird is born with feathers and the ability to see and walk around, what is it called?* It is called precocial. *Answer to the candling experiment question:* You should have seen that the old egg floated, but the new egg sank. If you didn't see that, let the old egg sit out for a few more days. The reason the old egg floats is because as time goes on, the air compartment grows. Thus, the old egg has more air in it than a fresh egg. This makes the old egg lighter, so it floats.

Lesson 7

Explain echolocation in your own words. Answers will vary, but they should describe how a bat makes sounds and waits for the sounds to come back. By analyzing the sounds and how long it took for them to come back, the bat can detect what is in front of it. *What are the differences between microbats and megabats?* Microbats are typically small and carnivorous, while megabats are usually larger and tend to eat pollen, nectar, and fruits. In addition, megabats resemble foxes (microbats don't) and fold their wings around them when they rest (microbats don't). *What beneficial tasks do bats perform?* Some eat insects, keeping their populations down. Others pollinate plants. *Where are some of the different places that bats roost?* Some roost in caves or other dark places. Others roost in trees. *What is interesting about bat hibernation and migration?* Unlike bears, bats are true hibernators. Their heartrate drops from about 400 beats per minute down to 25 while hibernating. Some bats migrate along the same paths as birds, and they often return to the very same spot they roosted the year before. *How do mother bats care for their pups?* The pups are kept in a nursery, and the mother bat goes out to feed and then visits the nursery to nurse, clean, coo to, and nurture her pup. *Why would you want to attract bats to your neighborhood?* They will keep the insect population down.

Lesson 8

Picture on page 126: This is a rhamphorhynchoid, because of the large teeth. *Explain what it is a like to be a paleontologist.* A paleontologist studies fossils to learn about extinct creatures. It is like looking at a picture of someone and trying to guess what the person was like. *Which ancient people wrote about animals that may have been pterosaurs?* The prophet Isaiah, Herodotus, and Josephus wrote about creatures that sound like pterosaurs. *Which modern day people talk about and draw pictures of animals that look like pterosaurs?* People in the jungles of Africa and South America have described and drawn pictures of what seem to be pterosaurs. *What are the two basic groups of pterosaurs?* The two basic groups are the rhamphorhynchoids and pterodactyloids. *Which group had the largest pterosaurs?* The largest pterosaurs were pterodactyloids. *Which group had the smallest?* The smallest pterosaurs were rhamphorhynchoids. *What were a pterosaur's bones like?* They were like bird bones: light and hollow. *What part of a pterosaur's brain is very large?* The flocculus, which helps the animal balance, was large in pterosaurs. *What does this tell us about pterosaurs?* It tells us that they were excellent fliers.

Lesson 9

Insect identification: A. Not an insect (too many legs) B. Not an insect (too many legs) C. Insect (6 legs) D. Not an insect (no legs). E. Insect (6 legs) F. Not an insect (too many legs) *How can you tell the difference between insects and other crawling creatures?* Count the legs. Insects have six legs. *What are the three segments of an insect's body?* An insect has a head, a thorax, and an abdomen. *What is interesting about an insect's eyes?* They are made up of many tiny lenses. *What are they called?* They are called compound eyes. *What are simple eyes?* Simple eyes are made up of only one lens. *What are the three kinds of insect mouths?* Insects can have chewing mouths, sucking mouths, or sponging mouths. *To what part of an insect's body are the legs and wings attached?* They are attached to the thorax. *How does an insect breathe?* Insects breathe through tiny holes, called spiracles, in the thorax and abdomen. *What is an ovipositor?* An ovipositor is on the abdomen of a female insect. She uses it to lay her eggs. *What are cerci?* Cerci are extensions on an insect's abdomen. They are used to give the insect a sense of touch at the back of the body.

Lesson 10

Explain what a lek is. It is a place where insects gather to find a mate. *What is complete metamorphosis, and what are its stages?* Complete metamorphosis is the life cycle of many insects where the juveniles look nothing like the adults. Its four stages are: egg, larva, pupa, adult. *What is the difference between complete metamorphosis and incomplete metamorphosis?* There is no pupa stage in incomplete metamorphosis, and the juveniles look similar to the adults. *What are the stages of incomplete metamorphosis?* The three stages are egg, nymph, and adult. *What is an immature dragonfly called?* It is called a naiad. *List the six different kinds of insect defenses that I discussed in this lesson.* The six defenses discussed in this lesson were: camouflage (crypsis), advertisement, mimicry, trickery, chemical defense, and bites or stings. *Explain how the bombardier beetle defends itself.* It has a chemical weapon that shoots boiling-hot, noxious gases.

Lesson 11

What is the job of a queen ant or bee? The queen lays eggs. *What is the job of a drone ant or bee?* The drone mates with the queen. *What are the jobs of the workers?* The workers do everything else, such as cleaning the nest, gathering food, taking care of the queen and drones, protecting the nest, etc. *Which are the males and which are the females?* Queens and workers are female, while drones are male. *Which insect do ants keep as "pets"?* They keep aphids. *Why do they do this?* They like to eat the honeydew that aphids make. *Explain some of the ways bees take care of the hive.* They feed the larvae and queen, make honey and cool the hive, repair the hive with wax, guard the hive, forage for flowers, and gather pollen and nectar from flowers. *Explain the bee dance and what it tells the other bees.* The bee dance is done by scout bees to tell gatherer bees where the flowers are. *How are bumble bees different from honeybees?* They are larger, and furry. The queen hibernates for winter and then starts a colony in the spring. The colony dies by winter, except for the queen. *How are Africanized bees different from honeybees?* They are more protective of the hive and more likely to sting. *What do social wasps make their nests out of?* They make their nests out of paper. *What is a solitary wasp?* It is a wasp that doesn't live in a colony. *How are termites different from bees and ants in the jobs each animal in the colony has and the social order of the colony?* Termites have different soldiers and workers, and the workers can be either male or female. The male works with the queen. *How do termites give evidence for creation?* They must have flagellates to help them digest wood. The termites and flagellates work together, which is evidence for design. *How can you tell termites from ants?* Ants have a petiole, while termites do not. The front wings of an ant are longer than the back wings, while termite wings are the same length. Ant antennae are usually bent, while termite antennae are usually not bent.

Lesson 12

Beetle identification: A. Beetle B. Not a beetle C. Not a beetle D. Beetle (You have to look close, but there is a line down the center of the back.) ***Robber fly/bee/wasp identification:*** A. Robber fly B. Bee C. Wasp ***How can you tell a beetle from other insects?*** Look for a line down the middle of the back where the wings meet. ***Which beetles are beneficial?*** Ladybeetles and dung beetles are beneficial. ***Describe the tip of a scarab beetle's antennae.*** The ends of a scarab beetle's antennae look like tiny fans. They can close to look like tiny knobs. ***What is the term that describes the way a firefly makes light?*** It is called bioluminescence. ***What is special about a firefly's light?*** It is cool and takes very little energy to make. ***How many wings do flies have?*** They have only two true wings. ***Where are their halteres and what do they do?*** They are behind the true wings and help in balance. ***Why do mosquitoes feed on human blood?*** Only female mosquitoes feed on human blood, and it is so they can produce eggs. ***What attracts them?*** They are mostly attracted by scent. ***How can you keep their population down?*** Get rid of any standing water in your area. ***How can you tell a robber fly from a wasp or bee?*** The eyes of a robber bee are raised above its head. ***What makes a bug a true bug?*** A true bug has front wings that are thick near the body and membranous near the tips. ***What makes water striders able to walk on water?*** A combination of water tension and the design of their feet make water striders able to walk on water. ***Why are giant water bugs sometimes called "toe biters?"*** They sometimes grab onto your toe with their front feet.

Lesson 13

Dragonfly/damselfly identification: The top picture is of a dragonfly, and the bottom picture is of a damselfly. ***Grasshopper/katydid/cricket identification:*** A. Katydid B. Grasshopper C. Cricket ***What is another name for a praying mantis?*** A praying mantis is also called a mantid. ***Explain the metamorphosis of a dragonfly.*** A dragonfly lays its eggs in the water, and the hatchling (called a naiad) is a water-breathing insect that lives underwater. After a few molts, it leaves the water, dries out, and the adult emerges from the naiad's exoskeleton. ***What is the difference between a locust and a grasshopper?*** A locust is a swarming grasshopper. A grasshopper that doesn't swarm is just a grasshopper. ***Where are a grasshopper's "ears"?*** They are either on the front legs or the front segment of the abdomen. ***How can you tell grasshoppers, crickets, and katydids apart?*** Grasshoppers are colored to blend in with the grass or brightly colored flowers, while crickets tend to be dark. Katydid wings often look like leaves. Katydids and crickets tend to have long antennae, while grasshoppers tend to have short ones. Grasshoppers are usually active all day, while katydids tend to be active in the late afternoon and evening. Crickets tend to be active at night. ***Which cicadas live for two years underground?*** Annual cicadas, sometimes called dog-day cicadas, live for two to seven years underground. ***Which cicadas live for 17 years under the ground?*** Periodical cicadas live for 17 years underground.

Lesson 14

Lep identification: A. butterfly B. moth C. moth D. skipper E. butterfly F. butterfly

Photograph and Illustration Credits

Photos and illustrations from www.clipart.com: 3, 8, 15, 16 (top), 23, 24 (bottom), 25, 30, 45 (bottom), 47 (top), 57, 60 (bottom), 62-64, 100, 106, 121, 122, 127, 131 (top), 137 (top), 140 (top), 147, 156, 159, 163, 166, 167 (bottom) 169, 171, 174, 223

Illustrations by Megan Whitaker: 7 (top), 43, 58 (top), 94, 105 (top), 123, 124, 161 (top), 173, 219

Photos copyright © Rusty Trump: 14, 26-28, 33 (top), 35, 42, 44, 45 (top), 46, 47 (bottom), 48 (bottom), 49, 53, 83, 86, 87, 89, 137 (bottom), 140 (bottom), 142 (top), 144 (both bottom), 152, 155 (bottom right), 158 (top), 160, 167 (top), 179 (top), 202 (top), 213, 214, 216 (middle), 217 (bottom) 221 (top), 226 (bottom left)

Photos copyright © Corbis Corporation: 4 (left), 75, 153 (left)

Photos copyright © IT Stock: 4 (right), 92

Photos copyright © www.focusnewzealand.com: 17

Photos copyright © Photodisc, Inc.: 12, 51 (bottom), 61, 90, 149 (middle)

Photos by Jeannie K. Fulbright: 1, 7 (bottom), 9, 11, 13 (top), 19, 37-40, 55-56, 72, 101, 103, 130, 146, 148 (bottom), 161 (bottom), 162, 175, 179 (bottom), 182, 198, 212, 222 (bottom), 228-230

Photo copyright © Gary Bell/oceanwideimages.com: 21 (top)

Photos copyright © Painet Photographic Arts and Illustration NETwork: 108, 115-117, 139, 148 (top), 150, 154, 157 (both bottom), 164 (bottom), 165, 177, 178, 187, 188

Photos from www.dreamstime.com: (copyright © holder in parentheses): 24 (Jan Tyler – top), 32 (Roger Otto), 172 (Stefan Sollfors), 227 (Newton Page)

Photos copyright © Comstock, Inc.: 41

Photos by Dr. Jay L. Wile: 48 (top), 76 (top), 119 (fossil replica), 125 (fossil replica), 126 (fossil replica), 128 (fossil replica), 204

Photos from www.istockphoto.com (copyright © holder in parentheses): 13 (Stan Rohrer – bottom), 16 (Matthew Dula – bottom), 21 (Richard Foote – bottom), 22 (Steffan Foerster), 29 (Peter Llewellyn), 31 (Eric Schmidt), 33 (Arpad Benedek – bottom), 34 (Peter Llewellyn), 52 (Janeen Wassink), 58 (Pamela Hodson – bottom), 66 (José Carlos Pires Pereira), 68 (Gigi B), 69 (Carolyn Mckendry – top, Rob sylvan – bottom), 70 (Loic Bernard), 74 (Alexander Mikula – top), 75 (Gertjan Hooijer – top), 76 (Paul Cowan – bottom), 77 (Peter Llewellyn), 79 (Marco Kopp), 84 (Mary Johnson), 91 (Colin Ochel), 99 (Maciej Sekowski), 105 (Julie De Leseleuc – bottom), 110 (Chris Pollack – right), 131 (Eric Forehand – bottom), 132 (John Shepherd – bottom left, Gilles Glod – bottom right), 133 (Matjaz Slanic), 134 (Paul Wolf), 135 (Rhett Stansbury), 136 (Chartchai Meesangnin), 138 (Stefan Klein – top), 142 (Rebecca Ellis), 144 (Audrey Roorda – top), 149 (Michael Ledray – left, Heather Ringler – right), 151 (Nancy Nehring), 153 (Brian Palmer – middle), 156 (Alex

Bramwell), 157 (David Philips – top left, Julie de Leseleuc – top right), 164 (Chartchai Meesangnin – top), 168 (Chartchai Meesangnin), 170 (Ruta Saulyte-Laurinaviciene), 203 (Eric Gagnon – bottom), 222 (Eric Shaw – top), 224 (Patrick Abanathy)

Photos from www.shutterstock.com (copyright © holder in parentheses): 51 (unknown – top), 65 (Loong Kok Wei), 67 (Halldor Eiriksson), 81 (Tony Campbell – top), 97 (Jack Scrivener), 104 (Paul Cowan), 107 (Jay Frater), 109 (Michael Lynch), 110 (Stephen Foerster – left), 112 (Stuart Elflett), 113 (Ginger Lash – top, montage from Linda Bucklin – bottom), 114 (Jenny Solomon), 155 (Carl Robison – top left), 176 (Montage from Rodney Mehring), 183 (Tyler Fox – top), 185 (Keith Naylor), 186 (Krzysztof Nieciecki), 189 (Glenn Frank – top, Peter Hansen – bottom), 190 (Heintje Joseph T Lee), 191 (Yanfei Sun), 192 (Uss Sergey Valentinovich) ,193 (Chia Yuen Che), 194 (Jason Ng – top and A, Stefan Sollfors – B, Jeff Lynch – C), 195 (Stuart Elflett – top, Koval – bottom), 199 (Micheal Ledray), 200 (Bruce MacQueen – top, Chua Kok Beng Marcus – bottom), 201 (Raymond Lin Wenwei), 202 (Steve Shoup – bottom), 203 (Evon Lim Seo Ling – top), 205 (Frank B Yuwono), 207 (Tan_Chuan-Yean – middle, Rui Vale de Sousa – right), 208 (Thomas Mounsey), 210 (Priscilla R. Steele), 215 (Erik H. Pronske, M.D.), 216 (WizData, Inc. – left, Newton Page – right), 217 (Chua Kok Beng Marcus – top), 218 (fotosav, Victor & Katya – bottom), 221 (Alexander M. Omelko – bottom), 225 (Andrew Snyder), 226 (McMac – top right), 226 (Chua Kok Beng Marcus – bottom middle, bottom right)

Photos copyright © Corel, Inc.: 73, 78, 80, 81 (bottom), 82, 95, 98, 132 (entire top row and bottom middle), 138 (bottom), 141, 153 (bottom), 155 (top right and bottom left), 183 (all but top), 184, 196, 206, 207 (left), 209, 218 (top), 220, 226 (top left, top middle)

Photos copyright © Hans and Judy Beste: 74, 93

Photos copyright © Creatas, Inc: 158 (bottom)

Illustration by PattyAnn Martirosian: 180

INDEX